Religious Ideology in American Politics

Religious Ideology in American Politics

A History

NICOLE GUÉTIN

McFarland & Company, Inc., Publishers
Jefferson, North Carolina, and London

An earlier, shorter version of this book was published in
French as *États-Unis: l'imposture messianique* (Paris: Éditions
L'Harmattan, 2004).

LIBRARY OF CONGRESS CATALOGUING-IN-PUBLICATION DATA

Guétin, Nicole.
    Religious ideology in American politics : a history /
Nicole Guétin.
        p.   cm.
    Includes bibliographical references and index.

    ISBN 978-0-7864-4193-8
    softcover : 50# alkaline paper ∞

    1. Religion and politics—United States—History.
2. Ideology—Religious aspects—History.   3. Ideology—
United States—History.   4. United States—Religion.
I. Title.
BL2525.G83   2009
322'.10973—dc22   2008052763

British Library cataloguing data are available

©2009 Nicole Guétin. All rights reserved

*No part of this book may be reproduced or transmitted in any form
or by any means, electronic or mechanical, including photocopying
or recording, or by any information storage and retrieval system,
without permission in writing from the publisher.*

On the cover: United States flag and church in North Dakota
prairie ©2009 Shutterstock

Manufactured in the United States of America

McFarland & Company, Inc., Publishers
  Box 611, Jefferson, North Carolina 28640
  www.mcfarlandpub.com

To my husband, Bernard

Acknowledgments

At the end of this study, I should like to thank first of all Denny Packard and Josette Jouas for their priceless contribution in commenting and proofreading this book. It is also with pleasure that I thank my good friend Dominique Faust, the Reverends David Bond and Emilius Kazooza for their judicious reflections. I am equally very grateful to my colleague Annette Almosen-Fazi who, through her vivid interest, encouraged me to pursue this research. Last but not least, I thank my husband, Bernard Guétin, for his patience, constant support and thoughtful suggestions.

Contents

Acknowledgments	vi
Preface	1
Introduction	5

PART I : THE IDEALIST VISION OF THE NEW WORLD

1. The Puritan Heritage	13
2. Religious Motivations in the American Revolution	30
3. The Emergence of a Collective Consciousness	46

PART II : THE AMERICAN POLICY OF CONQUEST

4. American Expansionism and Destiny	65
5. America: A God-Centered Nation	81
6. American Exceptionalism	97

PART III : THE FOREIGN POLICY OF THE UNITED STATES

7. The Monroe Doctrine	115
8. Racism and the Ethnocentric Debate	134
9. Civil Religion and American Messianism	154
10. Evangelism and Millenarianism	171

Conclusion	187
Chapter Notes	193
Bibliography	205
Index	211

Preface

This book belongs very much within the spirit of the times: It deals with the influence of religion on American political discourse. The work does not pretend to examine U.S. historical events in order to explain them from a new angle. It is simply an attempt to arrive at an understanding of the American mind through an examination of various phases in the country's history, and to illuminate an undeniable leitmotif lending coherence, character, and continuity to these historical events and the decisions that lay behind them.

From the colonial period to the present, political texts nationwide have been imbued with the spirit of a very specific religious rhetoric, one that reveals transcendental affiliations starting with the Puritan doctrine, moving to the concept of Manifest Destiny, and ending with the messianic vision of the world that characterizes the present day.

The terminology may have evolved over time but the associated expressive load seems to have been maintained. As Michael Kinsley writes in his article "God As Their Running Mate" in *Time* (September 17, 2007): "These days presidential candidates are required to wear their religion on their sleeve. God is a personal adviser and inspiration to all of them."

My particular intention is to discern and expose the consistency of this spiritual link that transcends American history from its earliest days to the present. The American forefathers undeniably played a determining role in the ideologies that have shaped the minds and acts of their successors. My first book on the subject, *États-Unis: l'imposture messianique*, published by L'Harmattan (Paris, 2004), was written for a French and European audience to acquaint them with the historical development of the American national ideology, and the impact it can have on today's international scene. To take one example, most Europeans have never heard the expression "Manifest Destiny," a concept which has underlain the political actions of the United States at all levels virtually since its birth. American and foreign intellectuals have focused their attention on this key element of American history, but often without picking out the links which give it coherence and unity throughout the centuries. I believe it is essential to describe and explain these transcendental and historical relationships.

I was first attracted by this subject while giving an aggregation course[1] on "Manifest Destiny: ideological and political aspects," at Caen University, located five hundred yards from the World War II American Memorial. I then realized the numerous common points connected with my thesis on *Anti-Puritanism in American Literature between the Two World Wars*. I became aware of the fact that the main tenets of the Puritan doctrine permeated not only the literary sphere but also the political. Certain American writers of the interwar period, such as Ernest Hemingway, F. Scott Fitzgerald or John Dos Passos, made their voices heard in response, as, having grown up on American soil, they had been nurtured by the culture of their motherland. According to them, Puritanism had overrated their idea of morality and curbed the free expression of modern art. Consequently, these literary dissenters showed a keen interest in Europe, which they considered a haven of liberty and creativity. Their works, many of them autobiographical, poured out harsh criticism of the Puritan tradition, whose effects, they claimed, could still be felt in the American psyche.

In this book, I seek to grasp the essence of a religious ideology, based on Puritanism, revealed through a significant number of American voices past and present. This may explain the decision to provide ample quotations. In this way one can demonstrate the true spirit that animated the discourse or reflections of these key American figures. If today, American religious-based nationalism tends to weaken among the population and certain political leaders, it appears that the notion of "destiny" remains embedded in the American psyche and that the American flag still holds a notion of "sacredness." This study is neither a book on the history of religion nor one on purely political issues in the United States. Countless numbers of works have already explored these subjects, but fewer have been published on the interaction between religion and politics, even where Manifest Destiny is concerned.

A few American intellectuals and writers have written on the "sacred" character of political life. I was thus able to acquire interesting documents, mainly at the University of Pennsylvania, in Philadelphia, the cradle of American political life. I also did some research at the American Library in Paris, which provides a good selection of historical works.

Books have been published on the religious aspect of political life and on Manifest Destiny. Among them are Albert K. Weinbergl, "*Manifest Destiny: A Study of Nationalist Expansionism in American History*; Anders Stephanson, *American Destiny: American Expansion and the Empire of Right*; Frederick Merk, *Manifest Destiny and Mission in American History*; Reginald Horsman, *Race and Manifest Destiny: The Origins of American Racial Anglo-Saxonism*; and Michael H. Hunt, *Ideology and U.S. Foreign Policy*. However, in my opinion, they emphasize political more than ideological aspects, and generally restrict their studies to the mid–1850s. I wished to expand my study beyond the period since I believe that the concept of Manifest Destiny encapsulates a complete range of religious and political concepts that extend before and beyond the limits of this particular period.

Introduction

America has always claimed to be "God's nation," and this work is an attempt to shed light on this bold assumption to which the country's history is closely linked. The most obvious manifestation of this idea lies in the intertwining of religious beliefs and political discourse, which often surprises a foreign observer. In official declarations, not only in Europe but also in international organizations such as the United Nations, people in the West are generally accustomed to the absence of religious terminology. History has taught Europeans that political systems based on a theocratic approach tend to result in dangerous absolutism, and Old Europe has retained the lessons of the past. However, this does not seem to be the case with the United States, whose political cohesion was truly achieved only after the Civil War, with the Northern victory favoring the emergence of a culture largely influenced by the Puritan, egalitarian and democratic New England states.

The origins of the American people are rooted in a particular historical context that Europeans must bear in mind if they want to understand the evolution of American mentality. Despite the threat of a French empire in America (Canada and the Louisiana Territory, bordering the thirteen colonies to the north and west) and a strong Hispanic presence on the West Coast and in the South, the first Anglo-Saxon communities formed the basic social fabric, even though many waves of immigration coming from various countries and ethnic groups modified its texture. After a long attempt at assimilating the immigrants of all the nationalities within the same culture, the U.S. now tends to preserve the traditions and habits of each ethnic group to become a multicultural nation. Ironically, with the gradual shift from a "melting pot" to a "salad bowl" over the centuries, it appears that American society is still in search of a national identity. At present, with the fusion of old and new immigrants, one may wonder what become of the Founding Fathers' idealistic vision.

In this historical perspective, it should be remembered that the first colonists had aspired to a country where all the citizens would engage, with a deep feeling of unity, in the fight for freedom and the creation of a new world, a genuine Promised Land. The freedom of religion, the first claim as they set foot on American soil, was soon contradicted during the period of religious turmoil. The first American Puritans, most of them of Calvinist origin, were convinced that this *terra incognita* was a place of exile allotted to them by God since the beginning of time, similar in many ways to the Promised Land of Moses. It was in this fervent spirit that in 1620, the Pilgrim Fathers signed a Pact of Union aboard the *Mayflower* to reinforce the strength of the community.

As a true code regulating the organization of daily life, this Pact of Union was deeply rooted in a religious tone. In 1630, John Winthrop, who was to become the first governor of the Massachusetts Bay Colony, declared to his fellow travelers:

> For we must consider that we shall be as a city upon a hill, the eyes of all people are upon us. So that if we shall deal falsely with our God in this work we have undertaken and so cause Him to withdraw His present help from us, we shall be made a story and byword throughout the world, we shall open the mouths of enemies to speak evil of the ways of God and all professors for God's sake, we shall shame the faces of God's worthy servants, and cause their prayers to be turned into curses upon us till we be consumed out of the good land wither we are going.[1]

Several decades later, a reflection by Pastor Cotton Mather (1663–1728) seemed to echo John Winthrop's statement:

> I write the Wonders of the Christian religion, flying from the depravations of Europe to the American Strand: And assisted by the Holy Author of that religion, I do, with all conscience of truth, requires therein by Him, who is the truth it self, report the wonderful displays of His infinite power, wisdom, goodness and faithfulness wherewith His divine Providence hath irradiated an Indian wilderness.[2]

Since then, the temporal and spiritual realms have never had genuine borders. This may explain why American politico-religious history was marked, later on, by an concept of major significance — Manifest Destiny — which has become a pillar of American ideology. The concept of Manifest Destiny appeared in the middle of the nineteenth century, but today is little known in Europe. This expression was coined by John L. O'Sullivan, editor of *The Democratic Review*, when, to justify the annexation of Texas in 1845, he advanced the idea of a divine right in the conquest of new American territories. One of his previous articles, "The Great Nation of Futurity," published in 1839,[3] contained the notion of Manifest Destiny. Amplified by the prophetic tone of its author, it announced "the era of American greatness," the destiny of "the nation of the nations," which was to "manifest to mankind the excellence of divine principles; to establish on earth the noblest temple ever dedicated to the worship of the most High — the sacred and the True." The biblical resonance inscribed in this religious

Introduction   7

attitude aimed at promoting "peace and good will among men."[4] An extract states:

> Our national birth was the beginning of a new history, the formation and progress of an untried political system, which separates us from the past and connects us with the future only; and so far as regards the entire development of the natural rights of man in moral, political, and national life, we may confidently assume that our country is destined to be the greatest nation of futurity.... The expansive future is our arena, and for our history. We are entering on its untrodden space, with the truths of God in our minds, beneficent objects in our hearts, and with a clear conscience unsullied by the past. We are the nation of human progress, and who will, what can, set limits to our onward march? Providence is with us.... The far-reaching, the boundless future will be the era of American greatness.[5]

A few years later, during the summer of 1845, it also appeared in the columns of *The Democratic Review*, where O'Sullivan developed his idea and used the expression "Manifest Destiny" for the first time. The text declared it was "our manifest destiny to overspread the continent allotted by Providence for the development of our yearly multiplying millions." This expression "was to some extent drowned" in an article justifying the annexation of Texas, which was simply entitled "Annexation" and which appeared at a politically critical moment. The British and the French opposed this annexation of Texas, and it is in this context that O'Sullivan reacted, condemning the interference of European states in American affairs. He reproached them for hampering American objectives and the achievement of Manifest Destiny:

> Away, away with all these cobweb tissues of rights of discovery, exploration, settlement, continuity, etc. To state the truth at once in its neglected simplicity, we are free to say that were the respective cases and arguments of the two parties, as to all these points of history and law reversed — had England all ours, and we nothing but hers — our claim to Oregon would still be best and strongest. And that claim is by the right of our manifest destiny to overspread and to possess the whole of the continent which Providence has given us for the development of the great experiment of liberty and federated self-government entrusted to us.[6]

This first use of the term "Manifest Destiny," as said above, went virtually unnoticed. It was only when the editor used it for a second time, six years later, in the *New York Morning News* that it found an echo. Meanwhile, public opinion had focused on the issue of the Oregon border, the object of a dispute with the British and a problem much more delicate to deal with than that of Texas because it implied a threat of war. O'Sullivan took the side of the expansionists who claimed "All Oregon," and this was again for him the occasion to state his dissatisfaction by invoking the Divine Plan. For O'Sullivan, the recognition of a divine right transcended all claims. The expression was taken up in political debates and became a true rallying cry, calling upon the British to soften their demands and, finally, cede Oregon to the United States.

A journalist of Irish origin, endowed with a rather jovial and optimistic temperament, O'Sullivan had been influenced (like many of his generation) by the romantic ideal of Jacksonian democracy. Indeed, President Andrew Jackson (1767–1845) embodied the American paradigm. The first president from the West, he was simple and natural, at ease with everyone and in any situation a true American gentleman. He was thus supported by all social classes: farmers, landowners, bankers, tradesmen and workers. In addition, Jackson saw the hand of Providence in the acts and will of the majority. When O'Sullivan founded *The Democratic Review*, his main objective was to awaken public opinion to democratic values based on these spiritual assumptions. The *Review* achieved remarkable success.

The concept of Manifest Destiny, of which O'Sullivan was made the best representative, was not only a rallying cry, but encapsulated an entire cultural heritage. The *Dictionary of American History*,[7] which includes a lengthy article on Manifest Destiny, mentions the "inevitable character" of the United States' territorial expansion. Although this concept was introduced at the time of the annexation of Texas, it was adopted again to justify many interventions in domestic and foreign affairs of the U.S. administrations in the second half of the nineteenth century. Those who believed in Manifest Destiny were also convinced of the superiority of American institutions.

The legacy of this ideological movement to American culture is of major importance because the idea of Manifest Destiny explains the propensity which Americans have to give a providential reading to their history, as well as to their future. In that sense, O'Sullivan exerted an influence beyond measure on generations of writers, historians, and politicians to come, who used this expression to such an extent that it became part and parcel of American idiomatic language.

According to him, the notion of Manifest Destiny did not include violence. In 1841, he was undoubtedly ahead of his time in proposing the creation of a Congress of Nations to resolve international conflicts. Besides, during his later commentaries in the *Morning News*, he stated that he was firmly opposed to the war with Mexico. Like many of his generation, he was a romantic and acted as their spokesman in his articles, especially when he discussed the issues of European monarchies. O'Sullivan refused all forms of allegiance, either individual or collective, and adhered to the "Spirit of the Age" that advocated freedom and progress, stating that only Americans could bring about their full accomplishment.

The editor's inflamed arguments not only defended the political interests of the United States but also recognized its literary and philosophical independence. In one of the issues of *The Democratic Review*, he wondered why American literature did not reveal the American soul, inspired by its imposing landscapes. In his vigorous style, he asked: "When would the country's literature imbibe the fresh enthusiasm of a new heaven and a new earth, and soar up upon the expanded wings of truth and liberty?"[8] Spokesman of the Romantic movement, O'Sullivan opened his columns to American men of letters, publishing writings by Nathaniel Hawthorne (a close friend of his), the poet Walt Whitman, Edgar Allan Poe, philosophers Henry David Thoreau and Ralph Waldo Emerson, and many others.

O'Sullivan seems to have been influenced by the famous philosopher Emerson, nicknamed the "Sage of Concord." Emerson was regarded as unrivalled in recognizing the "Spirit of the Age" and interpreting the mission of the United States. As one of the mentors of Transcendental thought, Emerson fashioned it into an ideological basis in the concept of Manifest Destiny. American Transcendentalism brought into light the role of Divine Providence in the future of the nation and in the progress of the human race. In 1844 Emerson gave a lecture in Boston, entitled "The Young American"; he drew young people's attention to the role they were to play in the fulfillment of a mission for their country. He declared that in the history of humanity some nations had had a paramount role in the propagation of universal values and that the United States had to ensure this mission as a country, free and responsible for new forces.[9] Furthermore, he encouraged young Americans to fully benefit from technological developments in the industrial and commercial fields. He finished his lecture by, stating that the United States was a nation "guided by a sublime and friendly Destiny."

At the close turn of the nineteenth century, another philosopher, John Fiske, reformulated the concept of Manifest Destiny in an article published in 1885, in *Harper's New Monthly Magazine*. It expressed the same premise as Emerson's, but was written in a more bombastic and emphatic style, giving it a somewhat imperialistic tone. Fiske announced the future preeminence of the Anglo-Saxon race in the cultural, economic and political spheres, stating that the language of Shakespeare would become a *lingua franca*:

> The language spoken by these great communities will not be sundered into dialects like the language of the ancient Romans, but perpetual intercommunication and the universal habit of reading and writing will preserve its integrity, and the world's business will be transacted by English-speaking people to so great an extent that whatever language any man may have learned in his infancy, he will find it necessary sooner or later to learn it to express his thoughts in English.[10]

Thus, O'Sullivan and his supporters condensed into a striking phrase the aspirations of a young nation filled with enthusiasm and the vision of a bright and providential future. Here, the mentality of a whole people is reflected, and this explains the longevity which the expression "Manifest Destiny" has witnessed. Still nowadays, it slumbers in the American collective consciousness and, if it is not clearly invoked any longer, the idea often underlies the political discourse of certain American leaders.

Part I

The Idealist Vision of the New World

1
The Puritan Heritage

The American cultural heritage has been shaped in a specific and determining way by the influence of Puritanism, even though the term has faded from modern language. However, today the idea of "messianism" cannot be understood without going back to the sources that have nurtured Puritan doctrine in the United States. To go back in time is thus necessary to define the religious principles which have characterized American culture. Without knowing the historical evolution of Puritanism, which emerged in Great Britain, and the influence it exerted in the United States, it is very difficult to understand the originality and the uniqueness of American thought.

Puritanism was born from the English Reformation through Henry VIII's initiative. When his wife Catherine of Argon failed to produce a male heir, he asked the Church of Rome for permission to obtain a divorce. After following the formal procedures with Rome to annul his marriage, Henry VIII faced the pope's firm refusal and thus decided to break with the Church of Rome. In his heart, the English sovereign wanted to remain a Catholic. But at the time, Luther's and Calvin's writings, introducing Protestantism in Europe, were widely read by the English clergy. The king's religious counselors began to adopt the new ideas and strongly supported the king in his decision to separate from the Roman Catholic Church. After long and various discussions between the two parties, the sovereign was excommunicated by Rome in 1533. The Act of Supremacy of 1534 proclaimed Henry VIII Supreme Head of the Church of England, and the Archbishop of Canterbury, Thomas Cranmer, newly appointed by the king, issued the Book of Common Prayer to be used exclusively for public worship.

Having repudiated his first wife, with whom he had only one surviving child, Mary (the others had died in infancy), Henry married Anne Boleyn, a charismatic lady who bore him another daughter, Elizabeth. Unfortunately for her, Boleyn was accused of adultery and Henry had her beheaded, as well as her supposed lovers. The king then married his third wife, Jane Seymour, one of the queen's ladies-in-waiting to whom he had shown some favors. Although a boy, Edward VI, was born from their union, the heir was too young to reign when his father died, so that regency was settled under the guidance of a council composed mainly of Protestants whose wishes were to spread Protestantism throughout the country. Young Edward, under the influence of his counselors, wished to exclude his half-sisters from the throne, especially Mary, a fervent Catholic, despite the Act of Succession passed by his father in 1544 designating both sisters as heiresses to the throne of England.

This unlawful political decision brought about an armed conflict at the end of which Mary came out victorious, as she had the massive support of the English people. Following the premature death of the young King Edward, Lady Mary was then proclaimed Queen and was crowned on October 1, 1553, by the Roman Catholic bishop Stephen Gardiner, whom she had delivered from imprisonment in the Tower of London. Mary Tudor devoted her reign to restoring the Catholic doctrine, and had Parliament abolish Edward's laws on religion. Her main political goal was to make Catholicism the state religion of England.

She also pursued a policy of repression against the Protestant leaders. Indeed, Bloody Mary, as she was called, was accused of many executions, among them that of Thomas Cranmer, Archbishop of Canterbury. Moreover, she had married the Spanish Catholic Prince Philip, which made her increasingly unpopular. The latter, succeeding to the throne of Spain in 1556, returned to his country fourteen months after having reigned with his wife as king consort. Mary Tudor's government met with important internal economic difficulties that prevented England from benefiting from the lucrative trade with the New World. Queen Mary died childless at the age of 42, and her half-sister Elizabeth succeeded her.

This period, during which England reconciled herself with the Papacy, is important since it triggered the inevitable conflict between Protestants and Catholics, as both religious groups were determined to dominate the political scene. Mary Tudor's reign brought forth the emergence of radical Protestants who strongly contemplated purifying the religion, hence the term "Puritans." Puritanism was never clearly defined since it was more a state of mind than an elaborate philosophical or religious doctrine but, given the historical background, Finlayson's definition seems very appropriate: "anti–Catholicism" would be a good substitute for this cloudy thing called "Puritanism."[1]

The Puritan movement really originated in England when Elizabeth I ascended the throne in 1558, reinforcing the hopes of the Calvinists, who longed for a Protestant England. Having suffered under the yoke of the former queen, these Calvinists believed they were going to see the end of their torments. However, there were still Catholic bishops in the country who remained attached to Roman obedience. Elizabeth I had to deal with these two opposing religious currents, and being a shrewd politician, tried to adopt an intermediate approach.

The publication of the Act of Uniformity (1559), making the sovereign supreme authority of the Church, could only satisfy the Calvinists as they were convinced that the Queen would not reiterate Mary Tudor's repressive policy. However, the revised edition of the *Book of Common Prayer*[2] inspired by the Reformation and originally published under Henry VIII, upset some of them, who protested against the surviving Catholic elements in this work. Thomas Cranmer, Archbishop of Canterbury under Henry VIII, had largely contributed to the *Book of Common Prayer*, which was to establish a compromise between moderate Anglicans and radical Calvinists. The objective of the new text was to correct the anti–Catholic tendencies, and as a result, the group of rebels, opposed to a consensual version of the *Book of Common Prayer*, founded to the Puritan movement.

When Elizabeth I came to power, the Puritans and several bishops criticized the revised edition, which particularly stressed the readings and the personal interpretation of the Scriptures, whereas the Puritans insisted on a comment or sermon because they believed it was the minister's duty to instruct the faithful. The queen herself sought to restrict the role of the preacher; she demonstrated this during a religious ceremony, where she permitted herself to challenge an eminent prelate several times, requesting him to return to the Scriptures. Extremely upset, the cleric could not complete his sermon!

The Puritans criticized other practices retained in the prayer book, such as the exchange of rings during the wedding ceremony, the celebration of saints, the titles of church leaders borrowed from Catholicism, etc. Moreover, the prayer for deliverance from the "Pope's tyranny, and all his detestable practices" had been eliminated. All these details took on considerable importance, and the bishops who surrounded the queen started to rebel. Becoming increasingly demanding, one of them, the Scot John Knox, even wrote a pamphlet entitled "The First Blast of the Trumpet of Judgment against the Monstrous Regiment of Women." The situation hardened in 1564 when the queen tried to put an end to the ongoing polemic on this subject and the crisis escalated when she asked her counselor Parker to enforce the regulation on church vestments, which the Puritans vehemently objected to.

This is a focal point in British and American history because it was during this period that Puritan ideology actually emerged. It began with the formation of a Puritan party, which, little by little, became a political and religious force in England. Elizabeth I had especially wanted to challenge the recalcitrant ones in order to make them aware of their narrow-mindedness, but they preferred to give up their offices rather than give in and acknowledge defeat. They published a document, registered in the Anglican Church's annals: "And if the Prince made the decision to order us what God did not order so that we cannot disobey him without incurring the rigors of the law, we must refuse to do what is prescribed by the Prince."[3]

Despite these clashes with the Puritan clergy, Elizabeth asserted the power of the Church of England and prevented her Catholic cousin, Mary Stuart, who pretended to be heir to the English throne, from usurping power. Following Mary Stuart's forced abdication as Queen of Scotland in 1567, several plots took place to eliminate the reigning queen, Elizabeth I, after which Mary was executed. This execution led Philip II of Spain to assemble his armada to invade England. The war against Spain lasted sixteen years and left the country with severe financial problems. These events marked the end of Elizabeth I's reign. She died childless and was succeeded by James I, the Protestant son of Mary Stuart.

Under James I, who reigned from 1603 to 1625, Catholic and Puritan tensions continued to grow. However, both religious groups had specific expectations from the new king: Protestants because the king came from Presbyterian Scotland (even though his mother had been a Catholic) and Catholics since James I's own wife, Anne of Denmark, had converted to Catholicism. Nevertheless, an incident provoked a wave of anti–Catholicism when Catholic dissenters, headed by Guy Fawkes, planned to blow up the House of Lords. The rebels were caught and executed, which amplified the anti–Catholic movement. Following this event, all the Catholic priests and Jesuits were ordered out of the country.

As to the Puritans' demands, they multiplied and created other conflicts on the ideological level. Their main demands focused on the withdrawal of the *Book of Common Prayer*, the removal of "popish symbols" such as wedding rings, and the ecclesiastical hierarchy to which they were vehemently opposed. Believing that the Anglican Reformation did not go far enough, they reproached it for deviating too much from the spirit of Calvinism. As a consequence, a split grew between the believers, who divided themselves into two groups: the Protestants and the Puritans. The situation worsened when King James sided with the Protestants, who intended to maintain the practice of sporting activities on Sundays, whereas the Puritans were strongly opposed to it.

To make themselves heard, the Puritan leaders wrote the Millenary Petition, collecting the signatures of a thousand ministers who asserted certain rights, in particular the discarding of Catholic practices. The Millenary Petition was a list of requests which included the removal of the sign of the cross at baptisms and the use of terms such as "priest," "absolution," etc. The dissenters also demanded more sermons and condemned traditional songs and music; above all, they requested the strict observance of the Sabbath, the day of rest.

One year later, the Hampton Court Conference (1604) was organized under the aegis of the king to focus on religious issues and try to bring the divergent points of view into line, but after numerous controversial arguments, James I refused to yield to the Puritans' demands. With regard to the ecclesiastical hierarchy, the king's formula, "No bishop, no king, no nobility," remained. Abolishing the episcopate meant abolishing royalty and nobility. The king needed them to extend his authority and therefore did not yield to their request. Only one decision was made — a single translation of the Bible for all churches and households in England, the King James Bible, which became an authoritative translation into English and a true bedside book.

King James I then published *The Book of Sports* (1633) to affirm his convictions and his authority, giving numerous details of what was permissible on Sunday, like dancing. It provoked the reaction of the great English poet and polemist John Milton (1608–1674), who accused the bishops of "drawing men from their most serious thoughts ... to throw them in the whirl of games, drinking and dances with women."[4] However, the Puritans did not yield. They tried to obtain from the king what they had not been able to obtain from Elizabeth I.

After a period of calm, the debate was rekindled again in 1621 when Prince Charles, the king's second son, contemplated marrying a Spanish Catholic princess. Parliament reacted by writing a petition, which the king rejected during a solemn meeting by dramatically tearing out the page on which it was inscribed. The king also prohibited the printing and importation of religious works, thus amplifying the crisis which took the shape of an ideological battle.

After the marriage of Charles I, who did not marry "his" Spanish princess but the sister of the French King (Louis XIII), Henriette-Marie, tensions between the two religious factions deteriorated. The Puritan nobility had been opposed to this marriage for fear the king would become too lenient towards Catholics, lifting their restrictions and undermining the role of the protestant Church of England; the conflict intensified when the royal court was invaded by the young queen's Catholic friends.

Furthermore, upon his accession to the throne in 1625, the young king sought to move away from the Calvinist doctrine that had permeated the English liturgy. He adopted a policy of repression against his subjects who were hostile to his religious policies and, in 1629, appointed the Archbishop of Canterbury, William Laud, as his political adviser. The latter resorted to the Court of High Commission for those who refused to comply with his directives and to the Court of the Star Chamber to inflict punishment, implementing draconian measures against the recalcitrant Puritans.

Failing to get along with the ruling class of Parliament on these important key issues, Charles' advisers began to lose ground as many members of the House of Commons criticized the king's abuse of power. Moreover, the latter had not succeeded in imposing his religious policy on Presbyterian Scotland, which made matters worse. Confronted with these issues that did not reach any solution, the king and Parliament refused to yield their position. As a consequence, Charles dissolved Parliament in 1629. Things worsened when, in 1637, Scotland refused to use the *Book of Common Prayer* intended to unify the traditional rite, which resulted in the revolt of Scottish bishops and led to the Bishops' War (1639–1640).

This political and religious crisis with Scotland put an end to Charles' eleven years rule and struggle for supremacy, and opened the way to civil war. Cavaliers (supporters of monarchy) and Roundheads (Puritan supporters of Parliament) began to arm. The Cavaliers underwent many defeats until Oliver Cromwell defeated them in 1645. A year later, the king surrendered to the Scots, who handed him over to the English Parliament. Charles I was put on trial for treason and was found guilty. During his trial, as an advocate of the Divine Right of Kings, he declared that "no court had jurisdiction over a Monarch."[5] He was executed in 1649, as his adviser, William Laud, had been in 1645.

Cromwell, the Puritan general, became Lord Protector of England, abolished the monarchy and proclaimed a republic. The Puritans then sought to approach the Scots, who were in the majority Presbyterian and whose theology rested upon Calvinist principles. They tried to found a Presbyterian Church in England and, to promote it, organized a synod, the Westminster Assembly, which made it possible for England to settle little by little into Presbyterianism based on Calvin's teachings. Questioned by a contemporary, Edward Symmons, as to why the parliamentary prisoners had taken arms against their sovereign, they replied: "They took arms against Antichrist and popery; for (said they) 'tis prophesied in the Revelation, that the whore of Babylon shall be destroyed with fire and sword, and what doe you know, that this is the time of her ruin, that we are the men that must help to pull her down."[6]

English Puritanism thus originated from important dissensions within the Christian Church in which Protestant Puritans, firmly opposed the Roman Catholic Church on small or fundamental issues. In the seventeenth century, the English penal code contained ferocious anti–Catholic laws which were applied on American soil during the colonial period, such as the 1704 Act which was destined to undermine the growth of popery. The most significant case concerned a law, passed in 1688 by Lord Bellomond in New York, that decreed the death penalty for Catholic priests.[7]

American Puritanism

The Pilgrim Fathers who landed in America on the *Mayflower* (1620) were not only Puritans fleeing the persecutions in their motherland, England, but also people who overwhelmingly believed it was their Christian duty to spread their faith. Most of them adhered to their millenarian fears, believing that the biblical events in the Book of Revelation were imminent and that the world was on the verge of collapse. They considered themselves the new "Army of Saints," fighting against the corrupt Anglican and Roman churches. They identified with the Hebrews in Exodus: "Recognizing that England belonged to the City of Man, yet insisting on the country's divine call, they distinguished themselves from other nations by 'resurrecting' (as Edmund Calamy boasted) the Hebrews' national or federal covenant."[8]

In their desire to restore the purity of the first-century Church, these immigrants adopted a strict religious ideology largely influenced by the main tenets of Presbyterianism. This particular Protestant denomination, linked to Reformation, first evolved in Scotland and was later established in England. John Knox, a member of the Scottish Parliament, was the first to spread the confession. Presbyterian principles were rooted in Calvinist theology, and its anti–Catholicism was mainly based on the rejection of ecclesial authority. Calvin himself, trained for Catholic priesthood, had become a reformed theologian, developing a doctrine that emphasized the sole authority of the Scriptures.

John Cotton (1584–1652), a distinguished figure of the Bostonian clergy and prolific writer, was well-known as a representative of American Puritanism. His main work *The Way of the Churches of Christ in New England* (1645) is still a good reference source concerning religion and politics in colonial times. Cotton was regarded as a staunch supporter of the Puritan theocracy; he stood for the intervention of civil officials in religious affairs. As a Congregationalist, he emphasized the Puritan resentment against Rome when he said: "The Holy Spirit makes no difference between the papist paganism and the paganism of the pagans. The Papacy is a refined paganism and the state of Papists dying in Papacy is more dangerous than the state of the pagans dying in ignorance."[9]

As mentioned above, during the period that preceded the Revolutionary War, the American colonists were subjected to the English penal code, which included harsh anti–Catholic laws. In all the northern colonies, Catholics did not dare proclaim their faith or practice their religion. There were no priests to celebrate Mass or administer the sacraments, and many laws were introduced to curb the practice of Catholicism. In schools, children were taught to sing:

> Abhor that arrant whore of Rome,
> And all her blasphemies,
> And drink not of her cursed cup;
> Obey not her decrees.[10]

As Theodore Maynard points out in his *History of American Catholicism*: "It is not impossible that two or three convicted New England witches went to the gallows for having recited a *Hail Mary* rather than conversed with Beelzebub!"[11] The Puritan doctrines of colonial times encouraged not only breaking with the Church of Rome but also returning to biblical sources. From this point of view and as exiles, the first New England settlers regarded themselves, as mentioned above, the Chosen People of God, comparing themselves with the Hebrews of the Old Testament. America was for them the New Jerusalem, a Promised Land, far from the corrupt world of Old Europe. It is important to note that, at the end of the seventeenth century, the French Calvinists also announced the fall of Babylon and the reestablishment of the true faith, their prophets serving as instruments of divine revenge.

If for the famous H. L. Mencken (1880–1956), an American literary and social critic of the twenties and thirties, Puritanism was only "the haunting fear that some one, somewhere may be happy," it was not the same for Perry Miller. Miller (1931–1963), a leading specialist in Puritanism in the United States, declared, "Without some understanding of Puritanism, it may safely be said, there is no understanding of America."[12]

Miller wrote two voluminous books on the Puritans in an attempt to rehabilitate the political, literary and artistic fields in which, according to him, Puritanism excelled. If he was aware of the Puritans' image as drawn by cartoonists in the 1920s—"a gaunt lank-haired killjoy, wearing a black steeple hat"— he noted that "any acquaintance with the Puritans of the seventeenth century" revealed "not only that they did not wear such hats, but that they attired themselves in all the hues of the rainbow, and furthermore that, in their daily life, they imbibed what seem to us prodigious quantities of alcoholic beverages, with never the slightest inkling that they were doing anything sinful."[13]

Miller quotes a dominant Puritan figure, Increase Mather, who said in one of his sermons: "Drink is in itself a good creature of God, and to be received with thankfulness, but the abuse of drink is from Satan; the wine is from God, but the Drunkard is from the Devil."[14]

Miller strongly advised his readers to try to free themselves from prejudices and misconceptions that tended to distort the true mentality of the first New Englanders. He regarded Puritanism as a kind of philosophy, a code of values imported to New England by the first colonists at the beginning of the seventeenth century, as well as one of the permanent factors of American life and thought, its influence extending well beyond the colonial period. It is true that, in all the spheres of activity, its imprint remained strongly engraved and shaped American culture, specifically in the political sphere.

As for the difference between English Puritanism and American Puritanism, Perry Miller explained that these two ways of thinking were from the same Protestant origin in that they affirmed an essential principle of Reformation theology, namely that "men are not saved by their acts but by faith alone, not by their deeds. The two sides could agree on the general statement that Christians are bound to believe nothing but what the Gospel teaches, that all traditions of men 'contrary to the Word of God' are to be renounced and abhorred."[15]

Indeed, in the beginning, the English and American Puritans concurred on a considerable amount of issues. Their movement gathered learned men and authors of academic works (Cambridge was the bastion of English Puritanism). These men were strongly opposed to what they called "the immediate revelation," that is to say, to all forms of direct communication with God: "The Puritans and Anglicans stood shoulder to shoulder" against any form of "enthusiasm."[16] They agreed in recognizing that God was the Creator of the world, that He governed by pouring out His grace upon men, but without deifying them. God's Word could only be recognized through the Bible, which was the only source of spiritual knowledge. The will of God was expressed through His Providence, which itself was discovered in the manifestations of the natural world. God did not address Himself directly to the human conscience: "He does not deify them or unite them to Himself in one personality."[17]

However, several painful events linked to Puritan intolerance came to disturb the relations between English and American Puritans and caused discord and dissension among them: first, the Hutchinson affair, which had great repercussions during colonial times. This event concerned a woman's personal revolt and led her to be the first defendant in a Massachusetts court. Emigrating from England in 1634, Anne Hutchinson arrived with her husband and their fifteen children in the colony of Massachusetts. Both she and her husband bore genuine respect and admiration for the Puritan preacher John Cotton, and followed him to the New World.

Anne Hutchison was welcomed and esteemed amid the Boston community, as she was a midwife, midwifery being highly respected in those days. She was also well read in theology and organized prayer meetings, which caused great unease among magistrates. As her popularity increased, she began to attract many people, including men, to her Bible study meetings, although it was highly inappropriate for a woman to speak in public, according to biblical teachings. What is more, she began to criticize the ministers' sermons and, worst of all, emphasized the role of God's spirit through individual intuition. This meant opposing Governor John Winthrop on important religious issues since direct revelation from God was considered a heresy in Massachusetts. Disputing the Puritan belief which did not admit such a conception of Christian doctrine, Hutchinson was considered all the more rebellious as she admitted having had a close relationship with Christ.

Winthrop and his supporters brought charges against Anne Hutchinson, and she was tried by the General Court of Massachusetts. The governor of Boston, who presided over the trial, accused Anne Hutchinson of having committed acts "not fitting for her sex."[18] At the trial, Anne defended herself and boldly answered all the questions. Governor Winthrop's biographer even reported that she was the governor's "intellectual superior in everything except political judgment."[19]

Anne Hutchinson, convicted, was banished from Massachusetts. Forced into exile, she settled in Rhode Island,[20] a refuge for those who could not accept the Puritan rigor. Since then, the Bostonian woman has become an emblematic figure. Joseph P. Lash, in his biography *Eleanor and Franklin* (1971), reported that Eleanor Roosevelt had put Anne Hutchinson at the top of her list of America's greatest women.[21] Today, Hutchinson is revered as a pioneer in the struggle for religious freedom in the United States and as an advocate of women's rights.

Roger Williams was another important person who marked the American collective consciousness (1603–1683) as a great representative of the Puritan world. As a well-known English theologian, Williams played an important role in England as well as in America. After having studied at Cambridge where he obtained his bachelor of arts degree, he chose to enter the Anglican Church, but he could not abide by Archbishop Laud's harsh administration. He became a dissenter and, discovering he had the heart of a Puritan, went into exile in America. However, when he arrived in Boston, he was asked to replace a pastor who was returning to London. Williams refused to join the congregation, which, according to him, was still strongly influenced by Anglicanism. Claiming that judicial power should be separate from religious power, he finally had a clash of opinion with Governor John Winthrop. In some ways, he was Thomas Jefferson's precursor in speaking of a "wall of separation" between religion and the political power.

He also rose against the idea that the saints of New England could be compared to Hebrews in the wilderness. Williams clearly stated that no one has a right to arrogate that identity, and his statement reflected and summed up a point of view that would be adopted by most enlightened minds:

Nature knows no difference between men ... in blood, birth, bodies, geography or political arrangements. Any state, in any land, was "a ship at sea with many hundred souls"—papists and protestants, Jews and Turks and Indians—"whose weal and woe is common." What, then, was all this talk of a "new found land of Canaan," divinely granted to a New Israel for their "everlasting possession"? To declare that prophecies were unfolding through the agency of "a *people*, naturally considered"—that a ship or state represented the millennial ark of Christ—"if this be not to pull *God* and *Christ* and *Spirit* out of Heaven, and subject them into natural, sinful, inconstant men ... let Heaven and Earth judge.[22]

In addition, Williams was concerned with the well-being of the Indians and took a stand against expropriations. He declared that the king had no right to deprive the Indians of their lands. As he was practically always at odds with the Massachusetts authorities, he was put on trial by the Salem Court for divulging "dangerous opinions," which led to his expulsion from the Massachusetts Bay Colony in 1635. After being sheltered by the Indians, he took refuge in Rhode Island with a dozen companions to establish a settlement.

He founded Providence with the firm intention to separate the civil sphere from the religious one. In 1644, he published a book that became a classic in Puritan literature: *The Bloody Tenet of Persecution for the Cause of Conscience Discussed*. He equally spread the Baptist faith,[23] which he left at the end of his life, declaring that churches did not have any legitimacy and that their imposed organizations were not compatible with the Gospel.

The famous Salem witch trials at the end of the seventeenth century also stamped American Puritan history, as they created a considerable stir among the new settlers. The episode originated with a family whose father was a minister, and whose young daughter and niece were raised by two black slaves, John and Tituba. Tituba told witchcraft stories to the girls, who a few days later were taken by tremors and convulsions, followed by other young girls. Due to these morbid symptoms and their blasphemous screaming, they were declared victims of demonic possession. To the doctor's question: "Who is tormenting you?" the young girls answered: "Tituba." But they continued by accusing female members of the Puritan congregation, one of whom, accused of bewitching the young girls, was tried in only one day. After a series of executions by hanging during the summer of 1692, a poor and unfortunate man was stoned to death for not having answered to accusations. These unhappy incidents were not only related to Puritanism, but also reflected the spirit of the time, when the boundaries between religion, superstition and magic were not clear-cut.

In the Puritan theology, the infernal forces were constantly at work, and the presence of Satan was suspected everywhere under one form or the other: "To men of the Reformation, to Protestants, the Devil was no abstraction; he was an ever-present force of evil, and to their eyes it seemed obvious that his last stronghold was the wilderness of America, inhabited by his imps."[24] Unfortunately, this psychosis involved many executions, the torture of fifty-five people and the imprisonment of one hundred-and-fifty others. Governor Winthrop started to worry when the charges targeted members of his own family, and a general amnesty was issued in 1693. The story of the Salem witch trials reveals the coercive aspect of the Puritan mentality in New England.

Despite these dark and painful events, most colonists decided to remain faithful to the Church of England, but progressively adopted their own ways of thinking. They founded religious communities headed by ministers who did not depend on ecclesiastical authorities. As Perry Miller stresses to understand Puritanism we must go back to an age when "the unity of religion and politics was so axiomatic that very few men would even have grasped the idea that Church and State could be distinct."[25] Consequently, the Church was considered the center of political and social life and gathered members who were granted civil rights. To join the congregation implied a ceremony, consisting, in particular, of a public confession and election by the "saints" of the congregation. This is how the regenerate men of New England imposed their rule and formed a kind of dictatorship, "not of a single tyrant or of an economic class, but of the holy and regenerate."[26]

Thus, at a time when religion and politics were inextricably bound, the Puritan leaders assumed the right to rule on private affairs. However, as time passed by, scandals, dissension and the arrival of new immigrants undermined the moral and religious rigor of American Puritanism. By the end of the seventeenth century, the theocratic system was abandoned, and every man who was a landowner or had small income was granted the vote, which progressively brought religious tolerance. New England Puritanism thus tended to lose its revolutionary character as a religious movement. Although it remained deeply entrenched in the American mind, the movement followed the motherland's political development under the influence of the "Levellers' party,"[27] which advocated the same rights for all. As Puritanism had become the dominant faith through the interplay of historical circumstances, it acquired a conservative coloring which time only accentuated. One may note that these immigrants, fleeing political and religious intolerance, displayed the same intolerance towards later immigrants. They were regarded as inflexible people as far as morality was concerned.

One of the catalytic elements that gave a new face to the Puritan philosophy was the Great Awakening of 1740, under the guidance of Jonathan Edwards. A Puritan minister and well-educated theologian, Edwards differentiated himself from his clerical colleagues by advocating the power of a personal experience in religion. This was a revolutionary idea for the majority of people who were accustomed to listening to interminable sermons without showing any emotional response. This great revivalist movement may well have been at the origin of the evangelical upsurge that has swept America up to the present day. Adopting a new form of religiosity, Edwards privileged the manifestation of God's spirit in human souls: "'Tis extraordinary as to the degree of gracious communications and the abundant measures in which the spirit of God has been poured out on many persons. Tis extraordinary as to the extent of it, God's spirit being so remarkably poured on so many towns at once and it's making such swift progress from place to place."[28]

On the other hand, Edwards remained strongly attached to his Calvinist and Puritan roots, given his convictions regarding the realization of biblical prophecies. The Congregationalist minister was convinced that the millennium was on the verge of happening in America: "the millennium state ... is NOW going to be introduced; yea, and [that] ... AMERICA is that Part of the World which is pointed out in the Revelation of GOD for ... the glorious Scene."[29]

However, while the forms of American Puritanism evolved over the centuries, the underlying spirit seemed a constant adaptable to each episode of the history of the United States. In the collective memory, the Puritans inherited from the Pilgrim Fathers the idea that they were the new "Chosen People" and that their mission was to found and establish an ideal society, an example for the world to come, comparable to the Hebrews under the leadership of Joshua in Canaan. Even if the Puritan tradition was not shared by all the immigrants, its imprint remained sufficiently strong to mark the American spirit and to pervade the traditions and habits. The Awakenings may well have constituted the best factors of the Puritan survival through the specific phenomenon of mass behavior which gradually became the mark of social pattern.

It would become necessary to wait until the end of the nineteenth century to see a phenomenon of protest against and rejection of this mentality, considered by the American writers of the inter–war period a harmful check on individual happiness. John Steinbeck, Ernest Hemingway, and William Faulkner, among others, vigorously denounced the Puritan rhetoric and mentality of their forbears.

Thus, little by little, the American identity began to take shape, derived from complex and different currents of thoughts. On the one hand, it was still marked by the Calvinistic concept of predestination involving the ideas of salvation and redemption. On the other hand, it was characterized by a more intellectual approach: an acute sense of responsibility towards the world, since the United States regarded its mission as a moral and spiritual duty.

When Congress celebrated the peace treaty with the United Kingdom, on December 11, 1783, the Reverend John Rodgers exclaimed in New York: "What great thing has the God of Providence done for our race! By the revolution we today celebrate, He has provided an asylum for the oppressed in all the nations of the earth."[30]

From the start of American colonization, the expression "an asylum for the oppressed" had become a true slogan and was often used in the sermons at the time of the Declaration of Independence. As time went on, the notion of refuge or haven for the oppressed remained associated with America. Another phrase was also evoked to emphasize America's responsibility towards the world: "the eyes of the world are upon you," a sentence with a biblical resonance which became the refrain of the Texas state anthem. From John Winthrop's time to the present day, these words have been used to highlight America's role as a model for all nations. This was emphasized by the British politician Charles Fox (1749–1806), before Parliament, when he declared that American resistance to British oppression had preserved the liberties of the whole of humanity.[31]

In his final speech, President Andrew Jackson (1767–1845) reminded Americans that Providence had chosen them to be "the guardians of liberty" and that they should always be aware of it in order to protect mankind.[32] At the time, most people believed that the example of America would be contagious and that all the nations of the world would follow it. This is what Abraham Lincoln meant when he said that America was "the last best hope of earth."

The New World was destined to become the new empire which God had set aside for America, nurtured by the aspirations and hopes of a "Chosen People." This messianic vision had already appeared in the course of the colonial period, but it was mainly at the time of the Revolutionary War that it began to surface again. Associated with the image of a glorious America, the expansionist doctrine gradually and implicitly asserted itself as the embodiment of a "Manifest Destiny." John Adams (1735–1826), second president of the United States, was convinced that the new nation was destined to cover "the northern part of that whole quarter of the globe." This idea was often underlined in the speeches and sermons of preachers during religious celebrations. On the occasion of the 1819 Treaty with Spain, David Trimble, a politician, stated: "The Father of the universe in his peculiar Providence has given natural boundaries to every continent and kingdom — permanent, physical, imperishable barriers to every nation, to shield it from invasion. God fixed the natural limits of our country ... and man cannot change them."[33]

Thus, expansionism was justified in the same way as the first settlements. However, the true objective of this campaign in favor of freedom was to undermine the threat which European despotisms might still exert.

Expansion could thus be regarded as a defensive measure to ensure greater safety to the citadel of liberty. Naturally, when expansion depended on the good will of neighboring states when they sought to join the union freely, there was no need to impose force. Samuel Cooper became the spokesman of this mode of adhesion to the federal state by declaring in 1780 during the inaugural ceremony of a new government in Massachusetts: "Conquest is not the aim of these rising states. Sound policy must even forbid it. We have before us an object more truly great and honorable." He added, "America should become the seat of knowledge and liberty, of agriculture and commerce, and of the arts, and what is more important than all, of Christian piety and virtue."[34]

As a rule, territorial expansion was based on the principle of freedom, given that the main principle of federalism entailed the free adhesion of the states. Since a constitutional amendment preserved local freedoms in most fields of everyday life, the scattered populations gathered around a federal government for the questions of general interest. After the Civil War, Andrew Johnson (1808–1875), seventeenth president of the United States, held federalism in such high regard that he thought the American political system would one day be able to extend to all the civilized nations of the world.[35]

America's mission and destiny were to influence and to set an example for the whole world. Unfortunately, the expansionistic policy was more concerned with protecting the country's interests than with exerting real philanthropy towards conquered countries. Yet the first settlers dreamed of a glorious and powerful America, and their enthusiasm was expressed by spokesmen whose eloquence reinforced these aspirations. Timothy Dwight, president of Yale University, evoked this somewhat lofty vision of American destiny in his farewell speech, on July 25, 1776, during which he described the American continent as an Eden, its the mild climate creating harmony between inhabitants who accepted the principles of civil government. According to him, never since the building of the Tower of Babel had the world known such a united people, and this fact could only lead to great benefits.

According to Dwight, the American empire was to be the last and most glorious on earth, raising human progress to the limits of perfection. Hidden by the Divine Hand until the collapse of European grandeur, this blessed place would testify to the "consummation of excellency." In an eloquent speech in the millenarian vein, the orator did not hesitate to quote Isaiah, comparing America to the wilderness that would "blossom like a rose" and become an "everlasting kingdom." When he addressed his students, he reminded them that they had to take part in the building of American glory, even though the future generations would collect the fruit. They had to lay the groundwork for American grandeur by sacrificing their individual interests and acting as "citizens of a world and like candidates for a name that shall survive the conflagration ... for the honor of mankind and your Maker."[36]

This speech encapsulated all the ideas that are contained in the expression "Manifest Destiny"; yet it dates back to a period prior to the coining of the term since the speech was delivered only several weeks after the signing of the Declaration of Independence. Moreover, the Revolutionary War itself had been interpreted according to religious principles. For most Americans, the afflictions and torments caused by the conflict were the result of acts committed against God's will. Nathaniel West, a notable public official at the time, spoke of public humiliation caused by moral transgressions, adding that God's punishment was to make people aware of the existence of national guilt: "God's purpose is to discipline us by national judgments into obedience to Himself."[37] This remark evokes a whole range of themes inscribed at the core of the biblical spirit: anger, judgment and redemption, purification, death, sacrifice and rebirth, baptism, etc. Later, Lincoln's assassination was also interpreted in a religious perspective with vocabulary borrowed from the New Testament, "the just dying for the unjust."[38]

If in England, Puritanism remained a marginal religious movement, in the United States, it participated in the construction of a national consciousness. The first wave of immigration left a deep imprint in the American culture insofar as, at the time of the Civil War, the great majority of the population was Anglo-Saxon. As Perry Miller noted, the vitality of Puritanism never really died and has always been present with its multifaceted aspects in the history of America. Let us note that on the ethical level, it participated in the positive characteristics of the American temper. The French essayist Hector Saint John de Crèvecoeur settled in America, and in *Letters from an American Farmer* (1782), he drew a moving and pleasant portrait of the first colonist, called "What is an American?":

> What attachment can a poor European emigrant have for a country where he had nothing? The knowledge of the language, the love of a few kindred as poor as himself, were the only cords that tied him: his country is now that which gives him land, bread, protection, and consequence:
> *Ubi panis ibi patria* is the motto of all emigrants. What then is the American, this new man? He is either a European, or the descendant of a European, hence that strange mixture of blood, which you will find in no other country. I could point out to you a family whose grandfather was an Englishman, whose wife was Dutch, whose son married a French woman, and whose present four sons have now four wives of different nations. *He* is an American, who, leaving behind him all his ancient prejudices and manners, receives new ones from the new mode of life he has embraced, the new government he obeys, and the new rank he holds. He becomes an American by being received in the broad lap of our great *Alma Mater*.[39]

If at present, American culture often appears cloaked in a Puritan ideology that seems to undermine its national ideal, let us not forget this notion of *alma mater* which ran through the centuries and played a crucial role in the birth of the American nation.

2

Religious Motivations in the American Revolution

During the eighteenth century, predication played a crucial role in the shaping of a revolutionary spirit. As tensions were growing between the colonists and the British, many preachers, especially the Congregationalists in New England, began to advocate political freedom in their sermons. In 1776, most evangelical clerics considered the Revolutionary War as a noble cause.

Linking biblical images to the Enlightenment, many of them approved of all political revolts if the governments did not fulfill their duties for the good of people; most people were convinced that American virtue prevailed over British corruption.[1] It was also believed that England and the European nations were still under the influences of dark forces, and that a break from such countries would bring some kind of spiritual liberation.

As a spirit of dissent pervaded the religious communities throughout the British colonies, the influence of the nascent Age of Enlightenment expanded in the intellectual circles. The American intelligentsia of the time put forward its ideas to which the Founding Fathers gave form in the wording of the Declaration of Independence. What is often refuted about these inspirers of the American institutional bodies is the religious basis underlying their political assumptions.

Nearly all eighteenth-century thinkers, the so-called Deists, were animated by strong religious feelings inherited from their cultural background and on which they founded their political theories. The majority of these thinkers adopted a "natural rights" philosophy, which rested on a transcendental vision of life. The seventeenth century English philosopher John Locke opened the path, to such an extent that, according to some historians, his political theory acted as a prelude to the writing of the American Constitution.

As Becker put it: "Jefferson copied Locke."[2]

Locke's Letter Concerning Toleration

Locke (1632–1704) was an English Protestant philosopher who wrote extensively on religion. He believed that "his writings would benefit true religions."[3] Although he was raised as a Puritan Presbyterian, he adopted a liberal theology which greatly influenced the Enlightenment French scholars, mainly Voltaire and Rousseau. Locke was viewed as a Christian humanist, and he was well aware of the difficulties emanating from the great variety of religious sects that had sprung up in his country since Reformation, leading to serious dissensions within the political sphere. Locke himself had to flee to Holland under false suspicion of involvement in a political plot, and grasped this opportunity to write his *Letter Concerning Toleration*. At the time, the Church of England was the official religion and dissenting Protestants were still subject to legal prosecution. In his work, he defined a line of theology which included the general principles that seemed to transcend all differences within these groups, namely, "the existence of God, his work as Creator, the duties owned him by mankind, and the expectation of reward and punishment."[4]

The main tenet of Locke's natural rights philosophy referred to a law of nature "writ in the hearts of mankind" a sort of "confident intuition of a universal order made by nature's God" which could be regarded as "the preamble to the political faith of the Dissenter, as of the subsequent Declaration of Independence."[5] Having witnessed his country's religious and political upheavals, he looked for a new form of relationship between religion and government. Locke argued that civil unrest was often due to the confrontation between both institutions and considered they should be separated. It was in that perspective that he wrote his *Letter Concerning Toleration*.

Locke's *Letter Concerning Toleration* was largely inspired by the Bible, from which he drew the foundation of the separation of the political body and the expression of personal faith. In his work, he emphasized that sovereigns should not be religious leaders or heads of a church, and that every man was allowed to adore God in the manner he thought to be most proper, respecting his own consciences. Locke invoked Matthew's words: "For where two or three gather together because they are mine, I will be right there among them" (Matthew 18:20).

The philosopher reminded his contemporaries that, in accordance with the biblical spirit, it was actually the Church that should be persecuted. This was Christ's message and the Gospel was very clear about it. The Church did not advocate tormenting or constraining people to accept its own beliefs or using weapons to convert them. Thus, it appeared that the Lockian theory was founded on Christian injunctions, although it excluded

Catholics and atheists! This fact may prefigure the shortcomings and paradoxes that underlay the American constitutional texts.

Locke's particular interpretation of the biblical text led to many objections from several scholars, given his environmental psychology based on an elitist vision of society: "Locke either invokes the traditional morality to win acceptance for a theory based upon hard self-interest, or ignored the traditional morality entirely. The former is exemplified by the chapter on property in the *Second Treatise*, which begins with the observation that God has given the earth to mankind in common and ends by rationalizing the unlimited accumulations of wealth."[6] The Protestant key to understanding the Scriptures according to which wealth is a sign of divine election finds an echo in this comment (Locke used to blame poverty on the poor). His theory, although resting on Christian principles, lacked spiritual dimension, preventing his arguments from being coherent with the true principles of an orthodox interpretation of the Sacred Book.

In spite of these theological ambiguities, Locke's conception of nature's God influenced Jefferson and the Founding Fathers, when they wrote the main articles of the Declaration of Independence. For the British, French and American philosophers of the Enlightenment, Christianity, orthodox or unorthodox, was socially useful, as it acted as a transcendent link that bound all people. In fact, what mattered was to find, in the word of God, just as Locke had done, the justification of ethical and political principles. "They had to demonstrate that 'life, liberty and the pursuit of happiness' were according to nature and the will of God, whereas tyranny and cruelty and the taking of property without consent were not."[7]

The Influence of the French Enlightenment on the American Revolution: Rousseau, Voltaire and Montesquieu

Rousseau's contribution to the spirit of the American Revolution came from his belief in the authority of reason in matters of faith and personal interpretation of the Scriptures. His spiritual inclinations carried him to trust his intuitions and made him aware of what was essential. As a deist in the broad sense of the term, like most of his intellectual fellow men, his main preoccupation was tolerance and benevolence as the two qualities were best embodied in the Christian faith. His *Social Contract* encouraged men, "in state of nature," to listen to their own consciences in the accomplishments of their civil duties. Ethical truths appeared self-evident to Rousseau, belonging to a transcendental logic. The reference to nature and nature's

God is echoed in the Declaration of Independence which strongly evokes Rousseaus theories:

> The preamble to the Declaration of Independence makes its case in universal terms. It appeals not to the British constitution, but to nature and nature's God. It speaks not of the rights of Englishmen known to lawyers but of rights of man self-evident to all. These qualities led an earlier generation of historians to assume that the Declaration of Independence had been influenced by Rousseau.[8]

The concept of "nature's God," often linked to Natural Law, took on an extreme importance in eighteenth-century philosophical thinking, but has always been very difficult to define. Indeed, even for Voltaire, who epitomized the spirit of the Enlightenment, this idea of nature's God was not really well defined; Voltaire often referred to the Christian teachings. Stating that Natural Law was that which nature clearly demonstrated to all men, Voltaire illustrated his point by referring to a biblical example—for instance, that men who had cultivated their land with their own hands had the right to harvest the products of it. Thus he believed that human rights could only be founded upon Natural Law. Nevertheless he reminded his audiences that the great rule which governed this concept throughout the world was the well-known divine injunction *Do unto others as you would have done unto yourself.* By quoting this sentence from the Gospel, Voltaire emphasized an implicit and innate propensity to humanize an abstract Deity devoid of compassion for mankind.

This transcendental shift in meaning from a watchmaker God to a more human God may also be perceived in Voltaire's own conception regarding the role of Reason. This "goddess" faculty, as he pompously called it, should be used to control men's passions when they are confronted by religious disputes within the political arena. For him, "the era of public harmony" could only occur through the "triumph of Reason." Citing as an example people who were compelled to flee their countries to avoid persecution, he noted: "It is in the interest of the State that exiled sons should be allowed to return, with humility, to their father's hearths; humanity demands it, Reason counsels it, and politicians need not be afraid of it."[9] Now, humility is a virtue inscribed at the heart of Christian ethics and does not flow from the principle of Natural Laws.

Regarding the use of Reason by politicians and citizens alike, Voltaire's major principle was based on the virtue of tolerance, guided by the "supreme faculty" in governmental affairs and public life:

> Is each individual citizen, then, to be permitted to believe only in what his reason tells him, to think only what his reason, be it enlightened or misguided, may dictate? Yes, indeed he should, provided always that he threatens no disturbance to public order.... The more the Christian religion is divine, the less does it belong. For a man is under no obligation to believe or not to believe. His duties are to

respect the law as and customs of his country, and if you claim that it is a crime not to believe in the prevailing religion, you are pointing the finger of accusation against our ancestors, the first Christians, and you are justifying the actions of those who were previously blamed for putting them to death.[10]

This universal injunction significantly influenced the theoretical background of the Declaration of Independence, even though Voltaire's arguments did not put forward original ideas, considering Locke's and other eighteenth-century philosophers' strong influence, also inscribed at the core of this institutional document. One may also notice that Voltaire's deistic thinking appears quite ambiguous, as his philosophical rhetoric often borrows biblical arguments. In a chapter of his *Treatise on Tolerance* entitled "The consequences of Intolerance," he insisted on the fact that Christian religion should be more divine, since intolerance produced only hypocrites or rebels. What emerges from these reflections is that the principle of tolerance is a fundamental element in eighteenth century Christianity. Here again, the idea of deism, which commonly defines the Maker of all things, the Supreme Being and not the Abrahamic God, leads to paradoxes and confusion. The last chapter of *Treatise on Tolerance* ends with "A prayer to God" which, for a deist, seems highly peculiar:

> May all men remember they are brothers! May they abhor the tyranny which would imprison the soul just as much as they execrate that highway robbery which makes off with the fruit of honest work and application. If the scourges of war are not to be avoided, let us at least not hate one another or tear each other apart in the midst of peace, but let us use the moment of our earthly existence to praise, in a thousand different but equal languages, from Siam to California, Thy goodness which has given us that moment.[11]

In this excerpt, one may wonder to which kind of God Voltaire was addressing himself. So-called Deists normally asserted that the Divine Entity did not intervene in worldly affairs, that He had created the world and human reason to recognize His creation. Let us not forget that Enlightenment thinkers were said to regard the world as a vast machine set in motion by its inventor, that unvarying laws (natural laws) revealed themselves through the light of reason and nature. Generally, these freethinkers professed no article of faith. Only human logic and common sense contributed to the understanding of their earthly existence. Under these conditions, was Voltaire a true Deist? This question is important since the Age of Enlightenment greatly inspired Jefferson and the framers of the American Constitution who were nevertheless categorized as Deists.

The concept of the Law of Nature was also present in Charles de Montesquieu's *The Spirit of Laws*. According to Montesquieu natural laws, emanating from a transcending power, protected man's natural rights. A French political thinker educated at the Catholic College of Juilly, Montesquieu

2—Religious Motivations in the American Revolution 35

achieved great success with the publication of his *Persian Letters*, a satire of the Parisian society seen through the eyes of a Persian visitor. His masterwork, *The Spirit of Laws* (1748) made him very popular in Great Britain and in America. Montesquieu, according to some American historians, had a powerful influence on the Founders, particularly on Jefferson and James Madison of Virginia, the "Father of the Constitution." The Declaration of Independence refers to these "inalienable laws" that are based on the acknowledgment of natural laws endowed by the Creator. In Book I, "Of Laws in General," of *The Spirit of Laws*, Montesquieu explains the notion of Natural Law, related to God as Creator:

> God is related to the universe, as Creator and Preserver; the laws by which He created all things are those by which He preserves them. He acts according to these rules, because He knows them; He knows them because He made them; and He made them, because they are in relation to His wisdom and power.... Thus the creation, which seems an arbitrary act, supposes laws as invariable as those of the fatality of the Atheists. It would be absurd to say that the Creator might govern the world without those rules since without them it could not subsist.[12]

Montesquieu's reflection is crucial, since it sheds light on the chiaroscuro and nebulous assumptions of the Enlightenment which focused on a clockmaker God, unable to interfere in human affairs. For Montesquieu, God is therefore responsible for these laws which do not proceed from the "big bang" of some Intelligent Designer. At the time, Montesquieu was extensively read by the American intelligentsia, and was frequently quoted on political issues in pre-revolutionary British America. His theory on the separation of powers to avoid the emergence of despotism largely inspired the framers of the American Constitution.

Yet, although Montesquieu believed in natural or physical laws sustained by God, he recognized that positive laws, instituted by fallible men, were necessary, even if they were "subject ... to ignorance and error, and hurried away by a thousand impetuous passions."[13] Furthermore, human laws and social institutions should be adapted to a variety of factors "to the people from whom they are framed..., to the nature and principle of each government ... to the religion of the inhabitants."[14] Like his contemporaries, Montesquieu considered religions as a check against despotic power. He did not go as far as Voltaire, who declared that religion was the opium of the people, but stressed that it had a beneficent influence on civil society when it was not an instrument of fanaticism and oppression.

The Spirit of Laws became an "American classic" as early as 1776 and at the time of the constitutional convention, in 1787, political debates seemed to unfurl under Montesquieu's eye. All the prestigious libraries, including those of Princeton and Yale, possessed copies of the work and people used it as a manual of political theory. Long extracts were published in newspapers: all revolutionary leaders acknowledged the French thinker as a great inspirer. The American historian George Bancroft reported that Washington himself possessed Montesquieu's main texts in his own library.[15]

Benjamin Franklin's Political Philosophy

As with his European counterparts, Benjamin Franklin's political philosophy was also pervaded by religious motives. He was regarded as a national icon by his fellow citizens; although many regarded him as a skeptical philosopher more attached to an ethos of self-interest than to the study of spiritual matters. Franklin's public statements are worth taking into account, in order to fully understand the depth of his political and religious motivations. As the most notable of the American delegates who participated in the elaboration of the American Republic, he (like his European counterparts) was labeled a Deist, believing in a transcendent Entity to whom the role of guide or Provider of graces was implicitly denied. Yet, if one reads his writings carefully, one notices that Franklin often refers to God's Providence, not only through his boundless generosity but most often to compensate for the misdeeds resulting from human failings.

Like most of his contemporaries, Franklin advocated the secular rationalism of Enlightenment. He nevertheless opened a breach to demonstrate that the practice of virtue tended to overlap the issue of natural rights, in the sense that all men were favored with a clear insight of Good and Evil and that, through the interplay of an inner light, they could grasp the advantages of being virtuous. The notion of "natural rights," he argued, was linked to the acknowledgment of virtues, which was a simple and natural way of respecting the rights of one's fellow men. Being good, temperate, honest, generous, frank and industrious was an implicit way of recognizing freedom and equality among men.

Virtue thus contained all the necessary conditions to become a good citizen and, moreover, encapsulated the seeds of private happiness. Franklin pointed out that discourtesy bred resentment and posed a threat to good relationships among men. Honesty and sincerity became the base of his self-improvement objective: "Use no hurtful Deceive," he noted in his *Autobiography*.[16] Of course, such intentions were not easy to realize, as human beings are generally inclined to look for their own interests. Raised in a Presbyterian family, Franklin was still influenced by the ambitious principle of the Puritan Doctrine of New England. In his writings one finds, at times, echoes of the English seventeenth-century author John Bunyan, who in his successful work *The Pilgrim's Progress*, depicted a protagonist who leaves his wife and children to go and combat, allegorically, all his vices, in quest of moral perfection. Franklin gives a good example of the zealous Puritan whose aim is to reach an angelic purity:

> It was about this time (in the early 1730s) that I conceived the bold and arduous project of arriving at moral perfection. I wished to live without committing any fault at any time; I would conquer all that natural inclination, custom, or company might lead me into. As I knew or thought I knew, what was right or wrong, I did not see why I might not *always* do the one and avoid the other. But I soon found I had undertaken a task of more difficulty than I had imagined. While my attention was taken up in guarding against one fault, I was often surprised by another. Habit took the advantage of inattention. Inclination was sometimes too strong for reason. I concluded at length, that the mere speculative conviction that it was our interest to be completely virtuous was not sufficient to prevent our slipping, and that the contrary habits must be broken and good ones acquired and established, before we can have any dependence on a steady uniform rectitude of conduct. For this purpose, I therefore contrived the following method.[17]

Then Franklin sets out to establish the list of thirteen virtues that he wished to practice in order to reach perfection and become a model of Christian charity: "Temperance, order, resolution, frugality, industry, sincerity, justice, moderation, cleanliness, tranquility, chastity and humility. Imitate Jesus and Socrates."[18]

All these precepts are inscribed at the core of the Christian faith. It is an idealistic vision of life and, obviously, no one knows to what extent the young Franklin honored these virtues! The modern reader is struck by this self-imposed discipline which embodies the strict and austere Puritan moral conduct. Many Puritan figures kept a diary where they noted all their human failings in order to better their religious and social behavior. Yet Franklin stretched his moral axioms and gave them a tone which seems universal to all religions. This may explain why Franklin's burial gathered a great assembly composed of different religious groups, Protestants from many established churches and denominations, Catholics and Jews. It is undeniable though that, gradually, Franklin escaped from the grip of Puritanism, to the bitter disappointment of his parents. Legend has it that once having come close to death at sea, he stated that if he had been a Catholic, he would have made the vow to build a chapel; as he was not, he mentioned a lighthouse. The myth of Winthrop's "City upon a Hill" is here again revived, evoking the biblical metaphor and the symbolic expression of America as a "light for the world."

Benjamin's resort to the practice of virtue, with the aim of bringing harmony and civility among citizens, remained a basis for his political philosophy. The theory of natural rights was tacitly expressed through an ethical dimension, but he was aware of the difficulty in safeguarding people's rights, since men often appeared fallible when their own interests were at stake. At the time of the Revolution, Franklin argued that the colonists were entitled to have representatives in the British Parliament and that they should enjoy the same rights as the British. He regarded these issues as worthy to be solved through peaceful negotiations, but as he gradually realized that such an approach became unrealizable between both parties, he turned towards his French friends. In 1776, as a delegate of the Second Continental Congress, he set sail for France, hoping to convince his allies to come to America's rescue.

In Franklin's opinion, the Revolutionary War was a necessity, but he sensed it as a painful experience since he always treated military interventions as foolish. The following excerpt of a letter written in 1783 testifies to his aversion for war: "At length we are in peace, God be praised, and long, very long, may it continue. All wars are follies, very expensive, and very mischievous ones. When will mankind be convinced of this, and agree to settle their differences by arbitration? Were they to do it, by the cast of a dye, it would be better than fighting and destroying one another."[19] Franklin's appeal for true reconciliation and proposal for an international peace between the belligerents arose from his deep sense of philanthropy, although he remained aware of the necessity to curb and undermine the expansionist policies of nations whenever possible.

During the drafting of the American Constitution, the presence of the 81-year-old Franklin was viewed as a favorable influence. He endeavored to help the delegates harmonize their points of view and played the role of a diplomat, using every means to bring about compromises. At the end of the Constitutional Convention, he stated that any form of government was a "blessing," if it was "well administered."[20] As Lorraine Smith Pangle notes:

> He urged from the outset that the delegates all regard themselves as representatives of the whole rather than of separate states, and during tense negotiations, his humour and gentle admonitions helped bring the fractious delegates together into difficult but necessary compromises. His charming speech at the close of the Convention, urging all to mistrust their own judgment a little, defer to the wisdom of the majority on the matters that still troubled them, and give the Constitution their unqualified support, ensured that it would be unanimously endorsed by the states represented and signed by all of the delegates except three.[21]

Therefore, Franklin's political ideas were based more on moral principles than on the respect of the citizen's civil rights, the ethical dimension prevailing on social constraints. Rationalism and reason emerged from two different sources: philosophy and ethics. Finally, Franklin opted for the second as it often sprang from a religious origin transcending the human limits of reason. He noted in his *Almanack*: "To lead a virtuous life, and go to heaven in season, you've just so much more need of Faith, as you have less of Reason."²² Nevertheless, he put aside the metaphysical issue of reason, focusing on its usefulness to establish concord and good relationships among citizens. Contrary to the main Protestant doctrine which stipulates that men are saved by their faith, he was convinced that good deeds were the surest means to obtain redemption. Consequently, a good pagan was more pleasing to the eyes of God than a bad Christian: "A virtuous heretic shall be saved before a wicked Christian: for there is no such a thing as voluntary error."²³

Franklin's religious approach seemed to forecast Jeremy Bentham's most influential philosophical system. Born in London in the mid–eighteenth century, Bentham originated a doctrine known as Utilitarianism: "This system was formed around the dual ideas that all reform should be dictated by the greatest happiness of the greatest number as a measure of right and wrong, and that human motivation was founded on self-interest. The coincidence of interest and duty became an ideal of social and moral reform."²⁴ In his writings, Franklin also put forward the idea of finding happiness emphasizing the notion of contentment and pleasure when one had accomplished an action in conformity with one's conscience. In nineteenth-century England this theme of "virtue rewarded" became preponderant during the Victorian era. During that period, another English philosopher, John Stuart Mill, stressed the importance of the moral improvement of mankind emerging from the right course of action.

Likewise, Franklin, in a letter to the *Pennsylvania Gazette* in April 1730, summarized his main political philosophy which was deeply inspired by religious arguments based on a utilitarian viewpoint. According to him, true wisdom came from a transcendental order, and governments have often relied on Divine intervention for the benefit of society. Ministers and the clergy, being His best representatives, deserved respect and consideration, as they should personify morality and truth. Their responsibility was great in the sense that if they failed in the accomplishment of their mission, they would be disregarded and scorned by the citizens:

> The wise men have in all ages thought government necessary for the good of Mankind; and, that wise governments have always thought religion necessary for the well ordering and well being of society, and accordingly have ever been careful to encourage and protect the ministers of it, paying them the highest public honors, that their doctrines might thereby meet with the greater respect among the common people; and that if there were no truth in religion, or the salvation of men's soul not worth regarding, yet, in consideration of the inestimable service done to mankind by the clergy, as they are the teachers and supporters of virtue and morality, without which no society could long subsist, prudent men should be very cautious how they say or write any thing that might bring them into contempt, and thereby weaken their hands and render their labours ineffectual.²⁵

This text is rooted in the American tradition and could have been written by Governor Winthrop one century earlier. It shows the extensive gap separating the French Enlightenment from the American Enlightenment. Considering these statements, the two countries stand far apart regarding their conception of political systems, as France succeeded in elaborating a secular political frame. In America, the notion of civil religion, which emerged during the twentieth century, stands as an effort to conciliate both politics and religion, but appears quite controversial in certain circles as it seems to infringe on people's convictions when they do not belong to any religious affiliations. At the same time, it contradicts the stance of the "good heretic," who may act according to ethical principles, in all honesty and sincerity.

While many historians reported Franklin's indifference to religious matters in his daily life and behavior, this apparent aloofness may be explained through the fact that he detached himself from the teachings of Calvinist Christianity. A friend of the evangelist George Whitefield, Franklin never shared his religious beliefs and convictions, even though he became his publisher. Franklin reported in his *Autobiography* that on one occasion, after Whitefield had given a homily, the preacher requested donations for charitable work. Franklin disagreed on principle and had decided that he would not give a penny. Having a few coppers, silver dollars and pistoles in gold in his pocket, he was determined not to soften. But as the evangelist went on preaching, he could not prevent himself from gradually emptying his pockets, starting with the pennies and ending with the pistoles of gold. This anecdote reveals Franklin's good temper and human generosity.

As regards toleration and freedom of religion, Franklin's position reflects his own personality: honest, frank and open-minded. If he favored both principles as a source of social harmony, focusing on their usefulness, he never criticized the multifaceted aspect of religion in the United States. All religious churches and denominations were founded on the acknowledgment of a common God. "The essence of religion," Franklin averted, "lies in the existence of a providential God who is to be served by doing good to men and the existence of an afterlife of rewards and punishments."[26] Franklin's reflection on God's providence is another sign contradicting his reputation as a freethinker or even a Deist. In a speech at the Constitutional Convention, he echoed not only a biblical sentence but also Shakespeare's line "There is Providence in the fall of a sparrow" (*Hamlet*), which in Franklin's words, became: "I have lived, Sir, a long time; and the longer I live, the more convincing proofs I see of this truth—that God governs in the affairs of men. And if a sparrow cannot fall to the ground without his notice, it is probable that an empire cannot rise without his aid."[27]

All in all, Franklin's spiritual and political legacy deeply affected the American spirit. Having struggled against all forms of corruption and wishing peace, justice and concord in the American political community, he reflected the social progress and improvement made since the colonial period through a jovial temper filled with optimism and faith, even though his liberal thinking did not always advocate the traditional interpretation of the Sacred texts.

Thomas Jefferson's "Wall of Separation between Church and State"

The principal author of the Declaration of Independence, Thomas Jefferson was also regarded as a Deist by American and European historians. Although he stood for the separation of politics and religion, the third president of the United States issued many momentous statements concerning his own religious convictions and beliefs, but for him, Deism stood for a theological approach rather than a religious doctrine. He was born in Albemarle County, Virginia, into a family belonging to the social and intellectual elite. Raised as an Anglican, before the Episcopalian Church was founded, he did not consider himself an Episcopalian. While many of his writings dealt with religious questions, Jefferson never affiliated himself with a specific denomination. Tempted at one time by the Unitarian faith, he never joined the church. However, in spite of Jefferson's non-affiliation to a specific religious group, his upbringing, culture and conduct did not reflect the distinctive traits of a liberal freethinker.

Jefferson recognized that Deism was a generic term expressing a philosophical movement based upon the belief in a transcendent God—the Supreme Being, the Sustainer of the Universe. He supported the advocates of the Age of Enlightenment, arguing that reason alone could grasp the idea of the existence and nature of God. He agreed with the Enlightenment thinkers who tended to view the universe as a "clock" set in motion by the Creator and regulated by natural law. Yet, he sustained the idea of a God-Providence who maintained the universe and kept it out of chaos:

> I hold (without appeal to Revelation) that when we take a new view of the universe, in its part general or particular, it is impossible for the human mind not to perceive and feel a conviction of design, consummate skill, and indefinite power in every atom of composition. The movements of the heavenly bodies, so exactly held their course by the balance of centrifugal and centripetal forces, the structure of our earth itself, with its distribution of lands, waters and atmosphere, animal and vegetable bodies, examined in all their minutest particles.... It is impossible! I say, for the human mind not to believe that there is, in all this, design, cause and effect, up to an ultimate cause, a fabricator of all things from matter and motion.... We see, too, evident proofs of the necessity of a superintending power to maintain the universe in its course and order.[28]

Deists rejected the mystical aspects of Christianity (miracles) and Incarnation. For them, Christ was a teacher of morals and his teachings matched the principles of natural law. They were interested in the figure of Christ as a human being because they were more attached to morality and ethics than to supernatural elements. Jefferson spoke their language on several of these points, but, generally speaking, he seemed to rely on a more "human" God. What is certain is that he too rejected Calvinism. In a letter to Ezra Stiles, dated June 25, 1819, he wrote a well-known sentence: "You say you are a Calvinist. I am not. I am of a sect by myself, as far as I know." He confirmed the statement in his correspondence with John Adams, declaring that he could never address Calvin's God, whom he considered an Atheist, adding that his religion was Demonism. These reflections illustrate the eighteenth century's growing lack of interest in radical Calvinism. In a sense, it brought religious relief to certain American Christians who felt liberated from the burden of spiritual determinism, the origin of which sprang from the complex understanding of the dogma of predestination.

What is worth noticing in Jefferson's behavior is not so much his personal feelings towards religion as his condemnation of the evils brought about by clashes among religions. His own creed was not what mattered; in a letter to the Danbury (Connecticut) Baptist Association on January 1, 1802, he said:

> Believing with you that religion is a matter which lies solely between man and his God, that he owes account to none other for his faith or his worship, that the legislative powers of government reach actions only, and not opinions, I contemplate with sovereign reverence that act of the whole American people which declared that their legislature should make no law respecting an establishment of religion, or prohibiting the free exercise thereof, thus building a wall of separation between Church and State.[29]

This metaphor of the "wall of separation" between Church and State has remained engraved in all memories. However, what appears paradoxical in the modern reader's eye is the fact that some of Jefferson's political rhetoric was imbued with religious assertions. In his short essay "The Philosophy of Jesus of Nazareth," inspired by his own experience of life and the teachings as given by Matthew, Mark, Luke and John, Jefferson was undoubtedly in search of spiritual models that could shed light on the way the Americans should conduct their lives in order to become respectful citizens. The fact that he had taken out all the passages relating to Jesus' miracles may be shocking to orthodox Christians, but what mattered to him was the evangelical message, devoid of supernatural events, as these, he argued, were intended to convince the unbelievers. Far from being an enemy to the traditional conception of the Christian faith, Jefferson intended to prove that the adhesion to such a religious creed would provide a frame in which the individual could easily follow the simple and clear message of the Teacher of "common sense."

However, in advocating the separation of Church and State, Jefferson did not seek to interfere with religion in general, regarded as a guarantee of moral conduct favoring the good relationship between citizens, but to draw a line between two different spheres. The *Jefferson Notes* contains myriads of statements emphasizing the fact that the intermingling of clerical institutions and public life was to be banished. Jefferson was very firm and clear about his governmental initiative:

> Because religious belief, or non-belief, is such an important part of every person's life, freedom of religion affects every individual. Religious institutions that use government power in support of themselves and force their views on persons of other faiths, or of no faith, undermine all our civil rights. Moreover, state support of an established religion tends to make the clergy irresponsive to their own people, and leads to corruption within religion itself. Erecting the "wall of separation between Church and State," therefore, is absolutely essential in a free society. We have solved, by fair experiment, the great and interesting question whether freedom of religion is compatible with order in government and obedience to the laws. And we have experienced the quiet as well as the comfort which result from leaving every one to profess freely and openly those principles of religion which are the inductions of his own reason and the serious convictions of his inquiries.[30]

From time immemorial, as Jefferson noted, freedom of religion has constituted one of the most delicate issues that confront human beings. In this paragraph, Jefferson truly deserves the title of "enlightened thinker," given the right tone and the clarity that pervade the text, the notion of toleration being expressed with an utmost gravity as a corollary to the respect of civil rights. The reference to the clerics relates Jefferson's own disappointment in his dealings with priests of whom he disapproved, on account of their authoritarian conducts. He considered them as "fallible" and "uninspired" men, having "assumed dominion over the faith of others." Most Protestant denominations have practically no ecclesial hierarchy, so the tendency was great for the ministers and preachers to impose their own views and religious directives. In the end, Jefferson could be regarded as a Christian humanist rather than a Deist, considering the core ideas of his political philosophy, condensed in his personal wish to allow his citizens to profess their own faith. Whatever has been said about Jefferson's personality, as a religious, philosophical or political figure, or even as a mere individual with his shortcomings and failings, the man breathed new life into the American community by brilliantly demonstrating the precious benefits of religious liberty.

From these observations, it appears that the eighteenth-century freethinkers, who originated the Era of Enlightenment, did not only base their argumentation on reason and personal experience to rationalize the existence of God, but also on biblical injunctions and moral principles. The age was often considered as a period of religious vacuum as many politicians strove to reach an ideal of liberty, seeking to drive sectarian violence away from politics. These English, French and American philosophers, labeled as Deists, did not only put forward human principles established by the goddess "Reason," but may well have echoed St. Paul's teachings when he said: "How far can man be ignorant of the natural law which is written in the human heart" (Romans 2:14). All these freethinkers had been raised in the Christian religion and implicitly translated the Christian thought into secular terms. Even if their own visions appeared unorthodox and contrary to the main Christian dogmas, they finally agreed to expound the crucial ideal concerning human rights. It is in that sense that they have been called "enlightened philosophers." Their outrageous statements were the result of exasperation when facing sectarian violence and humiliation. Benjamin Franklin was probably right when he said: "A virtuous heretic shall be saved before a wicked Christian!"

Yet a paradox exists regarding the American Declaration of Independence. Having worked at the building of a wall of separation between Church and State, Jefferson still mentioned "God" and the "God of Nature" as a crucial referent. This "God of Nature," derived from pure Deistic thinking, does not seem to correspond to the diverse religious assumptions advocated by the members of the Enlightenment. For most monotheist religions, the concept of "Inalienable Rights" derives from a Divine Entity whose immanence sustains and gives life to the vital principles.

Political institutions are thus transcended by a God with no substance and no spiritual reality—a God who has been conveniently elaborated to suit and protect everybody's interests in the political and social spheres. From this paradox a serious theological issue arises, as the Abrahamic God puts on many faces adopted by various religious groups each of which in turn proclaims that it possesses the "real" God. During the Civil War, both the North and the South claimed God on their side, thereby demonizing each other! This Manichean vision of Evil and Good might well come from the confused perception of the true Christian God who gradually lost his attributes as a triune God. The problem that arises from this idiosyncratic spiritual vision, transposed into the political sphere, seems to be the source of controversies and misunderstandings at the core of the American political life.

In the nineteenth century, Alexis de Tocqueville, in his "Essay on American Government and Religion," summarized these ambiguities, seeking to comprehend the place and role of Deism within the religious American communities:

It's incredible to see the infinite number of subdivisions into which the sects in America have split. Like circles traced successively about the same point, each new one a little farther away than the next. The Catholic faith is the immovable point from which each new sect separates a little further, while nearing pure Deism. You realize that such a spectacle can't fail to throw the mind of a thinking Protestant into inextricable doubt; and that's the emotion that I think I see in visible control at the bottom of nearly every soul. It seems clear to me that the reformed religion is a sort of compromise, a kind of representative Monarchy, a kind of religion that may well fill an epoch, serve as transition from one state to another, but which could never constitute a definitive state, and which is nearing its end.[31]

3

The Emergence of a Collective Consciousness

American national consciousness gradually took shape, drawing its own characteristics from the sources of English Puritanism while adapting itself to the new social, geographical and political environment. From the end of the seventeenth century, the religious and cultural independence of the young nation provided the foundations for its future identity. However, the wish of the first colonists who dreamed of a national religion was not fulfilled since Protestantism exploded into a multitude of denominations and sects. Nevertheless, as a free and tolerant country deeply permeated by the Enlightenment spirit, America could only favor the development of new religious communities. As a result, this development gave Puritanism a complex and many-sided dimension, while weakening its rigor and intransigence. The diverse American national identity was reflected in the religious, literary and artistic spheres.

Religious Incentives: The Rise of Methodism and Unitarianism

As far as religion was concerned, after colonial times two religious strands of thought, totally opposed to each other, began to surface: Unitarianism and Methodism. Both originated in England and ran parallel during the American postcolonial period, which explains Perry Miller's reflection that "Unitarianism was as much the child of Puritanism as Methodism."[1] The rise of these two evolving denominations entailed complexity and ambiguity in the understanding of the new American mentality that was stamped by both religious doctrines. Perry Miller focused on the dilemma:

> The Puritan philosophy, brought to New England highly elaborated and codified, remained a fairly rigid orthodoxy during the seventeenth century. In the next age,

3—The Emergence of a Collective Consciousness

however, it proved to be anything but static; by the middle of the eighteenth century, there had proceeded from it two distinct schools of thought, almost unalterably opposed to each other. Certain elements were carried into the creeds and practices of the evangelical religious revivals, but others were perpetuated by the rationalists and the forerunners of Unitarianism ... Puritanism itself became two distinct and contending things to two sorts of men. The most prevailing error arising from this fact has been the identification of Puritanism with evangelicalism in many accounts, though in histories written by Unitarian scholars, the original doctrine has been almost as much distorted in the opposite direction.[2]

As noted by Miller, Puritanism had begotten two offspring. From Methodism sprang the great Evangelical revivals of the eighteenth and nineteenth centuries, thus contributing to the evolution of Puritanism by means of a sentimental and emotional approach between the faithful and their Celestial Father. These revivals, aimed at reawakening the dormant faith of believers, were organized by Protestant ministers who left their parishes to go and make new converts. Such was the case of the well-known preacher John Wesley (1703–1791),[3] an English clergyman who founded Methodism, and gave 40,000 sermons in England and the United States. As an adventurous and daring evangelist, he did not seek, in the manner of Calvin, to elaborate theological doctrines but rather endeavored to promote a "religion of the heart." Much more flexible than Puritanism in its organization, and recognizing the intervention of a divine force in the human experience, Methodism[4] had a predominant influence on many Americans and contributed to the development of what was later called "Americanism."

English Methodism also spread throughout America thanks to George Whitefield during the First "Great Awakening,"[5] which lasted from 1720 to 1742. Whitefield first settled in New York to organize Methodist Societies, but moved away from the North, which, according to him, was too much of a Calvinist stronghold. He then headed for the southern states to propagate his movement. In their evangelizing throughout the colonies, the Methodists became "trappers of souls" and did not hesitate to brave bad weather to convert people in open-air meetings. (Hence the saying, "In such bad weather, you'll find no one outside except crows and Methodists!") Their methods were simple, but required a thorough knowledge of the Bible, talented orators, and a prodigious amount of energy. It was necessary to convince the sinner of his own misery and to offer him, according to the Calvinist tradition, the choice between damnation and redemption. He or she was offered the chance to be "born again" in order to escape the pangs of conscience and certain damnation. These practices led to innumerable conversions. Penitents saw their torments transformed into joy while the religious ceremonies and preaching continued.

The second Great Awakening, which took place in the 1820s and 1830s, also contributed decisively to the shaping of the American consciousness.

The population was largely influenced by bold and enthusiastic preachers who advocated the new religious trends through powerful and convincing rhetoric. These orators were interested in converting not only their fellow citizens but also the natives. During the conquest of the West in the 1840s and 1850s, several Protestant churches sent missionaries to convert the Indian populations. Rapidly, the West became the land of revivals and the kingdom of the preachers, who, with the Bible in their hands, organized camp meetings. It is related that some Indian tribes, probably also influenced by former Jesuit missionaries, asked the explorer William Clark, whom Jefferson had sent to Missouri, for the "Great Book of Heaven."

In the mid–1850s, the Methodist Church rapidly became the largest denomination in the United States, undermining the determinist and anti-democratic aspects of colonial Puritanism. This also implied the idea of a spiritual release, comparable to the political release from the supervision of an authoritarian state. The Methodists' stance towards politics revolutionized American culture, transforming traditional Protestantism into a populist religion by bringing spiritual egalitarianism into the different communities. Although the religious representatives of Methodism wanted to avoid politics, they preached hard work, philanthropy and civil righteousness using biblical language.

The second major denomination, Unitarianism, dates back to the period of the Protestant Reformation. A Unitarian is someone who does not believe in the Holy Trinity, rather believing that God exists only in one person. Theophilus Lindsey founded the first English Unitarian congregation in London in 1774, and it was introduced into America as early as the middle of the nineteenth century, influencing the rationalist movement that swept over America at the time. It was William Ellery Channing (1780–1842), an American pastor and philosopher, who strongly criticized the Calvinist doctrine and spread the Unitarian faith in Boston. According to his teaching, redemption was possible for all people and the Divine City was not exclusively reserved for the Puritan "saints." Channing attempted to convince the new pastors to discard the negative connotation attached to the "God of Wrath" and to advocate human compassion and love. In his combat against social inequality, the American pastor showed how the renewal of Protestantism had had a positive impact on political egalitarianism. These new religious assumptions underlay Channing's position in his struggle against slavery and in his defense of the working classes. Praising new ethics, Channing offered a convincing response to the spiritual expectations of his fellow men as materialism started to tarnish his country's moral and religious values. The philosopher believed in America's sublime role and wanted to preserve it from human perversion, which also explains his fight against the extermination of the Indians. In an open letter he wrote to Henry Clay, Channing expressed his disappointment relating to the deviated laws of American politics:

> It is often said that nations are swayed by laws, as unfailing as those which govern matter; that they have their destinies; that their character and position carry them forward irresistibly to their goals ... that, by a like necessity, the Indians have melted before the white man, and the mixed, degraded race of Mexico must melt before the Anglo-Saxon. Away with this vile sophistry! There is no necessity for crime. There is not Fate to justify rapacious nations, any more than to justify gamblers and robbers, in plunder. We boast of the progress of society, and this progress consists in the substitutions of reason and moral principle for the sway of brute force.[6]

Channing's arguments brought into relief the use of reason as a tool to combat the expansionists' destinarian tendency during the territorial conquest. As one of the foremost spokesmen of Unitarianism, he believed in the preeminence of human reason over the teachings of the Holy Scriptures, which he regarded as written by fallible men, holding that rationality was a revelation in itself. In that perspective, he extolled main tenets of the Enlightenment philosophers' rationalist thinking, who often mistook reasoning for rationalization. On the social and political level, Unitarianism was often associated with social reforms. Unitarians denounced the immorality of slavery, defended the cause of peace, and developed public education. Channing had a tremendous influence over religious and social life in New England particularly and America in general in spite of certain inconsistencies as his rationalist ideas often contradicted his platonic and transcendental vision of a world which could be envisioned as a sublime and pure reflection of the divine figure.

All in all, Methodism and Unitarianism retained some of the basic postulates of the Puritan doctrine, mainly the improvement of man's moral behavior in society, the importance of religious sermons by inspired ministers, and the ideas of redemption through *sola fide*. Yet both denominations discarded the dogma of predestination, rejecting the Calvinist doctrine of total depravity and divine election. American public opinion largely adopted these liberal theologies which developed side by side with the democratic principles of its Republic, giving them shape and substance in accordance with American pragmatism.

Influential Literary Strands of Thought in the Shaping of a National Consciousness

In the literary sphere, several nineteenth-century American writers undoubtedly stamped the national spirit as key figures who participated in the apparent metamorphosis of Puritan colonial America into a self-confident and more liberal nation. Among these were the novelist and short-story writers Nathaniel Hawthorne, the essayists Ralph Waldo Emerson and Henry David Thoreau, and the poet Walt Whitman. Their dissenting voices undermined the destructive driving force of Puritanism, denouncing its rigorous moralism and lack of aesthetics. As Richard Drinnon noted, "Individuals are the living substance of history, the carriers, the creators, sometimes, of the attitudes and ideas of their generations … they embody mainstream attitudes … or swim against the currents."[7]

In his writings, Hawthorne, whose great-grandfather was one of the judges at the Salem witch trials, chose the colonial period to stigmatize the Puritan conscience through his characters. In *The Scarlet Letter*, he uses evocative symbols and metaphors to emphasize the predicament of the sinners who feel less condemned by God's judgment than by a punitive society. Hawthorne's portrait of the two protagonists, Hester and Dimmesdale, creates an oppressive tension insofar as it implicitly denounces all the moral snares caused by guilt and remorse. The scarlet letter that Hester is compelled to wear on her chest symbolizes the moral aspect of historical Puritanism which, through its intransigence and punitive coercion, has become legendary.

Hawthorne's entire work reminds us that the first Puritan immigrants, victims of religious intolerance in their own country, had come to the New World to escape persecution, but when they first landed on American soil, they propagated the same inhuman practices they were subjected to in the decadent "Old Europe." Hawthorne became indignant at the Puritans' blindness, seeking to explain their inconsistency through Hester's behavior, who, despite being an adulteress, was transformed into a virtuous and free person. Indeed, if outwardly the protagonist submitted to American law, she valiantly challenged the religious society in which she lived, despising its rulers' self-importance and arrogant attitudes. In the end, she saves her reputation thanks to her courage and kindness, which she uses as a weapon to appease her enemies. Thus, bringing to light the dark side of Puritanism, portraying its Calvinist sense of inner depravity, the author conveyed the dramatic dimension linked to a dogmatic and ossifying doctrine. In addition, Hawthorne admitted that *The Scarlet Letter* had acted as therapy and exorcised his own feeling of guilt when he discovered his great-grandfather's participation in the Salem witch trials. Consequently, given the liberating influence his work produced on a community obsessed by the forces of evil, this personal therapy was transmuted into collective therapy. In "Hawthorne and His Mosses," Herman Melville, one of Hawthorne's great friends, tried to capture the novelist's literary genius:

Whether Hawthorne has simply availed himself of this mystical blackness as a means to the wondrous effects he makes it to produce in his lights and shades; or whether there really lurks in him, perhaps unknown to himself, a touch of Puritanic gloom, — this, I cannot altogether tell. Certain it is, however, that this great power of blackness in him derives its force from its appeals to that Calvinistic sense of Innate Depravity and Original Sin, from whose visitations, in some shape or other, no deeply thinking mind is always and wholly free.... Still more: this black conceit pervades him, through and through. You may be witched by his sunlight, — transported by the bright gildings in the skies he builds over you; — but there is the blackness of darkness beyond; and even his bright gildings but fringe, and play upon the edges of thunder-clouds. — In one word, the world is mistaken in this Nathaniel Hawthorne. He himself must often have smiled at its absurd misconception of him. He is immeasurably deeper than the plummet of the mere critic. For it is not the brain that can test such a man; it is only the heart. You cannot come to know greatness by inspecting it; there is no glimpse to be caught of it, except by intuition; you need not ring it, you but touch it, and you find it is gold.[8]

Indeed, in *The Scarlet Letter*, Hawthorne directly speaks to the human heart through the interplay of striking and impressive symbolism.

Two other literary figures also played an important role in building a collective consciousness: the Transcendentalist essayists Ralph Waldo Emerson and Henry David Thoreau. Both had an idealistic vision of America and considered their nation's mission and glorious destiny as the two pillars of the national identity. At the time, their respective works were permeated with the romantic spirit which was sweeping through the European continent.

A Protestant minister's son, Emerson was born in Concord, Massachusetts. After studying the classics in Boston and Concord, in which he did not really excel, he entered Harvard University to study theology. Four years later, he became a minister, but gave up his church after a short period of time. A Unitarian minister, he slowly abandoned the Unitarian doctrine to adopt the philosophy of Transcendentalism, regarding the dogmatic aspect of the religious institution as an imposture, preventing man from adhering to the true moral law — "the law of laws" — the law of Divine love. Emerson was especially attached to the notion of autonomy. As a rule, his natural disposition led him to prefer contemplation to active life, which led him to deepen his faith by adopting a pantheistic vision. Like most of his contemporary writers, Emerson was convinced that a break with the past was a necessary step to grasping the true originality of the emerging nation. During an annual speech to Harvard students in theology, he explained his anti-conformist position, the aim of which, he said, was "more to improve human nature rather than pursue and denounce evil."

After returning to America from a trip to Europe, Emerson gave numerous popular lectures. Audiences appreciated his speeches, which they perceived as in line with the expectations of a public ready to free itself from the fetters of Puritan tradition. In 1836, he founded the Transcendentalist Club, where people met to discuss the negative and disastrous effects of materialism, the rigidity of institutions, and also to ponder on the harmony between man and nature, as well as the manifestations of the "Oversoul," the spirit of the Universe.

In 1837, Emerson gave a lecture at Harvard University entitled "The American Scholar," which is generally regarded as the American declaration of cultural independence. He encouraged the students to set aside foreign literary works, declaring that only an American writer could contribute to the enlightenment of a true national literature, underlining the fact that America lacked thinkers and writers. In the same spirit, during a lecture before the Mercantile Library Association of Boston on February 7, 1844, Emerson presented his idealistic vision of a glorious America. The main themes of his discourse embodied in turn the emergence of a new American consciousness, the rise of patriotism and a deep faith in American destiny "through the design of the Spirit":

> I call upon you, young men, to obey your heart, and be the nobility of this land. In every age of the world, there has been a leading nation, one of a more generous sentiment, whose eminent citizens were willing to stand for the interests of general justice and humanity, at the risk of being called, by men of the moment, chimerical and fantastic. Which should be the nation but these States, Which should lead that movement but New England? Who should lead the leaders, but the young Americans? The people and the world are now suffering from the want of religion and honor in its public mind. In America, out of doors, all seems a market; in doors, an air-tight stove of conventionalism. Everybody who comes into our houses savors of these habits; the men of the market; the women, of the customs. I find no expression in our state papers or legislative debate, in our lyceums or churches, especially in our newspapers, of a high national feeling, no lofty counsels that rightfully stir the blood. I speak of those organs which can be presumed to speak a popular sense. They recommend conventional virtues, whatever will earn and preserve property.... Our houses and towns are like mosses and lichens, so slight and new; but youth is a fault of which we shall daily mend. This land, too, is as old as the Flood, and wants no ornament or privilege which nature could bestow. Here stars, here woods, here hills, here animals, here men abound, and the vast tendencies concur of a new order. If only the men are employed in conspiring with the designs of the Spirit who led us hither, and is leading us still, we shall quickly enough advance out of all hearing of other's censures, out of all regrets of our own, into a new and more excellent social state than history has recorded.[9]

The last reflections of this passage sum up Emerson's Transcendentalist vision of America, widely impregnated with the doctrine of Manifest Destiny. These ideas also evoke the elaboration of a new order in America, now ready to have its own national identity, even though this identity appears still based on the foundation myths of the Pilgrim Fathers, that is

3—The Emergence of a Collective Consciousness

to say, on the belief that America "should be inspired with the design of the Spirit." Finally, Emerson's text reiterates the same idealistic language as that of his ancestors from New England, only he appeals more to intuitive knowledge than to the logic of reason. His poetic imagination may have helped to bridge the gap between ancestral Puritanism and the rising mood of modern culture, but only on the surface, as the metaphoric image of a city upon the hill still lingers through the text.

In one of his essays, "The Poet," Emerson introduced the bard as a prophet who alone, can understand and grasp the meaning of spiritual realities. The poet has a sacred mission and as such can be considered as a pastor; it is in this perspective that Emerson (like Thoreau and many other intellectuals) took part in the major debates of the time over controversial subjects such as slavery, firmly condemning the inhuman laws applied to fugitive slaves. After giving countless lectures on the new and specific role of America, Emerson died in Concord in 1882.

Emerson was the first American writer to break with English traditions, especially those imbued with the harsh principles of an authoritative mentality. However, although a breath of fresh air permeated the stifling atmosphere still suspended over some American states, the Puritan legacy was still alive. God had not ceased to be the great Inspirer of the American destiny, the generous Provider of the Horn of Plenty, but within the religious communities feelings of anguish and guilt vanished to give way to a new ideal based on optimism and faith that, from then on, seemed to prevail over an austere vision of life.

Henry David Thoreau, Emerson's intimate friend and protégé, was another American essayist and philosopher who contributed to the development of a national consciousness. Born in Concord into a poor family, Thoreau obtained a scholarship to study at Harvard University and later became a schoolmaster. However, he refused to apply corporal punishment and was dismissed. Emerson allowed him to settle on his land, so Thoreau built a wooden cabin at the edge of a pond, where he lived alone for two and a half years, writing his masterpiece, *Walden*. Published in 1854, the work explores the benevolent effects of solitude from a Transcendental point of view. Like the Transcendentalists, Thoreau believed that spiritual reality (God) was embedded in physical reality (Nature). After a life of toil, the philosopher wrote, traveled and, following Emerson's example, gave speeches all over America, notably in favor of the poor and downtrodden. Thoreau died of tuberculosis in 1862.

Thoreau's philosophy rests on a mystical experience felt by certain individuals when contemplating the natural world. Rejection of rites and dogmas constitutes the key idea in his writings. He felt that man must acknowledge a whole system of intuitive moral laws. This philosophy was seen as sacred humanism in the sense that man, whose origin is divine, may grasp sufficient knowledge in order to be his own master and to act without deferring to other authorities. Thoreau's essential aim was to free man from all forms of tutelage. It is easy to understand how this liberal philosophy contributed to the formation of antislavery movements.

In 1849, Thoreau, who was imprisoned because he had not paid his taxes on account of his opposition to slavery and the Mexican War, wrote his essay "Civil Disobedience," adopting the motto: "Government is best which governs least." He aroused controversy about the right of conscience, and declared: "I think that we should be men first, and subjects afterward. It is most desirable to cultivate a respect for the law, so much as for the right. The only obligation which I have to assume is to do at any time what I think is right." His attitude of nonviolent resistance against unfair laws explains his passive reaction to imprisonment; in "Civil Disobedience," he described his experience in a simple and realist style, fraught with philosophical implications:

> I have paid no poll tax for six years. I was put to jail once on this account, for one night; and as I stood considering the walls of solid stone, two or three feet thick, the door of wood and iron, a foot thick.... I saw that if there was a wall of stone between me and my townsmen, there was a still more difficult one to climb or break through, before they could get to be as free as I was. I did not for a moment feel confined, and the walls seemed a great waste of stone and mortar. I felt as if I alone of all my townsmen had paid my tax.... I could not but smile to see how industriously they locked the door on my meditations.... I saw that the State was half-witted ... and that it did not know his friends from his foes, and I lost my remaining respect for it, and pitied it.[10]

Thoreau's example was followed by later civil rights activists. Gandhi told an American reporter that Thoreau's essay "Civil Disobedience" helped him in his fight for Indian independence. Martin Luther King also revealed that he was fascinated by Thoreau's refusal to cooperate with a wrong system. Considering Emerson's and Thoreau's involvement in civil affairs, Alfred Kazin noted in *On Native Grounds* (1942) that American writing "had always been more a form of moral propaganda than a study of esthetic problems" and that criticism "had usually sought ... to unite American writers in the service of one imperative ideal or another."[11]

The Transcendentalist doctrine of both philosophers reverberated widely on the spirit of the territorial expansion, having a substantial impact on American spokesmen such as John O'Sullivan, who thought that expansion ideally ought to be carried out in a peaceful way and only when territories were in favor of their annexation. Influenced by a philosophy which regarded the defense of individual rights as sacred, a number of political figures fought unyieldingly for the acknowledgment of these fundamental rights.

3—The Emergence of a Collective Consciousness

The emergence of a national spirit was also revealed through the works of America's first "poet of Democracy," Walt Whitman. Throughout his life, Whitman was concerned by politics and sought to spread his democratic ideas, especially his opposition to slavery. While the country's literature and intellectual life were still under the shadow of the motherland, Whitman's poems were devoted to praising the newborn American democracy. He considered himself a messiah-like figure in poetry[12] and certainly inspired the nascent national spirit. Like his fellow citizens, he favored a break with European culture and declared in his preface to *Leaves of Grass* (1876) that, during his lifetime, "The United States emerged from nebulous vagueness and suspense to full orbit."[13] Despite this slightly poetic arrogance, *Leaves of Grass* certainly responded to the new expectations of a people newly passionate with epic grandeur. It is therefore not surprising that he established symbiotic links with his readers. In his preface to the 1855 edition, Whitman wrote: "The proof of a poet is that his country absorbs him as affectionately as he absorbed it."[14]

Thus, like many of his American fellow men, Whitman believed that the only way for the United States to find a cultural identity was to eradicate any form of foreign influence. In one of his letters to Emerson (1856), he wrote that American literary genius outshone all foreign literary works of the past, which, although they were "majestic and proper in their own lands, became exiles in America."[15] The country had to free itself from ancient European ties to gradually discover a newborn nation's own aspirations because, Whitman argued: "Up to the present ... the people have no determined tastes, are quite unaware of the grandeur of themselves and of their destiny."[16] In other words, the American nation was still germinating and the poet resorted to a metaphor evoking God's Hand drawing the outlines of future America: "America is not finished yet, perhaps it never will be, now America is a divine sketch."[17]

Whitman went further, declaring that American poets were to reformulate the *tabula rasa* concept through their desire to totally erase all traces of former European literature. For them, the future could only be charged with new hopes. As they freely drew away from old traditions, just as the American political system had, American writers and literates, stated Whitman, "recognize nothing behind them superior to what is present with them."[18] A true rupture with the past represented a new step towards a bright future and the emergence of a new people. According to the poet, the United States had been designated to play a major role in the centuries to come:

> To me, the United States are important because they are unquestionably designed for the leading parts, for many a century to come. In them, History and Humanity seem to culminate ... not to become a conqueror nation, or to achieve the glory

of mere military or diplomatic or commercial superiority but to become the grand producing Land of Nobler Men and Women — of copious races, cheerful, healthy, tolerant, free — to become the most friendly Nation of Peace ... and not the Man's nation only but the woman's nation, a land of splendid mothers, daughters, sisters, wives.[19]

American genius did not reside in its institutions but in the people who enjoyed all the attributes of youth — enthusiasm, love of freedom and curiosity. When the people met the president, it was the president who tipped his hat at them, not the contrary: "The President takes off his hat to them, not they to him." This praise of the sovereign people revealed the poet's ideal vision that only a true democracy could confer faith and vigor to the young nation. However, this democracy was quite particular in the sense that, according to Whitman, it was built on specific ideological and religious foundations, as can be seen in the poem "Starting from Paumanok":

I say that the real and permanent grandeur of these states
  Must be their religion,
  Otherwise there is no real and permanent grandeur
  (Nor character nor life worthy of the name without religion, nor land
  nor man and woman without religion).

Whitman's focus on ethics and religiosity was an integral part of his conception of American democracy. By celebrating the virtues of the common man, Whitman's poetry was to build a spiritual community through vital principles found in the "pure ether" of the "divine All." His new literature was not "to pass away time, celebrate the beautiful, the refined, the past, or exhibit technical rhythmic, or grammatical dexterity — but a literature underlying life, religious, consistent with science, handling the elements and forces with competent power, *teaching* and *training* men."[20]

American democracy was to flower through the interaction between citizens and their beliefs, and religion was to play a central role through the intuitive power of poetry: "Religion must enter into the Poems of the Nation. It must make the Nation,"[21] Whitman wrote in *Democratic Vistas* (1871). Largely influenced by the Transcendentalist movement and the idea of an "Oversoul" permeating all earthly elements, including men, Whitman's poetry sought to capture the vital divine force, which would entail the acknowledgment of the "highest truths about human beings" and thus help them in establishing a true democratic religion. From the poet's point of view, traditional theology was declining. In his preface, he is quite explicit:

> For America, the supreme and final science is the science of God.... The people, especially the young men and women of America must begin to learn that Religion (like poetry) is something far, far different from what they supposed. It is, indeed, too important to the power and perpetuity of the New World not to be

consigned any longer to the churches, old or new, Catholic or Protestant — Saint this or Saint that ... it must be consigned henceforth to Democracy en masse and to Literature.[22]

In *Democratic Vistas*, his second major work after *Leaves of Grass*, Whitman expounded his political view in the form of a prose essay. Complex and lacking logic and clarity, the work is nonetheless a great piece of writing that does not leave the reader indifferent, for it condenses most of the idiosyncratic principles of American democracy in an energizing and exuberant style. Frequently marked by a certain dichotomy between Good and Evil in his thematic approach, Whitman's optimism always prevails over the dark side of his reflection. He stated, "The United States are destined either to surmount the gorgeous history of feudalism, or else prove the most tremendous failure of time,"[23] and thus announced the double-faced Janus aspect of his political theory.

Whitman longed for a democracy in which the "common man" would act individually, becoming an inspired good citizen through the means of great literature, which, understood by all, would be a catalyst: "Few are aware how the great literature penetrates all, gives hue to all, shapes aggregates and individuals, and, after subtle ways, with irresistible power, constructs, sustains, demolishes at will."[24] To him, the mission of government is not only to repress or exercise authority on its citizens, but also to "train communities" in order that each man can rule himself. As a consequence, Emerson's law of laws, brotherly love, will supplant civil law: "Would you have in yourself the divine, vast, general law? Then merge yourself in it."[25]

And this is valuable for all nations as these "alluring" aspects of American democracy can bring fraternity all over the world, "making the races comrades." The democratic system and people must be revitalized by religion, "For I say at the core of democracy, finally is the religious element." Whitman's insistent emphasis on the religious element derives from his belief in a kind of Deism that embraces all religions, but he nevertheless pointed out that to be "clothed in their resplendent beauty," these religious groups had to bear spiritual fruit.

And time was of the essence for American democracy to reach its flowering. Human institutions had to clear themselves from "fossilism" that tended to paralyze citizens, and the only remedy to replace these "morbitic matters" by "higher nutriments" was to resort to "goodness, virtue and law (of the very best,...)." In spite of menacing evils that existed in America, political democracy remained a "training-school for making first-class men."[26] Even though "the nation is still in a sort of geological formation state," Whitman argued, "the sublimest part of political history, and its culmination, is currently issuing from the American people."[27] In his grand and prophetic vision of America, the "Father of Democracy" also pondered on the issue of the gender role, praising the "divine maternity" of American women:

> Democracy, in silence, biding its time, ponders on its own ideals, not of literature and art only—not of men only, but of women. The idea of the woman in America, (extricated from this daze, this fossil and unhealthy air which hangs about the word lady,) developed, raised to become the robust equals, workers, and, it may be, even practical and political deciders with the men—greater than man, we may admit, through their divine maternity, always their towering, emblematic attribute—but great, at any rate, as man, in all departments; or rather, capable of doing so, as soon as they realize it, and can bring themselves to give up toys and fictions, and launch forth, as men do, amid real, stormy life.[28]

Whitman's treatment of Time in his conception of American democracy is not to be neglected, its fruition or accomplishment residing in the future when "it, with imperial power, through amplest time, had dominated mankind."[29] Still in its embryonic state in Whitman's days, democracy could only develop through the "production of perfect characters" and through the advent of "a sane and pervading religiousness."[30]

Despite the enthusiastic impulse that emanates from *Democratic Vistas* through the poetic prism of his genius, Whitman's holistic vision of democracy seems to rest on a conception of American society composed of different individuals whose spiritual maturity will never reach the same level, as the Puritans thought when they labeled themselves "saints." This utopian dimension, contained in his ideas of sanctified citizens, was part of the poet's dream of a perfect world. Whitman was aware of "many a deep intestine difficulty, and humane aggregate of cankerous imperfection,"[31] in American society, which demonstrates his realist approach to life. Yet his cosmic interpretation of the universe, imbued with a benevolent Divine Spirit, is linked to the old myth of the Promised Land in the sense that both assumptions rest on the eventuality of paradise on earth.

Thus, under the influence of these literary and philosophical trends, America witnessed the rise of a national spirit in the construction of its identity. Always imbued with religiosity and a new metaphysics found in Transcendentalists, the American mind was influenced by a literature celebrating the ambitious and utopian ideals of the young American republic. Hawthorne, Emerson, Thoreau, and Whitman contributed to the development of this national mentality that led to the emergence of an "inspired" democracy. They all played a crucial role in this ideological shift which disrupted the Founding Fathers' firm and clear religious assumptions. It can be noted that these views developed in parallel with political and economic movements as they were in line with historical requirements.

Painting as an Emblematic Sign of American Glory

Literature was not the only artistic domain in which the ideological vision of America was reflected. Painting also evoked the aspirations of a people fascinated by images portraying their country's grandeur and ambitions. Thomas Cole (1801–1848) was one of the most representative painters of that time and was called "the Father of the Hudson River School," the American art movement known for its magnificent landscapes. Obsessed with the grandeur and fall of empires, he used his artistic technique to moralize. The comparison between America and the Roman Empire had been a common idea in the United States as early as the eighteenth century.

The pictorial genre became very popular in the United States, as the country was now anxious to celebrate Manifest Destiny through sublime and imposing images while the frontier advanced towards the shores of the Pacific Ocean. Cole intended to reveal the transcendental majesty of American sites through technical and artistic devices. In his book *The Magisterial Gaze: Manifest Destiny and American Landscape Painting*,[32] Albert Boime describes the links that exist between painting and Manifest Destiny by evoking a specific vision that he calls the "Magisterial gaze," the gaze of a person who dominates a vast panorama. This technique sought to illustrate the territorial ambition which corresponded to the national ideology.

In his series *The Course of Empire*, Cole was concerned with perspectives that gave the impression of dominating a landscape. His painting *River in the Catskills*, in which a young farmer contemplates the landscape from a hilltop, is a good example of his practice. The background is strewn with thickets and uprooted trees, and symbolizes lands to conquer. Boime explains that the "magisterial gaze" embodies a desire for power and attests to America's social and political ambitions. He compares it to the "reverential gaze" technique, which produces the opposite effect and is found in classical painting.[33] Regarding the allegorical dimension of such paintings, Boime noted:

> Most of this should be familiar to students of American culture, but until now there has been no systematic attempt to comprehend the landscape schools in a theoretical perspective through analysis of their formal structures and their signification. Thus far the most illuminating scholarly research in the realm of landscape has emphasized the relation of landscape painting to the myth of the wilderness and the West in terms of historical narrative and content. The myth of nature and its conversion into religious doctrine has centered on the need to resolve the antinomy between nature and culture, between the Virgin land and its deflowering. In this scenario, the painters are reduced to impotent spectators passively documenting a passing scene. I intend to argue just the opposite, that

far from being passive recorders, they participated in the very system they condemned and projected it symbolically in their work.[34]

The truth of this reflection is difficult to establish, as it was reported that "Cole felt it his duty to depict nature, especially American nature, as the "visible hand of God."[35] What is certain is that Cole was a romantic painter prone to enhance reality, conferring to it the magic halo of a transcendental presence.

America is also depicted through symbols and allegorical images, such as the personification of American progress in the form of a woman rising in the air, her forehead crowned with a wreath adorned with a star, the Empire star. The woman is moving west to civilize the Indians who are fleeing, panic-stricken, as John Gast's painting *American Progress* shows.[36]

While the American landscape became a source of contemplation, a new artistic style developed: Luminism, seeking to reflect the many-sided aspects of American glory. Its founder, Frederick Edwin Church (1826–1900), strove to highlight the spirit of the expansionist doctrine inspired by Manifest Destiny. Most of his works were characterized by elements that evoked God's presence in the natural world. Luminism was often compared to Transcendentalism, as both endeavored to stress the evidence of a spiritual dimension in the American natural world. The effects of light created a soft and hazy atmosphere propitious to reflective meditation on the supernatural world.

A key figure in the Hudson River School, and the best-known pupil of Thomas Cole, Church was "always concerned with including a spiritual dimension in his works."[37] Sketching and painting the mountains of New England, like most of the painters of his generation, Church revealed landscapes veiled in transparent radiance, suffused with supernatural light; he sought to capture the unutterable truths which lie behind the beauty of the natural world. Thus snowcapped mountains symbolized the pure and dazzling light of the divine spirit. The blurred and distant details of his pictures that seemed to melt with this poetic vision unified the scenery and served as a symbiotic process to show that Nature and God were one.

Church did not restrict himself to drawing pastoral and bucolic scenes charged with a touch of mystic quietness. He also painted storms with menacing clouds as if to introduce the forces of darkness into the peaceful garden of the Promised Land. In his canvas *Storm in the Mountains*, one perceives the disrupted elements wrapped in the somber atmosphere that invades the remaining white spaces, forming a mysterious and threatening chiaroscuro. Through his impressive and majestic canvases, Church epitomized all the characteristics of a glorious and blessed America. As Dr. Carr, author of a catalog of Church's paintings, noted:

3—The Emergence of a Collective Consciousness 61

Much of Church's artistic appeal stems from the vivid imagination implicit in his painted images, as well as their apparent authority and variety. Put another way, his paintings regularly possess strength, seeming self-sufficiency, and multiformity identifiably his own. One of those strengths is "magnitude," impressiveness," "grandeur," "power," "opulence," and concomitant nobility Church intended to be inviting, and which most viewers find just that. Amplitude is his ally, in two, three, and four dimensions. The formats of his largest canvasses, *The Heart of the Andes*, of 1859, ..., *The Iceberg*, of 1861..., and *Niagara Falls from the American Side*, of 1867..., are spacious enough to walk into.[38]

Two of Church's emblematic paintings, *Our Banner in the Sky* (1861) and *Our Flag* (1864), are linked to the Civil War; *Our Banner in the Sky* was drawn in support of the Northern side. It conveys the dramatic aspect of the conflict through the white streaks of the flag appearing in the reddish sky and rising on a wasteland. The patriotic message is obvious, symbolizing the strength and victory of the Union. *Our Flag*, depicting the American flag planted on a sturdy rock, Carr noted, "proclaimed Church's three-pronged patriotic message: the North is rock-solid; the North has weathered the storm; the North will emerge triumphant."

The glorious representation of the New World, reflected in both literature and painting, helped to highlight the deep meaning of Manifest Destiny. From its inception, American culture was nurtured by a dream born in the first settlers' imagination. Anxious to live in the sanctuary of a bounteous God, they endeavored to build a New Jerusalem, a model of democracy for European nations and a refuge for the oppressed of the world. This celestial and shining city was reflected in all the facets of American culture. God's subliminal image permeated all artistic fields; He left His print through the inspired American minds of the time who considered themselves as prophets and instruments of His divine will.

Part II

The American Policy of Conquest

4

American Expansionism and Destiny

The Louisiana Purchase: A Good Deal

When Thomas Jefferson[1], the key author of the Declaration of Independence, was sworn in as the third president of the United States, the Union was composed of sixteen states, whose number Jefferson very much intended to add to. During his two terms of office (1801–1809), the face of America was dramatically transformed. The government became more democratic as the new president's electorate attracted different social classes, essentially small farmers and workers who outnumbered the traditional elites and wealthy landowners. Jefferson's vision was to encourage the development of agriculture in order to make citizens independent, happy and free through the cultivation of the land. This ambition was part of his agrarian philosophy, which had been influenced by the eighteenth-century French philosophers whose works he had read and whom he had met during his long stay in France.

Indeed, Jefferson had spent some time as minister to France, just before the French Revolution (1785–1789), and some of the French thinkers' ideas underlay his own philosophical vision. For example, Voltaire's *Candide*, whose theme is connected with the return to natural and simple life, advocating to "cultivate one's own garden," had a strong impact on Jefferson's conception of life. The symbolic evocation of gardens might represent some kind of celestial paradise where men and women are able to rediscover the simple joys offered by the natural world. This idea runs through Jefferson's utilitarian writings as he idealized the farmers' genuine virtues by giving them a religious, biblical echo:

> Those who labour in the earth are the chosen people of God, if ever he had a chosen people, whose breasts he has made his peculiar deposit for substantial and genuine virtues.... Corruption of morals in the mass of cultivators is a phenomenon of which no age nor nation has furnished an example.[2]

The conquest of new lands was thus a new opportunity for Jefferson to spread his religious and visionary goals. He opened the way to territorial expansion with the Louisiana Purchase in 1803, which was followed in turn by the annexation of Florida (1819), Texas (1845), Oregon (1846), the Mexican Cession (1848) and finally Hawaii, Puerto Rico, and the Philippines (1898), all marked by the seal of Manifest Destiny. The new territories were not acquired without conflicts despite Jefferson's wish for peaceful expansion. Indeed, from the beginning of the territorial expansion, Jefferson had planned to buy these lands from the Indians and then to assimilate the natives into the mass of American people.

However, the Treaty of Paris (September 1783), which ended the Revolutionary War, did not mention any Indian policy. Jefferson, in his Second Inaugural Speech, insisted on the fact that he had regarded with commiseration the native Indians who were "endowed with the faculties and the rights of men." As a humanist, he believed that the natives should be encouraged to learn "agriculture and domestic arts," which alone could help them in maintaining "their place in existence." Jefferson also emphasized that the federal government's role was to educate the Indians and convince them not to remain "as their Creator made them," since ignorance and lack of knowledge would undermine their safety.

However, as everyone knows, territorial expansion unfolded through dramatic events and wars; the American government often attempted, with or without a reason, to justify this expansion by Divine intervention. The new land became a "God-centered nation" inspired by various American statesmen, including Presidents Thomas Jefferson, Andrew Jackson and James Polk, and other political figures, particularly Henry Clay, John Calhoun and Daniel Webster. These statesmen played an important role in the rise of American nationalism, insofar as they advocated patriotic pride opening the way to expansionism and to what was later called American exceptionalism.

These emblematic figures were not the only personalities to express nationalistic points of view, nor were they fully representatives of the spirit of Manifest Destiny, but their voices were widely heard, given the political role they played at the time. One must also add that expansionism in the 1840s had been analyzed according to divergent criteria:

> Many historians have argued that the spirit of manifest destiny or pioneer restlessness was the primary cause of expansion. Other scholars have asserted that expansion was the product of a governmental policy. Finally, there are those historians who reject both of these extremes or somehow combine them.[3]

The Louisiana Purchase, effected by Jefferson, who opened the era of territorial expansion in 1803, seems to relate to the first argument of this analysis since the spirit of Manifest Destiny did underlie the western conquest. With this agreement between France and America, Napoleon, who had recently come to power and was in great need of funds, was able to balance France's budget. He was also very happy to place this land safely beyond the grasp of a covetous England, his rival at war. He reportedly confided to his finance minister, "This accession of territory affirms forever the power of the United States, and I have just given England a maritime rival that sooner or later will lay low her pride."[4] For the modest sum of 15 million dollars, Jefferson fulfilled his dream of a great continental nation and doubled the size of the Union.

The Louisiana Purchase was Jefferson's greatest achievement during his presidency and earned him popular acclaim. In truth, the president had sent envoys to France to acquire the port of New Orleans, as American merchants were interested in the site for storing agricultural goods and shipping them to different parts of the United States. Jefferson had not actually planned to purchase the Louisiana territory, as no provision existed in the Constitution for acquiring such an enormous tract of land. He was therefore extremely surprised when the American negotiators returned with an agreement to buy the entire territory, which of course he hastened to sign.

Robert Livingston, the American ambassador who negotiated the purchase from France, made this famous statement, now carved in stone beside the main entrance of the Louisiana State Capitol Building: "We have lived long but this is the noblest work of our whole lives.... The United States take rank today among the first powers of the world." In addition, the acquisition of the Louisiana Territory triggered a certain fascination with exploring the western parts of America, and embodied the concept of Manifest Destiny which included, among other elements, the desire to link the Atlantic and Pacific coasts.

Annexation of Florida: The "Destined Use of the Soil"

The acquisition of Florida (1819) which followed was more painful because of its racial overtones, since large territories were occupied by Indians who enjoyed certain autonomy. It was during that time that the concept of a "destined use of the soil," imagined by Albert Weinberg, was made explicit. It is worth noting that in 1786, Jefferson had written, "It may be taken for granted that not a foot of land will ever be taken from the Indians without their own consent."[5] Unfortunately, such was not the case since the Indian populations were constantly made to move west and the occupation was often justified by the so-called "providential design" which pervaded colonial Puritan doctrines. Indeed, in his *Conclusions for the Plantation in New England*, John Winthrop, New England's first governor, based his arguments on the biblical precept "Be fruitful, and multiply, and replenish the earth, and subdue it" (Genesis 1:28) in order to legitimize the occupation of Indian lands. According to this prominent Puritan leader, the land was to be divided into two parts. The first part was to become hunting grounds for Indians who were unsuited to cultivation, and the second part was destined for white settlers to transform the soil into agricultural land.[6]

Referring to biblical scriptures, the first Puritans maintained that any land which was not exploited was available to become the property of those who were able to cultivate it. Native Americans, above all hunters, were thought unfit for agriculture, and this explained why they had to give up their land. However, Indians, too, had religious beliefs, as the following reflection testifies. The speaker was a Pawnee chief who addressed President Monroe in 1822:

> The Great Spirit made us all — he made my skin red and yours white; he placed us on this earth and intended that we should live differently from each other. He made us, redskins, to rove through the uncultivated woods and plains; to feed on wild animals and to dress their skins. He also intended that we should go to war, steal horses from and triumph over our enemies — cultivate peace at home and promote the happiness of each other.[7]

Like the white Americans, the Indians were not reluctant to defend their rights by using religious arguments.

Another thesis, which sought to justify the eviction of Indians from their land, consisted in sublimating the role of American civilization. The question put by the governor of the Indiana Territory, William Henry Harrison, confirms this approach:

> Is one of the fairest portions of the globe to remain in a state of nature, the haunt of a few wretched savages, when it seems destined by the Creator to give support to a large population and to be the seat of civilization, of science, and of true religion?[8]

These religious arguments explained why, convinced of their legitimate rights endowed by the Creator, American leaders used an internal rebellion in 1810 as a pretext to occupy part of western Florida; then, in 1813, they annexed a small strip of land extending from Mobile Bay to the Perdido River. Claiming the need to pacify the border, General Andrew Jackson seized the opportunity to invade Florida in 1817, making several incursions into the region and becoming quite popular through his pursuit of those he called the "wretched savages." He considered himself "the instrument of an avenging God" and stated at the end of the conflict: "The hand of heaven has been pointed against the exciters of this war; every principle [sic] villain has been killed or taken."[9] This occupation had not been authorized by the government, but Congress did not renounce it, and Spain finally ceded Florida for the sum of 5 million dollars by a treaty signed in 1819 and ratified two years later (the Adams-Onis Treaty).

Secretary of State John Quincy Adams had declared that Spain's inability to maintain order in this region justified Jackson's incursion. Thanks to this treaty, the United States was now in possession of the entire territory extending from the Atlantic to the Rocky Mountains. Politicians and statesmen gave religious-based arguments to legitimize this conquest, notably Congressman George Strother, who declared during a House debate in 1819:

> The Western frontier is that portion of the world where civilization is making the most rapid and extensive conquest of the wilderness, carrying in its train the Christian religion and all the social virtues. It is the point where the race is most progressive; establish but the principle, that the God of nature has limited your march in that direction—that the Indian is lord paramount of that wide domain, around which justice and religion have drawn a circle that you dare not pass— the progress of mankind is arrested and you condemn one of the most beautiful and fertile tracts of the earth to perpetual sterility as the hunting ground for a few savages.[10]

The concept of the God of nature in this statement is quite problematic, as Strother has just mentioned the Christian religion. As we have already noted, the apparent antagonism between a "God of Nature" and a "God of Providence" is difficult to grasp in a purely theological and Christian perspective. Serge Ricard notes, not without a certain irony, that in the expansionists' minds, "Nature and Providence were happily married to beget a wonder child: geographical predestination, fed on the marvelous alibi of territorial contiguity. The Floridas, Texas, the Rockies, the Pacific coast and even the Isthmus of Panama could be claimed, and Cuba, the West Indies and Hawaii become natural appendages of the North American continent."[11]

The acquisition of Florida was followed by the first organized Indian removal to the west of the Mississippi River, even though Indian tribes could legally assert their right of refusing to give up their land. The Cherokees, who had set up a constitution modeled on the American one, became the main victims of the Indian removal policy, whose goal was to put into practice one of the Puritan axioms: "Carrying the Indian away was to preserve barbarity at the expense of industry and thrift."[12]

Texas and the Emergence of Manifest Destiny

The annexation of Texas was of prime importance since it was during its acquisition that O'Sullivan used the expression "Manifest Destiny" to legitimize its occupation. Both terms, "Manifest" and "Destiny," had already appeared in one of O'Sullivan's articles in 1839 under the title "The Great Nation of Futurity," published in *The Democratic Review*. The text conveyed the spirit of American exceptionalism: "The far-reaching, the boundless future will be the era of American greatness. In its magnificent domain of space and time, the nation of many nations is *destined* to *manifest* to mankind the excellence of divine principles."[13]

In this excerpt, as we may notice, the religious terminology is quite expressive and evokes the main tenets of the Puritan ideal, since America's destiny was to show the world the preeminence of "divine principles." In addition, a strong vein of the newly arising Romantic movement also ran through the text of his 1839 editorial. Evocative images such as the "roof of firmament" and "star-studded heavens" are linked to the lyrical exaltation which contributed to the new strands of thought that characterized the "Spirit of the Time." O'Sullivan's first article had a prophetic tone; the 1845 editorial in which the expression "Manifest Destiny" appeared gave it reality. From then on, the expression became a rallying cry to promote the settlement of the West, offering a deterministic vision of history ruled by Divine power.

The opening line of O'Sullivan's second article — "It is time now for opposition to the annexation of Texas to cease" — referred to Texas' situation in the 1840s. Texas had been colonized by Spain, which had built several missions from the end of the seventeenth century until 1821; nonetheless, the Spanish population was quite scarce and composed of practically only farmers and rangers. The other inhabitants, among them Mexicans and Indians, had also settled this vast land. But gradually Mexicans began a rebellion against the Spanish authorities that lasted over ten years, at which time Mexico expelled the tiny Spanish population and took over Texas in 1821. However, when the Spanish left, the Mexicans allowed an American businessman, Stephen F. Austin, to settle there with an American community, provided they converted to Catholicism and did not practice slavery. Some of the American planters refused such ideological and religious constraints, which triggered conflicts with the Mexican authorities. In addition, American settlers had been attracted to buy land in Texas as prices were very low, which resulted in substantial growth in the population. At length, a conflict broke out between the American colonists and Texas, still legally belonging to Mexico. The colonists, who by far outnumbered the Mexicans, finally declared Texas independent in 1836.

President Andrew Jackson, who was in office at the time, recognized the independence of the Texas republic, which had drawn up its own constitution and chosen a flag that was distinguished by having only one star, hence the name, "The Lone Star Republic." Texans, the majority of whom

4—American Expansionism and Destiny

had been born in the United States and still considered themselves Americans, requested that the state be annexed to the country of their birth. But the Senate refused to ratify the admission of Texas as a state because it would upset the balance between the slave states and the free states. Yet, the majority of the Americans took an interest in its annexation since those living in the South considered the expansion of slavery into these new territories vital to its economic, cultural, and political survival, while people living in the North looked forward to establishing new trade relations.

At the time, the abolitionist movement was gaining support in the North, and the admission of Texas as a slave state would give the slave states a majority of the seats in the Senate, a development the North was determined to prevent. The Federalists, who in their great majority were opposed to slavery and expansionism, wished first to strengthen the existing states before launching into perilous expansionist adventures. O'Sullivan's 1845 article was first addressed to them, as he tried to convince these opponents to rally to his cause. He said, "It was time for the common duty of Patriotism," adding that it was "common sense to acquiesce with decent grace in the inevitable and the irrevocable." He also wanted to draw their attention to the meddling of other nations in American affairs, and their "spirit of hostile interference against us, for the avowed abject of thwarting our policy and hampering our power."

The notion of "Manifest Destiny" appeared at this crucial point, carrying with it the whole issue concerning the justification of the territorial conquest. As mentioned above, O'Sullivan, before publishing his well-known article in December 1845, stated:

> Anyone who casts a glance over the map of North America would see that Texas was a huge fragment, artificially broken off from its proper continental setting, a setting symmetrically planned and adapted in its grand destiny and duly in the possession of the race sent there for the providential purpose.[14]

Here, as already stressed above, the concept of Manifest Destiny refers not only to a Divine Order issued to open and give legitimacy to territorial expansion but also to the idea of a superior race chosen to fulfill this task. This idea emerged in the 1840s, after the British and the Americans had put forward several theories on the genetic superiority of the white race, seeking to justify the racial conflicts that punctuated territorial expansion. This subject underlay many ambiguous controversies; for example, O'Sullivan, Jackson's loyal supporter, declared that he "had to stand aloof from the delicate and dangerous topic of slavery and abolition."[15] At the time, O'Sullivan adopted a rather current attitude, reflecting the specific vision of Manifest Destiny:

> The last order of civilization, which is the democratic, received its first permanent existence in this country …, a land separated from the influences of ancient

arrangement, peculiar in its position, productions, and extent, wide enough to hold a numerous people, admitting, with facility, intercommunication and trade, vigorous and fresh from the hand of God, was requisite for the full and broad manifestation of the free spirit of the new-born democracy. Such a land was prepared in the solitudes of the Western hemisphere.[16]

Democracy was thus the American people's prerogative, a godsend from heaven destined to extend and develop over the years. Democracy already implied the idea of a promising future when human progress could be fulfilled only through the American experience. The past was a bygone issue from which lessons might be drawn. However, it could not shed light on national destiny because the despotic and tyrannical political system of monarchy, which had marked the history of the European nations, must not be reproduced on the virgin soil of the United States. As a new people, American citizens were deeply attached to these founding principles and, as far as authority was concerned, depended only on their Creator.

The Texas annexation of 1845 exemplified the expansionists' arguments as stated by O'Sullivan, who regarded this region as providentially included in the American continent and belonging to the race sent there to possess it. Despite the firm opposition of the Mexican leader Antonio Lopez de Santa Anna, and the rejection by the Senate of President Tyler's treaty of annexation in April 1844, Congress, supported by President-elect Polk, approved annexation in February 1845.

"All Oregon"

Manifest Destiny went on "manifesting itself" with the annexation of Oregon in 1846. This new acquisition was geographically important, as the nation for the first time opened a door to the Pacific Ocean. The British and the Americans had jointly administered the region since 1818 and had concluded a vague political agreement in which neither party had exclusive rights. The British Hudson Bay Company administered the northern and western parts of Oregon and the Americans controlled the remainder of the territory. This American population, after a massive migration along the Oregon Trail, including explorers, merchants and farmers, soon surpassed the English settlers in number. Around 1845, Oregon's population numbered 750 British citizens and 5,000 Americans. Tensions within the two communities occasionally erupted into conflicts, the more so as the British still represented the somewhat tyrannical motherland.

James K. Polk's election to the presidency was going to play an important part in the Oregon annexation, as his supporters had advocated the occupation of the region. In his inaugural speech, on March 4, 1845, Polk affirmed his intention to annex Oregon, considering this right as "clear and unquestionable":

> Nor will it become in a lesser degree my duty to assert and maintain by all constitutional means the right of the United States to that portion of our territory which lies beyond the Rocky Mountains. Our title to the country of the Oregon is "clear and unquestionable," and already our people are preparing to perfect that title by occupying it with their wives and children. But eighty years ago our population was confined on the west by the ridge of the Alleghenies. Within that period — within the lifetime, I may say, of some of my hearers — our people, increasing to many millions, have filled the eastern valley of the Mississippi, adventurously ascended the Missouri to its headsprings, and are already engaged in establishing the blessing of self-government in valleys of which the rivers flow to the Pacific. The world beholds the peaceful triumphs of the industry of our immigrants. To us belongs the duty of protecting them adequately wherever they may be upon our soil. The jurisdiction of our laws and the benefits of our republican institutions should be extended over them in the distant regions which they have selected for their homes. The increasing facilities of intercourse will easily bring the States, of which the formation in that part of our territory can no longer be delayed, within the sphere of our federative Union. In the meantime every obligation imposed by treaty or conventional stipulations should be sacredly respected.[17]

Throughout this speech, Polk's expansionist rhetoric expresses the distinctive elements inherent in Manifest Destiny, namely the notion of inevitability relating to the integration of Oregon into the American continent, the mention of the increasing population to legitimize the settlement of people "engaged in establishing the blessing of self-government" and the idea of sacredness attached to the respect of stipulations.

Other incidents in Polk's policy corroborated his religiously inclined self-assurance. Negotiations with the British were long and difficult, as the latter did not wish to yield the entire region; consequently, both parties started to agree on partition. However, this decision did not fully satisfy Polk's ambitions, and the president grew increasingly impatient to the point of retracting a proposition he had made to the British. As nearly all conciliatory approaches ended in failure, the dispute reached a critical stage and war with England was even contemplated. Polk declared to his Secretary of State that if there was a war, the United States would "stand in the right in the eyes of the whole civilized world, and ... England would be in the wrong."[18]

Britain finally ceded Oregon to the United States in 1846 after a long debate over the territory's borders. It was important for the president to settle this issue because he wanted to concentrate his full attention on Mexico. On this Oregon issue, President Polk had been supported by a large majority in Congress, and *The Washington Union* reported that when Polk claimed Oregon in its entirety, shouting "All Oregon," Congress hastened to answer "Amen!," which resounded as a clear echo of Manifest Destiny right at the core of the federal government. At the same time, *The Democratic Review* published a lyrical ode "to the coming fusion of England manufacturing and American agriculture" to emphasize the fact that the two parties sealed their destiny into a single community. In the end, the Oregon issue had tightened the link between the Americans and the British, since both communities belonged to the Anglo-Saxon race from which "prosperity would ensue."[19]

The U.S.–Mexican War: A Mission of Regeneration

After the annexations of Texas and Oregon, some Americans, especially Whigs like Henry Clay, thought the nation should gather strength and consolidate before expanding further. They feared this expansion would jeopardize the delicate balance of interests within the Union between pro-slavery and free states. In 1847, a Whig congressman addressed the expansionists with what proved to be prophetic insight: "You are rushing headlong and blindfolded upon appalling dangers; you are rekindling the slumbering fires of a volcano."[20] Indeed, such a clear-sighted statement foreshadowed the American Civil War.

After settling the Oregon question, Polk turned his attention to the American West, particularly to cities such as San Francisco and San Diego, which offered business opportunities. These territories belonged to Mexico, but American settlers had gradually invaded the Sacramento and San Joaquin valleys via the Santa Fe Trail. As a consequence, Mexico, which had not recognized Texas' independence, broke off diplomatic relations. At that time, most expansionists adhered to the common belief that the United States had a God-given right to extend its power to civilize Native Americans or Spanish-speaking Mexicans. Consequently, they were ready to follow Polk and his government into a military enterprise in order to expand the American territory from "sea to shining sea."

Several Democrats supported the president after he issued his war message in Congress, arguing that a war with Mexico would enhance the U.S. image abroad. One of the congressmen, Cass, told the Senate: "The present is a most important crisis which is perhaps, to affect our character and our destiny for a long series of years." Another deputy, Bennett, added that war could be an excellent opportunity for the United States to "teach foreign powers to dread the free people of this republic." Finally, at the beginning of the hostilities in 1847, a third congressman, Ritchie, stated that "the

United States had been at peace for a considerable portion of a century; our deeds of military prowess had been forgotten; our capacities, either to defend ourselves or to assert our rights and honor by arms, were almost unknown."[21] The same Ritchie noted at the end of the war: "The military prowess of our people and of our institutions has excited the astonishment and won the admiration of the world."[22] It was in this particular context that the conflict burst out, Polk himself having backed his supporters' statements before the beginning of the conflict, noting that "European and other foreign powers entertained imperfect and erroneous views of our physical strength as a nation and of our ability to prosecute war, and especially a war waged out of our own country."[23] Convinced of their exceptional virtues as a nation, the United States entered war with Mexico.

The U.S. Mexican war broke out in April 1846 when an incident occurred on the borders of the Rio Grande. Mexican cavalry forces attacked American troops on territory south of the Nueces River in Texas, which both the United States and Mexico claimed. President Polk ordered General Zachary Taylor and his army into this region to defend the border. During this time, he sent an envoy, John Slidell, to Mexico to conduct negotiations in order to annex these territories. To this effect, Slidell offered the Mexican government the cancellation of its debts in exchange for Texas' independence, which, as previously noted, had still not been recognized by the Mexican authorities. Slidell also asked Mexico to sign an agreement detailing the borders of the Rio Grande. Moreover, President Polk was interested in purchasing California and part of New Mexico, for which he offered the sum of 30 million dollars. Not only did the Mexican government turn down Slidell's offer, but General Mariona Paredes, the new head of state, refused to receive him. Slidell was outraged and returned to Washington convinced that the Mexicans would not give up an inch of their territories unless they were "chastised."

Polk responded to the situation by ordering General Zachary Taylor to advance to the Rio Grande, bringing fear to the Mexicans who crossed the river on April 25, 1845, to attack an American patrol. Polk asked Congress for authorization to declare war, stating that "war exists," but before the latter could respond, he sent more troops to the front. Within a week, American troops pushed the Mexicans back, inflicting heavy casualties. After defeating the Mexican forces, Taylor won a series of victories in California, seizing Los Angeles and Monterey. The number of dead and wounded reached a thousand, while the American losses did not exceed fifty.

Yet on the political level, Polk began to worry about the widening opposition to war among the American public. People living in the northern states feared the expansion of slavery and some, including a young Whig congressman from Illinois, Abraham Lincoln, accused Polk of betraying Congress and playing the role of an aggressor. But Polk's plan, which consisted in driving the Mexicans away from Texas, invading California and New Mexico, and then marching on Mexico City, imposed itself, as it seemed to pursue the irresistible appeal of Manifest Destiny. The Mexico City campaign, which had been launched to take the capital, was the most difficult of all the other war objectives, and Polk, having doubts about General Taylor's competence, replaced him with General Winfield Scott, a decorated hero of the War of 1812 against the British. Scott laid siege to Mexico City and entered it on September 14, 1847, but the Mexicans, although defeated, refused to capitulate. The city was so devastated that Scott feared for a moment that no one would be left to sign the treaty. Finally, the Treaty of Guadalupe Hidalgo was signed in February 1848, granting the U.S. the region of the Rio Grande bordering Texas, New Mexico and California.

Thus, the acquisition of these new territories seemed to bring Manifest Destiny to fruition with the United States stretching across the North American continent. Following these annexations, the U.S. government had to deal with the problems of assimilating these new foreign populations. Racial controversies developed as the expansionists sought to convert these former enemies so they could enter the "sanctuary of American democracy."[24] An American citizen, Justin Smith, conducted a study of the Mexican War and declared that Providence had entrusted the Americans with the task of "regenerating" the decadent Mexican population. Obviously, the anti-expansionists did not share this line of thinking, which (according to them) restricted the idea of true democracy. Nonetheless, it was at the time of the annexations of Texas and Oregon that Smith's opinion was expressed with greater force through the words of Congressman Duncan, who extolled the exceptional quality of Anglo-Saxon institutions compared to Spanish and French institutions which had slowly faded away, given their inability to enact "liberal and equal laws."[25]

In return, the Mexicans took their revenge by treating the Yankee planters as a "degenerate part of the English race." Americans hardly tolerated such insults, and it is often said that those who supported the war were not only motivated by expansionism but also by the idea that the Mexicans' folly and arrogance had to be "punished," as Slidell remarked. Walt Whitman, the great American poet, had himself declared, "Yes, Mexico must be chastised,"[26] adding that Americans were as capable of "crushing the enemy as to conquer territories."

The theory of "regeneration," widely proclaimed during the Mexican War and in the debates that followed, also permeated the press. For instance, *The Illinois State Register* asked of its readers: "Shall this garden of beauty be suffered to lie dormant in its wild and useless luxuriance?" *The New Her-*

ald echoed: "This territory belongs not to indolent Mexico but to the people who would use it to scatter God's blessings to mankind." As for *The Democratic Review*, it issued the following statement: "The process which has gone through the North, of driving back the Indians, or annihilating them as a race has yet to go through the South."[27]

The Imperialist Urge: Annexation of Hawaii, Cuba and the Philippines

With Manifest Destiny "still running loose,"[28] the last decade of the nineteenth century was dominated by the emergence of an imperialistic foreign policy. Islands in the mid–Pacific started to attract diplomatic and military personnel, as they could be used as stations for improving trade with China and as eventual bases for the American merchant marine. The young politician Albert J. Beveridge voiced these political ambitions:

> American factories are making more than the American people can use; American soil is producing more than they can consume. Fate has written our policy for us; the trade of the world must and shall be ours.... We will establish trading-posts throughout the world as distributing points for American products. We will cover the ocean with our merchant marine. Great colonies governing themselves, flying our flag and trading with us, will grow about our posts of trade. Our institutions will follow our flag on the wings of commerce. And American law, American order, American civilization, and the American flag will plant themselves, on the shores hitherto bloody and benighted but by those agencies of God henceforth to be made beautiful and bright.[29]

All the ingredients of the expansionists' destinarian vision were inscribed in this text. President William McKinley, a Republican, who held office from 1897 until his assassination in 1901, together with members of his administration, realized that Hawaii indeed offered a very good geographical and commercial position for American interests. The islands had weathered a revolution in 1893, during which the rebels asked for American assistance, but the U.S. government, headed at the time by President Grover Cleveland (1893–1897), refused to commit the country's forces in the region. However, shortly after McKinley became president, the government of Hawaii on April 3, 1897, officially asked the United States to open negotiations for eventual annexation. The Japanese navy was anchored near Hawaii, and McKinley, fearing a Japanese invasion of the islands, hastened to sign a treaty on June 6.

The Japanese protested because the status quo in Hawaii was essential to the good relations between the nations and their interests in the Pacific Ocean. McKinley resisted and the Japanese government abandoned its claims after a series of diplomatic notes. The treaty required a two-thirds majority to be ratified by the Senate, but met with conflicting positions. The opposition came mainly from Democrats, who were concerned by the racial composition of the Hawaiian population. Failing to obtain the required two-thirds majority, McKinley declared to his personal secretary, George B. Cortelyou, in March 1898, "We need Hawaii just as much, and a good deal more, than we did California. It is manifest destiny."[30]

During the Hawaiian revolution, the magazine *Harper's* published an article entitled "Manifest Destiny" authored by Carl Schurz, who reported "the acquisition of such territory, far and near, as may be useful in enlarging our commercial advantages, and in securing to our navy facilities desirable for the operations of a great naval power."[31]

After the signing of the treaty with Hawaii, Congressman Mitchell stated that people had been more convinced of the justification of annexing Hawaii by the slogan of Manifest Destiny and the "logic of events" than by rational arguments. However, opponents of its annexation reacted by saying, "Never should such a scurvy thing as this Destiny be running around the universe loose. Signs should be erected everywhere to shoot it at sight."[32]

Concerning the term "destiny," it must be noted, as already mentioned above, that its semantic meaning derived from a religious concept was altered under the influence of the scientific era, which marked its beginning during this period, and the word became related to the determining aspects of nature and progress. Before being appointed as Lincoln's secretary of state, Senator William Seward, seeking to justify the American commercial interests in the Pacific Ocean, noted: "Our course has been shaped not so much by any self-guiding wisdom of our own, as by a law of progress and development impressed upon us but nature itself."[33] Indeed, in the 1890s, the expansionists declared that the annexation of Hawaii was considered by the American statesmen as a "contingent necessity."[34]

Many people argued for the annexation of Cuba, considered as Spain's treasure chest and located only a short distance from Florida, claiming that Manifest Destiny and common sense connected the two pieces of land. The island's strategic and commercial links with its Yankee neighbor seemed obvious. So when Cubans started to revolt against Spanish oppression in 1895, after the Ten Years' War (1868–1878), American intervention was welcomed by the rebels. During a previous conflict on the island under President Ulysses S. Grant, a man from Kentucky had written a letter arguing, "For God's sake, let us go in, and Cuba, voluptuous Cuba will be the reward."[35] This revolt against Spain resulted in many casualties, and the Cuban economy, in which U.S. businesses had a controlling interest, began to deteriorate, which led the United States to take notice. In 1895, public opinion, inflamed by the press and supported by big business, began supporting the idea of liberating the island from Spain. Ohio Senator John Sherman boldly stated, "No earthly power would keep the United States out of Cuba."[36] On April 4, 1896, the U.S. government declared that Spain did not have any claim on Cuba, but required of the Cubans to cease the rebellion. President Grover Cleveland announced that American troops would intervene only once the ultimatum had expired. During these talks, the press played an important role, highlighting (and often exaggerating) the atrocities of the rebellion and mobilizing public opinion in favor of intervention. Walt Whitman encouraged U.S. intervention in Cuba: "It is impossible to say what the future will bring forth, but 'manifest destiny' certainly points to the speedy annexation of Cuba by the United States."[37]

In February 1897, McKinley expressed his opinion in a document entitled "The Untried Alternatives in Cuba," in which the echoes of Manifest Destiny were clearly expressed: "If it shall hereafter appear a duty imposed by our obligations to ourselves, to civilization and humanity to intervene with force, it will be without fault on our part and only because the necessity for such action will be so clear as to command the support and approval of the civilized world."[38]

McKinley's decision to intervene militarily in April 1898 was based on the idea that the United States had a role to play as *guardian* of civilization. This idea marked the beginning of the Spanish-American War, the "splendid little war" as Secretary of State John Hay liked to call it. After three months of fighting, the aim of the combat purportedly being to protect American citizens who had settled in Cuba, the island was freed and obtained its independence before being made a protectorate of the United States in 1901.

As for the acquisition of the Spanish-held Philippines, the Manifest Destiny theme went almost unnoticed, since hardly anyone in America was aware of the existence of these "obscure and unknown" islands. And the people who had heard of them generally thought that they might eventually be invaded by Russia or Japan. Yet Senator Henry Cabot Lodge contemplated not only annexing Hawaii but also expanding the Navy, maintaining American influence in Samoa, building the Panama Canal, and acquiring a large naval base in the Pacific Ocean.[39] In reality, it was a group of naval officers who proposed their plans to McKinley in 1897 after drawing up a war strategy. Congress was in favor of their objectives, most members believing that Spain had to give up her colonial empire as a war indemnity.

When Admiral George Dewey won the first victory in Manila in May 1898, it was a surprise for all those who were unaware of the existence of these distant islands. Once the Philippine Islands had been invaded, a debate arose about their fate. After many hesitations as to whether to conquer part or all of them, McKinley declared, "Duty requires us to take the archipelago." Several options were duly studied: should the United States keep only a naval base, establish a protectorate, or divide the archipelago into several zones of influence? But President McKinley suggested that it was the role of Providence to decide. "Congress can declare war," he said, "but a higher power decrees its bounds and fixes its relations and responsibilities."[40] As the president was interviewed by a delegation of Methodists in 1899, he developed this pious reflection:

> I walked the floor of the White House night after night until midnight; and I am not ashamed to tell you, gentlemen, that I went down on my knees and prayed Almighty God for light and guidance I went down more that one night. And one night, it came to me this way—I don't know how it was, but it came. (1) That we could not give them back to Spain—that would be cowardly and dishonorable; (2) that we could not turn them over to France or Germany—our commercial rivals in the Orient—that would be bad business and discreditable; (3) that we could not leave them to themselves—they were unfit for self-government—and they would soon have anarchy and misrule over there worse than Spain's was; and (4) that there was nothing left for us to do but to take them all and educate the Filipinos, and uplift and Christianize them, and by God's grace do the very best we could by them, as our fellow-men for whom Christ also died.[41]

President McKinley's words mirror most of the popular ideas of the time combined in the catchphrase Manifest Destiny, namely, religious belief, intense nationalism and America's mission in the world. Since the beginning of the territorial conquest, the U.S. expansionist policy was stamped by these key themes which punctuated each stage of the westward movement. It was clear that Jefferson's dream of a united and single nation in which all populations would merge peacefully had not been realized, given all the pains and bloodshed that were inflicted on the Native Americans and Mexicans.

Likewise, beyond North America, in the last decade of the nineteenth century, while the revival of the term Manifest Destiny occurred to promote overseas expansion, notably in Hawaii, Cuba and the Philippines, a wave of criticism arose. One of its strong opponents, William Jennings Bryan, wrote: "Destiny is not as manifest as it was a few weeks ago!"[42] However, it seems that the idea of a Manifest Destiny "allotted by Providence" never ceased to haunt the American psyche in its justified or unjustified political and military interventions. During World War I, President Woodrow Wilson spoke of the purity and spiritual power of democracy, stating that the United States was "in the presence of the realization of the destiny which we have awaited, its manifest destiny."[43]

5

America:
A God-Centered Nation

Presidents and Ideals

American nationalism not only took shape through the main events of the westward expansion but was also encouraged by presidents and prominent political figures of this period, among them Thomas Jefferson (1743–1826), author of the Declaration of Independence, who was elected president at the beginning of the nineteenth century. As a political theorist, Jefferson supported ideas based on agrarian philosophy, which were already imbued with the spirit of Manifest Destiny. Jefferson feared that ongoing urbanization and industrialization would undermine citizens' rights: "Industry creates degrading living conditions, whereas farmers, owners of their lands and thus enjoying freedom, had better living conditions."[1] The statesman believed that the development of farming would favor men's happiness, making them more virtuous; he had advocated colonial expansion to encourage the creation of a real "Arcadia" where everyone would cultivate his own garden. When the president purchased the Louisiana territory, doubling the area of the United States, he fulfilled what is often called the "Jeffersonian dream." As he was considered the great inspirer of the Declaration of Independence, having advocated individuals' inalienable rights (life, liberty, the pursuit of happiness, etc.), his political actions and writings always emphasized a democratic ideal based on man's fundamental dignity and equality. Largely influenced by the Enlightenment philosophers and John Locke's writings, Jefferson believed in a kind of "public felicity" stemming from a moral and philosophical approach to political life and based on a social contract between citizens and responsible governments. In addition, Jefferson appeared as a precursor to the transcendental ethics inscribed at the core of Manifest Destiny, as this statement from his inaugural speech testifies: "America, favored by the numerous virtues of a diversified religion, acknowledged the capital role of Providence in the prodigality that she exerted on men in this world and in the other world."[2]

Andrew Jackson (1767–1845) embraced the Jeffersonian spirit and adhered to this specific vision of America. As presidents, both concentrated on the restoration of American democracy. Like Jefferson, Jackson's ambitions were to defend the "common man" against aristocracy. As an ardent nationalist, he defeated the English in 1815 and fought the Indians in the southern states. What is more, Jackson shared his forbears' mythical ideas about God's providential benevolence to his Chosen People. During one of his military campaigns, Old Hickory, as Jackson was commonly called, wrote a letter to his wife, telling her that he had occupied an Indian town and was given "a few cattle, and about three thousand bushels of corn ... this was a providential supply, the truth is that we have been fed like the Israelites of old in the wilderness."[3]

Contrary to the presidents who preceded him and whose families came from the Virginian elite, he considered himself the best representative of the people. The following anecdote illustrates his ardent desire to adopt his people's religious convictions. As he was living with a woman who had left her husband on account of his cruelty and disturbed mind — and not legally divorced — Jackson received a pamphlet from his political opponents, asking, "Ought a convicted adulteress and her paramour husband be placed in the Highest office of this free and Christian land?"[4] Jackson quickly married, for he did not wish to betray the religious ideal of a country whose values he wished to support. Indeed, the new president had a populist approach and shared most of his constituents' concerns, particularly regarding issues related to the Native Americans. His Indian policy made him very popular but, at times, testified to dramatic and unconscious blindness.

During his two terms, 90 treaties were signed with Indian tribes, but, gradually, they were forced to abandon their land to the ever-growing number of advancing white settlers. To palliate the painful situation, the president created an Indian territory in Arkansas and, in 1836, the Bureau of Indian Affairs, in charge of settling disputes. A few months after the vote on the Removal Act (1830), Congress passed a law to relocate Native American tribes living east of the Mississippi River. In his second annual message (December 6, 1830), Andrew Jackson gave his personal version of the "successful" enterprise through a rhetoric fraught with bare contentment towards the Native Americans: "Towards the aborigines of the country, no one can indulge a more friendly feeling than myself, or would go further in attempting to reclaim them from their wandering habits and make them happy, prosperous people."[5]

Jackson's discourse was equally pervaded by a utopian and romantic vision of life, arguing that "it was a source of joy" to see that America's young population, "unconstrained in body and mind," could develop "the power and faculties of men to the highest perfection."[6] A feeling of national self-righteousness also ran through the text as he tried to compare the Indians' plight to the migrants' exodus from Europe. Evoking the Europeans' departure from their homelands, heading for "an unknown land," abandoning their belongings to "seek new home in distant regions," Jackson focused on the Indians' fate. He declared: "If the offers made to the Indians were extended to them (the Whites), they would be hailed with gratitude and joy ... the policy of the General Government toward the red man is not only liberal but generous."

One also finds a certain racial antagonism in the way Jackson expressed himself regarding the civilized world versus the world of the "savages." Wishing to uplift the aborigines' morals, he imagined them as a "dense and civilized population covering large tracts of country now occupied by a few savage hunters," adding that "it will separate the Indians from immediate contact with settlements of Whites." In the same manner, Jackson noted that their savage habits should be cast off so that they would be able to form an "interesting Christian community." Finally, Jackson's insistent emphasis on racial discrimination relates to the notion of home: "And is it supposed that the wandering savage has a strongest attachment to his home than the settled, civilized Christian?" All these comments must be understood in their historical context, of course, but their incisive resonance still affects the modern reader's sensitivity.

The Indians' plight is connected to the doctrine of Manifest Destiny in the sense that it includes a determinist factor, as the inevitable move of the white population cannot be restrained: "The waves of population and civilization are rolling to the westward, and we now propose to acquire countries occupied by the red man of the South and the West by a fair exchange, and at the expense of the United States, to send them to a land where their existence may be prolonged and perhaps made perpetual." The inexorable character of the removal of Indian populations is also stressed by Jackson's bold rhetoric when he put the question: "Can it be cruel in the Government when, by events which it can not control, the Indian is made discontented in his ancient home to purchase his lands, to give him a new extensive territory, to pay the expense of his removal, and support him a year in his new abode?"

The strongest moral incentive that stood out to justify the Indians' displacement, and which underlay Jackson's speech, may be found in the religiously inclined Puritan doctrine, according to which Native Americans descended from a cursed tribe of ancient Israel. Thus, they had to be converted to enter the American Holy Shrine, the citizens of which would unite to "open the eyes of the children of the forest to their true condition, and by a speedy removal, to relieve them from all evils, real or imaginary, present or prospective, with which they may be supposed to be threatened."

The removal of the Native Americans beyond the Mississippi River began in the 1830s, and is generally called the Trail of Tears. One in four of the travelers never arrived; several thousand Indians died during this doleful exodus, due to disease, exposure and exhaustion. At the time, because of his relentless involvement in subduing Native Americans, Jackson was referred to as Sharp Knife. Yet the seventh president of the United States remained convinced of his positive role in the building of a republic, "studded with cities, towns and prosperous farms, embellished with all the improvements which art can devise or industry execute, occupied by more than twelve million happy people, and filled with all the blessings of liberty, civilization, and religion."[7]

Despite his successful national deeds, Jackson's policy concerning the Indian issue to "extend the area of freedom" was severely criticized by several Democrats whose views were less nationalistic and who did not assent to the credo of Manifest Destiny. One of them, in a Fourth of July speech to the trade unionists of Boston in 1834, reminded the audience that "Patriotism consists in nothing but a brotherly affection, an extensive love toward the whole human family."[8] In the same spirit, Staughton Lynd cited Seth Luther's words in his *Address to the Working Men of New England* in 1833, underlining the fact that "national glory often covered human suffering," adding "Did not the Bible say that God had made the nations of one blood, a truth confirmed by the Declaration of Independence? Lafayette, Pulaski, Steuben and others had help in the Revolution." Stressing the negative role of extreme chauvinism, Seth Luther further declared: "It is this damnable principle [of nationalism] which has desolated the earth for centuries," and "made our beautiful earth one vast slaughter house."[9] These dissenting voices catalyzed strong opposition against the exacerbated nationalism within the political and intellectual arenas. However, in spite of these conflicting views in the Democratic Party, President Jackson delivered his farewell address stressing America's unique destiny, among nations, allotted by Providence:

> You have the highest of human trusts committed to your care. Providence showered on this favored land blessings without number, and has chosen you as guardians of freedom, to preserve it for the benefit of the human race. May He who holds in His hands destinies of nations, make you worthy of the favors He has bestowed, and enable you, with pure hearts and hands and sleepless vigilance, to guard and defend to the end of time, the great charge He has committed to your keeping.[10]

After Jackson, American political life experienced a period of relative serenity, and the part played by the presidents of the United States, in home or foreign affairs, was generally less noteworthy, although the national feeling remained an emblematic trait of American politics. Martin Van Buren held office from 1837 to 1841. In line with the nationalistic ideal of the time, the eighth U.S. president mentioned the American experiment as an example to the rest of the world in his inaugural speech on March 4, 1837: "The power and influence of the Republic have arisen to a height obvious to all mankind." He further declared that the American Constitution was a "sacred instrument."[11] But less than three months later, the financial panic of 1837 tarnished his mandate, as it was a severe blow to American economic prosperity. His successor, William Henry Harrison (1841), died from pneumonia one month after his inauguration, which thrust the country into a political crisis. The following president, John Tyler (1841–1845) vetoed a new bank bill that had been passed by Congress, causing most of his cabinet members to resign. Concerning the issue on the interaction of religion and politics, it should be noted that on July 10, 1843, President Tyler wrote a letter to Joseph Simpson, which included the following text on the separation of Church and State:

> The United States has adventured upon a great and noble experiment, which is believed to have been hazarded in the absence of all previous precedent—that of total separation of Church and State. No religious establishment by law exists among us. The conscience is left free from all restraint and each is permitted to worship his Maker after his own judgment. The offices of the Government are open alike to all. No tithes are levied to support an established Hierarchy, nor is the fallible judgment of man set up as the sure and infallible creed of faith. The Mohammedan, if he will to come among us would have the privilege guaranteed to him by the Constitution to worship according to the Koran; and the East Indian might erect a shrine to Brahma if it so pleased him. Such is the spirit of toleration inculcated by our political institutions.... The Hebrew persecuted and down trodden in other regions takes up his abode among us with none to make him afraid ... and the Aegis of the government is over him to defend and protect him. Such is the great experiment which we have tried, and such are the happy fruits which have resulted from it; our system of free government would be imperfect without it.[12]

Tyler's text reflects the true spirit of the Enlightenment philosophy and should be remembered for its clear-sightedness and integrity. As a philanthropist and due to his consideration of the people, Tyler was nicknamed Honest John. Vice president at the death of Harrison, he was also dubbed His Accidency because no one expected him to take office. Finally, his third nickname, The Veto President was given to him on the grounds that he had vetoed many laws.

With Polk's election in 1845, the Democrats returned to power and the new president played a major role on the political scene. Under his presidency, the idea of Manifest Destiny flourished through three episodes of territorial expansion: the annexations of Texas and Oregon, and during the Mexican War. Polk's strong will and determination to annex these territories were criticized as he was often accused of a lack of integrity and of having strong financial ambitions. To justify the annexation of Texas, President Polk stressed the inevitable character of the westward movement: "Texas had been absorbed into the Union in the inevitable fulfillment of the general law which is rolling our population westward ... it was disintegrating from Mexico in the natural course of events, by a process perfectly legitimate on its own part, blameless on ours; and in which all the censures due to wrong, perfidy and folly, rest on Mexico alone."[13]

The annexation of Texas was of prime importance since it opened up the route to the West, which was to become the new El Dorado of the American adventurers, the discovery of gold leading to the well-known Gold Rush. Curiously, the annexation of Texas took place under unexpected circumstances—its proclamation of independence, the Texas Declaration of Independence, written in haste in a single night and modeled on the American Declaration of Independence, concluded as follows:

> We are, therefore, forced to the melancholy conclusion, that the Mexican people have acquiesced in the destruction of their liberty, and the substitution therefore of a military government; that they are unfit to be free, and incapable of self-government ... and, conscious of the rectitude of our intentions, we fearlessly and confidently commit the issue to the decision of the Supreme arbiter of the destinies of nations.[14]

Similarly, Polk's ambiguous attitude during the Mexican War raised many heated debates, and it has often been said that Polk was always looking for pretexts to invade Mexican territory. Thus as he accused the Mexicans of having crossed the American border, "...invaded our territory and shed American blood upon American soil,"[15] an internal source reported that the day before the Mexican attack, Polk had already prepared his message requesting a declaration of war. The crisis took the form of a popular cause despite the opposition of many diplomats and politicians who doubted Polk's sincerity. Congressman and former president John Quincy Adams condemned the declaration, calling this conflict "a most unjust war," and Senator John C. Calhoun, fearing a war of aggression, voted against it.[16]

In his second annual message to Congress, on December 8, 1848, war with Mexico having been declared after the failure of the Slidell mission, Polk endeavored to justify the war by giving a detailed list of its causes. The president began to evoke the irresistible development of the American grandeur, gradually unveiling his nationalistic vision of the United States, stressing the historical role of the nation: "The process of our country in her career of greatness, not only in the vast extension of our territorial limits and the rapid increase of our population, but in resources and wealth and in the happy condition of our people, is without an example in the history of nations."[17]

The many occurrences of the term "civilized" in his speech reinforced the idea that, compared to Mexico, America was an important country among modern civilized nations. Polk tried to justify his military intervention by saying: "After years of endurance of aggravated and unredressed wrongs on our part, Mexico, in violation of the solemn treaty stipulations and of every principle of justice recognized by civilized nations, commenced hostilities, and thus, by her own act, forced the war upon us."

President Polk also praised America and the inestimable value of its citizens, speaking of "the great body of our people" who acquiesced to the war, being "eminently patriotic" to protect their country's honor and interest by scarifying themselves, entailing a feeling of "national pride and exultation" for himself and within the governmental sphere: "The alacrity and promptness with which our volunteer forces rushed to the field of their country's call prove not only their patriotism, but their deep conviction that our cause is just."

According to President Polk, Mexico initiated the war when its cavalry forces attacked American troops south of the Nueces River in Texas, which both the United States and Mexico claimed. It was equally Mexico which "started the system of insult and spoliation," said Polk, noting that American citizens "engaged in lawful commerce were imprisoned," that "American vessels were seized" and the American flag "insulted." Worst of all, "Mexico herself became an aggressor by invading our soil in hostile array and shedding the blood of our citizens."[18]

Polk emphasized that America's attitude was irreproachable and sought to prove his point through various elements of justification: "We might appeal to the whole civilized world for the justice of our cause." Striving to convey America's sense of self-righteousness, Polk boasted American virtues such as "the love of peace" and its "magnanimous moderation." His speech constitutes an important page of American history, since it reflects the deep nationalistic motives that animated the expansionist leaders of those days, marked, at times, by racial inflections, as suggested by Anders Stephanson's ironic remark: "The degraded Mexican-Spanish race was in no state to receive the virtues of the Anglo-Saxon race."[19]

The "Great Triumvirate"

Several prominent American statesmen played key roles in shaping the American national spirit. Among them were John C. Calhoun, Henry Clay, and Daniel Webster. Through their actions and speeches, these important figures greatly contributed to the American national ideology that pervaded American history insofar as the three were undoubtedly influenced by the notion of Manifest Destiny. Merril D. Peterson focused on their role in the particular political conjuncture:

Webster, Clay and Calhoun: the destinies of these three men who met in Congress in May 1813 were intertwined. Their arrival on the political stage announced a new era of American statesmanship, and their departure forty years later brought it emphatically to a close. They were representatives, spokesmen, ultimately personifications, of their respective sections: East, West, and South. Intensely ambitious, they were more often political rivals than friends; and although each would be disappointed in his quest for presidency, they were widely regarded at home and abroad as the foremost American statesmen of this age. In 1832, when they came together in the Senate for the first time and coalesced in opposition to the president, Andrew Jackson, the idea of "The Great Triumvirate" was born. It was the offspring of the feverish Jacksonian imagination, for the prospect was very small of these master spirits—Caesar's death.[20]

Henry Clay, the oldest of the three, was born in Hanover County, Virginia in 1777. After studying law, he became a brilliant lawyer and was appropriately nicknamed the "Orator of the Age." It is said he never lost a case. One day, after defending a murderer who came to thank him, he responded, "Ah, Willis, poor fellow, I fear I have saved too many like you, you ought to be hung!"[21] Clay was a charismatic statesman, filled with enthusiasm and optimism. Endowed with a lively temper, his warmth and generosity attracted a large audience, as he knew how to charm and enrapture people. An outgoing personality, he enjoyed drinking, playing poker, and telling stories. Moreover, clever, open-minded and a fervent nationalist (like his colleagues), he bluntly stated to a gathering of American senators: "I love true glory. It is this sentiment which ought to be cherished, in spite of cavils and sneers and attempts to put it down, it finally conducted this nation to that height to which God and nature have destined it."[22]

Clay was a well-known conservative who for thirty years defended his ideas in the Senate, resorting to a vivid and enflamed style. But despite several attempts, he never succeeded in winning the presidency. On the issue of slavery, his views remained firm and rested on religious principles. During one of his election campaigns when he gave his personal opinion on slavery, a Quaker strongly reacted to his views, telling him that as a patriot, a philanthropist and, a Christian, he ought to free his slaves in order to set an example for his pro-slavery constituents. Clay answered that, in his view, equality was an abstract principle, adding: "I look upon slavery as a great evil ... what would be the condition of the two races in those slave States upon the supposition of an immediate emancipation? Does any man suppose that they would become blended in one homogeneous mass? Does any recommend amalgamation, that revolting mixture, alike offensive to God and man?"[23]

Clay's theory was based on the fact that there were too many differences between the races. His idea was to gradually emancipate black people and send them back to Africa in order to avoid potential tragedies and racial conflicts in the future. His answer to the frustrated Quaker citizen expressed a certain amount of irritation and aggressiveness: "Go home, and mind your own business, Mr. Mendenhall, and leave other people to take care of theirs. Limit your benevolent exertions to your own neighborhood. Within that circle you will find ample scope for the exercise of your charities. Dry up the tears of the afflicted widows around you, console and comfort the helpless orphan, clothe the naked, and feed and help the poor, black and white, who need succor; and you will be a better and wiser man than you have this day shown yourself."[24]

Henry Clay died on June 29, 1852. The same day, Lincoln, who had called him a "beau ideal of a statesman," had a public tribute organized for the outstanding orator. During this tribute, he delivered a moving eulogy, noting about Henry Clay that "The spell — the long enduring — with which the souls of men were bound to him" was "a miracle." Lincoln further commented:

> He was surpassingly eloquent ... yet, Mr. Clay's eloquence did not consist, as many fine specimens of eloquence do, of types and figures — of antithesis, and elegant arrangement of words and sentences; but rather of that deeply earnest and impassionate tone, and manner, which can proceed only from great sincerity and a thorough conviction, in the speaker of the justice and importance of the cause. This it is that truly touches the chords of sympathy; and those who heard Mr. Clay never failed to be moved by it, or ever afterwards, forgot the impression.... Mr. Clay's predominant sentiment, from first to last, was a deep devotion to the cause of human liberty — a strong sympathy with the oppressed everywhere, and an ardent wish for their elevation.... During its delivery [of speeches] the reporters forgot their vocations, dropped their pens, and sat enchanted from near the beginning to quite the close.[25]

Regarding the issue of slavery, Lincoln reminded the public that Clay's position was to be respectfully understood, as Clay thought there was a "moral fitness in the idea of returning to Africa her children, whose ancestors have been torn from her by the ruthless hand of fraud and violence." Clay believed that, once settled in their native land, they would draw profit from the rich and fruitful experience they had acquired on the American soil. He thought this might be part of the great designs of the Ruler of the universe, transforming thus "an original crime, into a signal blessing to that most unfortunate portion of the globe."[26] Lincoln concluded his speech by encouraging Americans to "strive to deserve, as far as mortals may, the continued care of divine Providence, trusting that, in future national emergencies, He will not fail to provide us the instruments of safety and security."

The second member of the triumvirate, John Calhoun, was born in 1782, in South Carolina, and became a typical southern leader, as he claimed: "There is my family and connections. There I drew my first breath; there are all my hopes. I am a planter — a cotton planter — I am a southerner man and a slaveholder — a kind and merciful one, I trust and none the worse from being a slaveholder."[27] Calhoun was of Scotch-Irish descent and was raised as a Calvinistic Presbyterian, following his father to the frontier in his relentless fighting of Indians. The child had no formal schooling but read extensively thanks to a nearby library. Life at the Calhouns' was far from being joyful and fancy, and induced the youngster to spend his time reading: "Having skipped the slow, hesitant, dreamy learning of childhood, with all its innocent fantasies and pleasures, Calhoun suddenly vaulted into the realm of the philosophers."[28]

At his father's death, the young man was obliged to take over the farm, but people around him, aware of his intellectual abilities, advised him to pursue a classical education, which eventually led him to Yale University. After graduating from Yale, he was elected senator in 1811, and often expressed his nationalistic ideas in Congress where he was widely supported by his peers. This political backing opened a new career for him, as it contributed to his appointment as secretary of war. Calhoun was considered a clever and learned man, but had a reputation for making blunders; a British observer once noted that his knowledge of human nature was somewhat limited. Nonetheless, Calhoun's mind and character, "hard — grave, inflexible —" were all one. Morally and temperamentally, he was more Puritan than the Puritans. The purity of his private life, conceded by all, tended to elevate his public life, placing it above suspicion of mere selfishness, at least in the eyes of his admirers."[29] Defeated in the presidential election of 1824, he assumed the vice presidency, during which term he expressed his views on slavery, often referring to religious principles underlying the doctrine of Manifest Destiny. Calhoun had closely followed the development of the anti-slavery movement from the first polemics to the abolitionists' petitions. Opposed to these anti-slavery claims, he attempted to have his proslavery resolutions adopted by the Senate in order to hamper the progress of the abolitionist movement, but his efforts were often unsuccessful.

Calhoun's governing idea was that individual rights prevailed over those of the local community, which in turn took precedence over those of the state, which themselves surpassed the nation's rights. The federal Union was necessary because it protected the states, but it was not created to promote conformity — rather, to allow diversity. This line of thought could also be applied to slavery, which Calhoun considered the touchstone of social order, since this institution protected the liberties of the southern white population. Material success being the reward (and outward sign) of a good and honest life (according to the old Puritan principles), many colonists saw in slavery a divine decision in favor of the Chosen People. As the slaves were not included in this social group, they were regarded as the Chosen

People's servants. According to these assumptions, the South Carolinian senator regarded this practice as the surest and strongest base of all the free institutions of the world. During a vehement speech in Congress, Calhoun indicated that by emancipating the slaves, the American people would be degraded and that America would become "the permanent Mexico abode of disorder, anarchy, poverty, misery and wretchedness."[30]

The Mexican War also contributed to revealing Calhoun's ideas on racial questions. Opposed to the Mexican cession, he informed Congress in January 1848 that he was concerned about the Mexican population. In a lengthy speech, he declared that half of the Mexican population was of Indian origin with mixed blood, adding: "I protest against the incorporation of such a people. Ours is the government of the white man ... are we to overlook this great fact, are we to associate with ourselves, as equal companions and fellow citizens, the Indians and the mixed races of Mexico?"[31] Calhoun answered his own question, saying that such an association would be degrading for Americans and would deal a fatal blow to their institutions.

What explained Calhoun's stance as regards his proslavery arguments may be found in his own interpretation of the Declaration of Independence. He contested one of its main principles, namely, "all men are created equal." He called it a "false and dangerous proposition," declaring "this assertion had its origin in the writing of Locke and Algernon Sidney, which assumed hypothetical states of nature that had no bearing on the actual condition of society."[32] Indeed, Calhoun impressed his audience when he gave a lecture, the "Oregon Bill Speech" (1848) on this topic. Through his self-assured tone of voice and his orator's gift for communication, he criticized Jefferson's "glittering generalities." Here is the entire text, in order to retain the true essence of Calhoun's arguments:

> The proposition to which I allude, has become an axiom in the minds of a vast majority on both sides of the Atlantic, and is repeated daily from tongue to tongue, as an established and incontrovertible truth; it is that "all men are born free and equal." I am not afraid to attack error, however deeply it may be entrenched, or however widely extended, whenever it becomes my duty to do so, as I believe it to be on this subject and occasion.
> Taking the proposition literally (it is in that sense it is understood), there is not a word of truth in it. It begins with "all men are born," which is utterly untrue. Men are not born. Infants are born. They grow to be men. And concludes with asserting that they are born "free and equal," which is not less false. They are not born free. While infants they are incapable of freedom, being destitute alike of the capacity of thinking and acting, without which there can be no freedom. Besides, they are necessarily born subject to their parents and remain so among all people, savage and civilized until the development of their intellect and physical capacity enables them to take care of themselves. They grow to all the freedom of which the condition in which they were born permits, by growing to be

men. Nor is it less false that they are born "equal." They are not so in any sense in which it can be regarded; and thus, as I have asserted, there is not a word of truth in the whole proposition, as expressed and generally understood.

If we trace it back, we shall find the proposition (that "all men are born free and equal") differently expressed in the Declaration of Independence. That asserts that "all men are created equal." The form of expression, though less dangerous, is not less erroneous. All men are not created. According to the Bible, only two, a man and a woman, ever were, and of these one was pronounced subordinate to the other. All others have come into the world by being born, and in no sense, as I have shown, either free or equal. But this form of expression being less striking and popular has given way to the present, and under the authority of a document put forth on so great an occasion, and leading to such important consequences, has spread far and wide, and fixed itself deeply in the public mind. It was inserted in our Declaration of Independence without any necessity. It made no necessary part of our justification in separating from the parent country, and declaring ourselves independent. Breach of our chartered privileges, and lawless encroachment on our acknowledged and well-established rights by the parent country, were the real causes, and of themselves sufficient, without resorting to any other, to justify the step. Nor had it any weight in constructing the governments which were substituted in the place of the colonial. They were formed of the old materials and on practical and well-established principles, borrowed for the most part from our own experience and that of the country from which we sprang.

If the proposition be traced still further back it will be found to have been adopted from certain writers in government who had attained much celebrity in the early settlement of these States, and with whose writings all the prominent actors in our revolution were familiar. Among these, Locke and [Algernon] Sidney were prominent. But they expressed it very differently. According to their expression, "all men in the state of nature were free and equal." From this the others were derived; and it was this to which I referred when I called it a hypothetical truism. To understand why, will require some explanation.

Man, for the purpose of reasoning, may be regarded in three different states: in a state of individuality; that is, living by himself apart from the rest of his species. In the social; that is, living in society, associated with others of his species. And in the political; that is, being under government. We may reason as to what would be his rights and duties in either, without taking into consideration whether he could exist in it or not. It is certain, that in the first, the very supposition that he lived apart and separated from all others, would make him free and equal. No one in such a state could have the right to command or control another. Every man would be his own master, and might do just as he pleased. But it is equally clear, that man cannot exist in such a state; that he is by nature social, and that society is necessary, not only to the proper development of all his faculties, moral and intellectual, but to the very existence of his race. Such being the case, the state is a purely hypothetical one; and when we say all men are free and equal in it, we announce a mere hypothetical truism; that is, a truism resting on a mere supposition that cannot exist, and of course one of little or no practical value....

But to call it a state of nature was a great misnomer, and has led to dangerous errors; for that cannot justly be called a state of nature which is so opposed to the constitution of man as to be inconsistent with the existence of his race and the development of the high faculties, mental and moral, with which he is endowed by his Creator.

Nor is the social state of itself his natural state; for society can no more exist without government, in one form or another, than man without society. It is the political, then, which includes the social, that is his natural state. It is the one for which his Creator formed him, into which he is impelled irresistibly, and in which only his race can exist and all its faculties be fully developed.

Such being the case, it follows that any, the worst form of government, is better than anarchy; and that individual liberty, or freedom, must be subordinate to whatever power may be necessary to protect society against anarchy within or destruction from without; for the safety and well-being of society is as paramount to individual liberty, as the safety and well-being of the race is to that of individuals; and in the same proportion, the power necessary for the safety of society is paramount to individual liberty. On the contrary, government has no right to control individual liberty beyond what is necessary to the safety and well-being of society. Such is the boundary which separates the power of government and the liberty of the citizen or subject in the political state, which, as I have shown, is the natural state of man — the only one in which his race can exist, and the one in which he is born, lives, and dies.

It follows from this that all the quantum of power on the part of the government, and of liberty on that of individuals, instead of being equal in all cases, must necessarily be very unequal among different people, according to their different conditions. For just in proportion as a people are ignorant, stupid, debased, corrupt, exposed to violence within and danger from without, the power necessary for government to possess, in order to preserve society against anarchy and destruction becomes greater and greater, and individual liberty less and less, until the lowest condition is reached, when absolute and despotic power becomes necessary on the part of government, and individual liberty extinct. So, on the contrary, just as a people rise in the scale of intelligence, virtue, and patriotism, and the more perfectly they become acquainted with the nature of government, the ends for which it was ordered, and how it ought to be administered, and the less the tendency to violence and disorder within, and danger from abroad, the power necessary for government becomes less and less, and individual liberty greater and greater. Instead, then, of all men having the same right to liberty and equality, as is claimed by those who hold that they are all born free and equal, liberty is the noble and highest reward bestowed on mental and moral development, combined with favorable circumstances. Instead, then, of liberty and equality being born with man; instead of all men and all classes and descriptions being equally entitled to them, they are prizes to be won, and are in their most perfect state, not only the highest reward that can be bestowed on our race, but the most difficult to be won — and when won, the most difficult to be preserved.

They have been made vastly more so by the dangerous error I have attempted to expose, that all men are born free and equal, as if those high qualities belonged to man without effort to acquire them, and to all equally alike, regardless of their intellectual and moral condition. The attempt to carry into practice this, the most dangerous of all political error, and to bestow on all, without regard to their fitness either to acquire or maintain liberty, that unbounded and individual liberty supposed to belong to man in the hypothetical and misnamed state of nature, has done more to retard the cause of liberty and civilization, and is doing more at present, than all other causes combined. While it is powerful to pull down governments, it is still more powerful to prevent their construction on proper principles. It is the leading cause among those ... which have been overthrown, threatening thereby the quarter of the globe most advanced in progress and civilization with hopeless anarchy, to be followed by military despotism. Nor are we exempt from its disorganizing effects. We now begin to experience the danger of admitting so great an error to have a place in the declaration of our independence. For a long time it lay dormant; but in the process of time it began to germinate, and produce its poisonous fruits. It had strong hold on the mind of Mr. Jefferson, the author of that document, which caused him to take an utterly false view of the subordinate relation of the black to the white race in the South; and to hold, in consequence, that the former, though utterly unqualified to possess liberty, were as fully entitled to both liberty and equality as the latter; and that to deprive them of it was unjust and immoral. To this error, his proposition to exclude slavery from the territory northwest of the Ohio may be traced, and to that of the ordinance of '87, and through it the deep and dangerous agitation which now threatens to ingulf, and will certainly ingulf, if not speedily settled, our political institutions, and involve the country in countless woes.[33]

This speech appears as a very elaborate and clever exercise of rhetoric that could flatter the mind. While this reasoning may have been attractive to many Americans at the time, it is obviously biased, since Calhoun focused more on the letter than on the spirit of the Declaration of Independence.

The third Great Triumvirate figure is Daniel Webster, who was born in 1782 in New Hampshire. Although Webster was brought up on a farm and was the son and grandson of pioneers, he received an excellent and thorough education. Since books were rare, the young man often learned texts by heart, memorizing long passages of Milton's *Paradise Lost*, which was a classic of Puritan literature. In 1805, after studying law at Dartmouth College, Webster settled in Boston as a lawyer before launching into politics and joining the Federalist Party. Like his colleagues Calhoun and Clay, he had strong nationalist convictions and regarded the American Constitution as "the sacred and inviolable palladium of American liberty."[34] Moreover, Webster clung to the idea that religion constituted a strong medium to support politics: "The altar of our freedom should be placed near the altar of our religion,"[35] he declared.

When he was elected to the House in 1823, Webster had already acquired a solid reputation as a lawyer, and his nationalist ideas, based on the Manifest Destiny tenets, were often imbued with a transcendental spirit expressed in an immoderate and pompous style. Called the "Yankee Demosthenes,"[36] he delivered speeches pregnant with suggestive metaphors, and echoed the prominent Greek politician's rhetoric. During one of his speeches (January 26, 1830), Webster emphatically invoked the fate of the Union, indicating that he did not wish to see it betrayed by internal quarrels, but glorified throughout the whole world. In his passionate discourse on the Union and Liberty, the American flag became the sacred emblem of Liberty and the Union:

While the Union lasts we have high, exciting, gratifying prospects spread out before us, for us and our children. Beyond that I see not to penetrate the veil. God grant that in my day at least that curtain may not rise! God grant that on my vision never may be opened what lies behind! When my eyes shall be turned to behold for the last time the sun in heaven, may I not see him shining on the broken and dishonored fragments of a once glorious Union; on States dissevered, discordant, belligerent; on a land rent with civil feuds, or drenched, it may be, in fraternal blood! Let their last feeble and lingering glance rather behold the gorgeous ensign of the republic, now known and honored throughout the earth, still full high advanced, its arms and trophies streaming in their original luster, not a stripe erased or polluted, not a single star obscured, bearing for its motto, no such miserable interrogatory as "What is all this worth?" nor those other words of delusion and folly, "Liberty first and Union afterwards"; but everywhere, spread all over in characters of living light, blazing on all its ample folds, as they float over the sea and over the land, and in every wind under the whole heavens, that other sentiment, dear to every true American heart, — Liberty and Union, now and forever, one and inseparable![37]

This statement touched people's hearts and further nurtured their minds with vivid symbols that were to remain, as Webster stressed, sacred emblems in the American psyche. As to the man, he remained one the greatest statesmen and orators of the nation. A sincere Christian, he felt a great responsibility in the fulfillment of his national duty. An anecdote reveals the depth of his involvement in the Christian faith. When he left the Capitol to spend his summer vacation with his family in a remote region, he used to go to the small country church. When his niece asked him why he seemed to pay more attention to the country pastor's homily than to the sermons in Washington, he answered: "In Washington, they preach to Daniel Webster the statesman. But this man has been talking to Daniel Webster, the sinner, and telling him of Jesus."[38]

Webster, like Clay and Calhoun, never attained presidency. Nevertheless, the three experienced high esteem and great fame. As a new generation of American leaders, they stamped national politics with their ardent, not to say, flamboyant, political and religious arguments. Giving a new impetus to nationalistic feelings, they knew how to convince American citizens through their fiery rhetoric, fraught with evocative symbols and often permeated with sentimental religiosity. Resorting to poetry and oratory, they contributed, with Jefferson, Jackson and Polk, to the building of the American country as a "God-centered Nation," the goals of which were to make people happy and free, here and now. The memory of the Great Triumvirate never faded in American history. In 1847, when Webster traveled through the South, the *Charleston Daily Courier* praised, in somewhat bombastic prose, the three celebrated statesmen:

And ours is indeed a fortunate country — Ireland has her O'Connell, England her Peel, France her Louis Philippe — but we can happily point out on our roll of free citizenship to a triad of living greatness—Clay, Webster and Calhoun are the three GREAT MEN OF AMERICA—each in his section or sphere towering in colossal proposition and pyramidal eminence above all rivalry; and when grouped on the national canvass, forming a picture and a spectacle of moral and intellectual grandeur, for the world's admiration and the national pride. They have each stood beyond compeer Senators in the State House ... co-equals in greatness, but each having a greatness peculiarly his own ... and each of whom, although he may never be destined to climb the Presidential step, is crowned with a loftier, wider and more valuable fame than the Presidency can bestow—for they preside in the admiration and the hearts of their countrymen.[39]

Adding to all these considerations conferred by America's nineteenth-century intelligentsia, President John Adams' words summarize and confirm the postulates of the American national spirit as a Puritan-based ideology. On November 13, 1813, Adams, aged 78, wrote to his former adversary Jefferson, "Many hundred years must roll away before we shall be corrupted. Our pure, virtuous, public spirited, federative republic will last forever, govern the globe and introduce the perfection of man."[40]

6

American Exceptionalism

An Imperialistic Vision of the American Nation: Frederick Jackson Turner

The historian Frederick Jackson Turner (1861–1932) viewed the conquest of the West as the principal component of American national identity. Born in Wisconsin, he was from a family whose origin can be traced back to English Puritans. After earning his master of arts degree in history, he received his doctorate at Johns Hopkins University where he became assistant professor. At the time of the closing of the frontier, Turner took the opportunity to study the effect it had on American thinking. On July 12, 1893, only one year after the frontier was officially declared closed, he underlined its specific character at a high-level conference of international historians in Chicago. Turner surprised the audience with his interpretation of this historical episode: the concept of Manifest Destiny, such as it was perceived by O'Sullivan, lost its original meaning and took on a new meaning that seemed to stray from religious overtones, while keeping certain of its elements. Indeed, Turner's basic conception of the frontier remained strongly attached to the inevitable character of Manifest Destiny, but the historian upheld that the democratic ideal, based on equal opportunity, found its origin in the experiment of the frontier.

Territorial expansion, he argued, by gradually reducing the extent and boundaries of the virgin lands, constituted a determining factor in the economic and social development of the United States. Turner noted the continuous renewal of the American experience and reiterated the need to break with the constraints of the past. The frontier which had produced Andrew Jackson, said Turner, was "free from the influence of European ideas and institutions. The men of the 'Western World' turned their backs upon the Atlantic Ocean, and with a grim energy and self-reliance began to create a society free from the dominance of ancient forms."[1] The pioneers, moving through the untamed continent, far from bondage, had forged their own identity as a people, since they were forced to rely on strong energy and efficient pragmatism. However, as he observed, war with the indigenous people was the only way to conquer these newly discovered lands. As a consequence, American settlers would have to subdue not only the large open spaces but also hostile natives, who were viewed as natural obstacles that had to be removed in the irresistible push westward. Turner noted:

> The Indian was a common danger, demanding united action. Most celebrated of these conferences was the Albany Congress of 1754, called to treat with the Six Nations, and to consider plans of union. Even a cursory reading of the plan proposed by the congress reveals the importance of the frontier. The powers of the general council and the officers were, chiefly, the determination of peace and war with the Indians, the regulation of Indian trade, the purchase of Indian lands, and the creation and government of new settlements as a security against the Indians.[2]

In fact, the racial problem arising from Western expansion was closely linked to the concept of Manifest Destiny inasmuch as it reverberated in the mentality of people that formed the frontier communities. Turner himself had spent his childhood in one of these western settlements and had implicitly adhered to the Puritan doctrine concerning the American aborigines. For these pioneers, still influenced by a "providentialist" reading of the Holy Scriptures, mankind was divided into two parts: the "Children of Light," generally found among the civilized people who lived in conformity with the Gospel, respecting institutions and order and the "Children of Darkness," the savages who lived in darkness, paganism and ignorance, "like wild beasts with their dark skins and being confused with the thick forests that had to be cleared."[3] In the American mind, still impregnated with religious and biblical culture, the Children of Darkness were identified with the Philistines, who were believed to have been an uneducated and barbarous people.

This metaphysical and dualistic vision of mankind increasingly colored the principles of national American ideology and widely contributed to the shaping of the political, economic and social structures of the country. Although these religious assumptions were generally shared by the American public, they were often discussed and met with strong opposition in literary circles. The Englishman Rudyard Kipling, for example, addressed the theme in one of his poems, "The White Man's Burden," published in 1899, exposing the feelings of guilt harbored by Americans with regard to their policy on the assimilation of minorities. Other writers, notably Eliza Lee, described the conquest of the West in a more painful way, by movingly evoking the image of the vanishing Indian: "One by one, they perish like the leaves of the forest; they are effaced from the earth by an inexorable destiny."[4]

Despite the "inexorable destiny" of the Indian people, Turner saw the move westward as a founding process in the building of American democracy. Indeed, because the wilderness released individuals from social constraints, they did not depend on anyone. As Turner noted, "We have the complex European life sharply precipitated by the wilderness into the simplicity of primitive conditions,"[5] which meant that the pioneer had to provide for his own needs since he could not count any longer on the services of an organized society. He was willing to live under such precarious conditions because he believed his efforts would one day be rewarded. This optimistic and romantic attitude seemed to be in phase with the spirit of the age.

Central to Turner's essay was the notion that the frontier was an evolving social process thanks to several factors. Firstly, this evolution was due to American institutions: "Behind institutions, behind constitutional forms and modifications, lie the vital forces that call these organs into life and shape them to meet changing conditions."[6] Secondly, these changes were rendered easier thanks to the ability of the pioneers to adapt to a return to primitive conditions when facing the hazards of the wilderness: "American development has been continually beginning over again on the frontier."[7] By emphasizing "this perennial rebirth" and "fluidity of American life," the historian pinpointed the main characteristics of the frontier spirit.

Adhering to Jefferson's agrarian theory in the elaboration of an ideal society where people would have their own farms, Turner revived the "myth of the garden." This concept was deeply anchored in the nineteenth-century national consciousness, despite the onset of the industrial age. He saw the development of society following three stages, like the "waves of the ocean" which "have rolled one after the other." The first stage concerned the pioneer who "depends for the subsistence of his family chiefly upon the natural growth of vegetation." The pioneer paid no rent and felt "as independent as the 'lord of the manor.'" The following wave of immigrants bought the lands, extended the fields, planted trees, cleared out roads and built wooden houses with windows, schools and courthouses, and displayed "the picture and forms of plain, frugal, civilized life." The last wave of migrants, Turner explained, would come ever nearer to an Eldorado thanks to their endeavors and perspicacity in business:

> The settler is ready to sell out and take the advantage of the rise in property, push farther onto the interior and become himself, a man of capital, and enterprise in turn. The small village rises to a spacious town or city; substantial edifices of brick, extensive fields, orchards, gardens, colleges and churches are seen. Broadcloths, silks, leghorns, crapes, and all the refinements, luxuries, elegancies, frivolities, and fashions are in vogue. Thus wave after wave is rolling westward; the real Eldorado is still farther on.[8]

Turner was equally persuaded that the frontier had promoted a certain form of nationalism because the pioneer needed the government's help to deal with issues in the public sector, to improve relationships with the other pioneers, and to settle problems regarding territorial statutes. He explained that by being "precipitated by the wilderness into a kind a primitive organization," the first settlers tended to live secluded from one another and fear any authoritative body: "The tax-gatherer," he wrote, "was regarded as a representative of oppression." Only a national government could help the pioneers administer the public sector and improve contacts between the different communities.

Accordingly, precarious living conditions favored the promotion of the common man and abolished class distinctions; at the same time, the new settlers developed a democratic policy that extended the voting rights to all the citizens without reference to race, heredity, nationality or religion. Turner's thesis, the aim of which was to praise and assert that American democracy originated from the frontier spirit, exalted the national sentiment and emphasized the exceptional nature of *Homo Americanus*:

> The result is that to the frontier the American intellect owes its striking characteristics. That coarseness and strength combined with acuteness and inquisitiveness; that practical inventive turn of mind, quick to find expedient; that masterful grasp of material things, lacking in the artistic but powerful to effect great ends; that restless, nervous energy, that dominant individualism, working for good and for evil, and withal that buoyancy and exuberance with come with freedom — these are traits of the frontier, or traits called out elsewhere because of the existence of the frontier.[9]

The originality of Turner's description of the frontier was equally expressed through the factual analysis of the environment. From this viewpoint, the historian remained faithful to his time, since the nineteenth-century American strand of opinion manifested great interest in the historical and biological sciences. He asserted that a study of local history was a true source of knowledge, and his methodology was based on experimental research and evolutionist investigations, which consisted in comparing society to an organism in mutation reacting to external pressures. At the turn of the twentieth century, he abandoned the Romantic vision that placed the American destiny in an epic and messianic perspective to favor the scientific method based on the biological study of man. From then on, he joined his fellow historians, who were inclined to believe that it was no longer the God of the Puritans who was in charge of American destiny, but the God of Nature.

Thus, Turner's study on the frontier epitomized nineteenth-century cultural and intellectual trends in the sense that his enthusiastic and bold hypothesis remains the most influential piece of writing about the West. He supported ideas that formed the backbone of American national identity, among them the rejection of European political and social traditions. Like many of his contemporary peers, he wished to initiate a new way of life: the American way of life. He participated in the Romantic movement by borrowing its fanciful vision of the world as a mythic and heavenly garden, mystical reminiscence of a lost paradise. Finally, Turner was a man of his time when he adopted the main tenets of Manifest Destiny, which underlie the following lines:

> Since the days when the fleet of Columbus sailed into the waters of the New World, America has been another name for opportunity, and the people of the United States have taken their tone from the incessant expansion which has not only been open but has been forced upon them. He would be a rash prophet who should assert that the expansive character of American life has now entirely ceased. Movement has been its dominant fact, and, unless this training has no effect upon a people, the American energy will continually demand a wider field for its exercise.[10]

Through his evocative lines, Turner expressed the geographical determinism that strongly marked the ideology and metaphysics still slumbering at the heart of American collective desires. He foresaw the expansionist impulse in the U.S. nationalistic ideal that would find no barriers to stop its progress in the name of "Mighty Destiny." Yet it seemed that a barrier was erected by Native Americans, through the voice of Sioux Chief Standing Bear who voiced the Indian Manifest Destiny: "Before the white man came, the earth was bountiful and we were surrounded with the blessing of the Great Mystery."[11]

Naturally, referring to the Indian issue, how not to mention Wounded Knee, emblematic place of the last conflict between the Indians and the Americans? It is noteworthy to study the origin and causes of the Wounded Knee Massacre, on the grounds of its link with religion. It is necessary to focus on the Indian policy from its beginning to understand the slow process that culminated in the final drama.

The Indian Removal Act, signed in 1830 by President Andrew Jackson, marked the first phase of the U.S. Indian policy. After the Civil War, the government resorted to a policy of forced assimilation, but this new strategy was difficult to enforce due to the Indians' strong resistance. Deeply hurt, frustrated and discouraged, the Native Americans had no hope of remaining free. Some took refuge in the consolations of the spiritual world. One of them, Wovoka, whose father had been a religious leader, worked in the Nevada district for a rancher, David Wilson. The latter, a devout Presbyterian, profoundly influenced Wovoka (who called himself Jack Wilson). The Indian had many opportunities to hear Bible parables and was quite impressed by the supernatural world.

Two years before the Wounded Knee Massacre, Wovoka revealed to his people that he had had a prophetic vision: he had seen all his ancestors and dead relatives coming to life again and the departure of whites from America. The Indian prophet informed Native Americans that, for this vision to come true, they had to practice the Ghost Dance as a religious ceremony. Wovoka's message, called the "Messiah Letter," reads as follows:

> When you get home you must make a dance to continue five days. Dance four successive nights, and the last night keep up the dance until the morning of the fifth day, when all must bathe in the river and then disperse to their homes. You must all do in the same way.
>
> I, Jack Wilson, love you all, and my heart is full of gladness for the gifts you have brought me. When you get home I shall give you a good cloud [rain?] which will make you feel good. I give you a good spirit and give you all good paint. I want you to come again in three months, some from each tribe there [the Indian Territory].
>
> There will be a good deal of snow this year and some rain. In the fall there will be such a rain as I have never given you before.
>
> Grandfather [a universal title of reverence among Indians and here meaning the messiah] says, when your friends die you must not cry. You must not hurt anybody or do harm to anyone. You must not fight. Do right always. It will give you satisfaction in life. This young man has a good father and mother. [Possibly this refers to Casper Edson, the young Arapaho who wrote down this message of Wovoka for the delegation].
>
> Do not tell the white people about this. Jesus is now upon the earth. He appears like a cloud. The dead are still alive again. I do not know when they will be here; maybe this fall or in the spring. When the time comes there will be no more sickness and everyone will be young again.
>
> Do not refuse to work for the whites and do not make any trouble with them until you leave them. When the earth shakes [at the coming of the new world] do not be afraid. It will not hurt you. I want you to dance every six weeks. Make a feast at the dance and have food that everybody may eat. Then bathe in the water. That is all. You will receive good words again from me some time. Do not tell lies.[12]

Wovoka exhorted his people to peace, preaching nonviolence among themselves and towards the Whites. The Ghost Dance movement propagated very quickly among the Indian tribes. Unfortunately, the ritual was misinterpreted by members of rebel tribes who, still embittered by their plight, perceived it as a war dance. In addition, Wovoka also informed his people that wearing a white shirt would make them invulnerable to rifle bullets. Federal officials reacted with fear to these practices and, on the request of government employees working in the Sioux Reservation of South Dakota, the Indian Bureau in Washington sent cavalry and infantry troops on the spot. An overwhelming force of soldiers confronted the Native Americans at Wounded Knee. Fighting between the two parties led to the killing of more than 200 people, including women and children. On December 29, 1890, after many years of resistance, America had ceased to be the land of Indians. This dramatic event left a deep scar on the page of American history and is often remembered during a moving ceremony, the site being designated as a National Historical Landmark.[13] Wovoka's peaceful admonition contained striking millennial overtones. One finds in his text several of the spiritual ingredients connected with St. John's apocalypse. In the Indian psyche, this message of deliverance takes on a quasi-universal dimension, given its religious and political implications.

Turner's thesis, written three years after the Indian heart had been "buried," appeared as a successful achievement: young America had mastered its own continent and could now claim that its geographical and political ambitions had been realized. Among expansionist adepts, a sentiment of triumphalist elation comforted them as their destinarian objectives had been reached. The promotion of the frontier in Turner's narrative paved the way for the emergence of a new concept characterizing the American national identity—exceptionalism.

American Exceptionalism

Jan Willem Schulte Nordholt evoked the notion of American Exceptionalism (born under the pen of Alexis de Tocqueville) in his article entitled, "The Turner Thesis Revisited," published in 1994. Nordholt attempted to explain how the American syndrome of exceptionalism gradually emerged,[14] reminding readers that, even though Turner's theories gave rise to heated debates and critical polemics among Western historians, it was not wholly forgotten, and still lingered in American mentality. Engraved in the collective memory, Turner's hypothesis regarding the frontier has not ceased to strike the imagination of Americans who often tended to idealize the New World's civilization. However, Turner's ideological premises rested on a tragic element, which Nordholt called the "American fate." Turner, he argued, like his predecessors, advocated the rejection of all European culture and sought to rediscover the tradition of innocence. But in Nordholt's opinion, there is a link between innocence and tragedy, which generates a paradox: "There is still another word that we might use for the same problem, the word paradox. It is the paradox of a people who believe that they are able to make a new beginning in the history of the world, but who, at the same time, assert that they are the heirs of the cultural tradition of all mankind."[15] Thomas Jefferson, Nordholt wrote, once declared in a letter to a friend that one could no longer say "nothing is new under the sun," since "the whole chapter in the history of our republic is new." This statement did not prevent Jefferson from giving his own house the appearance of a Greek temple!

Turner was one of Jefferson's great admirers, but by implicitly bringing into play the tradition of innocence likely to initiate a new civilization in the wilderness, he merely reproduced a model already contended with over the centuries. Nordholt explained that this paradox was already noticeable in the writings of J. Hector St. John de Crèvecoeur, in his *Letters from an American Farmer*. Quoting two contradictory sentences in the French author's work, he emphasized this apparent incoherence. Indeed, Crèvecoeur stated that the American was "a new man who acted upon new principles," entertaining "new ideas and new opinions," but wrote in the same passage, that Americans were "the western pilgrims" who had imported "that great mass of arts, sciences, vigor, and industry which began long since in the East."[16]

The idea that man is able to regenerate himself in Mother Earth, observed Nordholt, is firmly rooted in the old traditions of western Europe. Indeed, this topic was taken up again by Michel de Montaigne who, in *Of Cannibals* (1595), preached the return to the invigorating source of the natural world: "After all, it would hardly be reasonable that artificial breeding should be able to outdo our great and powerful mother, Nature. We have so burdened the beauty and richness of her works by our innovations that we have entirely stifled her. Yet whenever she shines forth in her purity she puts our vain and frivolous enterprises amazingly to shame."[17] Similarly, Jean-Jacques Rousseau, among others, had praised the idea of the "noble savage," uncorrupted by the impact of civilization, in the first sentence of his *Emile* (1762): "Everything is good in leaving the hands of the Creator; everything degenerates in the hands of man." Nordholt equally referred to Jefferson who "himself gave it a pastoral charm," when he confessed his belief that "those who labor in the earth were God's chosen people."[18] Nevertheless, at the end of the nineteenth century, the idea of innocence evolved and was transformed into a kind of romantic emotion, which made the paradox more poignant insofar as nostalgia for a lost paradise was confronted with the lure of material progress.

Despite this paradox, Nordholt argued, Turner's hypothesis had far-reaching consequences on the American mind because it gave an exceptional character to American democracy. Turner refused to accept the Teutonic theory, in vogue at Johns Hopkins University, which claimed that the foundations of American democracy originated in Germanic culture. This theory explained how the Germanic peoples, or Teutons, had invaded the greater part of England, exterminating most of the Celts. America, mainly peopled with these Anglo-Saxons (or former Teutons) had preserved their customs which influenced American institutions. The American scholars termed their theory the "germ" system, for they professed that the origin of American democracy came from the forest of Germany.[19]

The exceptional character of the American identity was then vigorously defended by Turner, for whom the western frontier, cradle of democracy, transformed the plain American into a new man, a self-made man, and a true democrat: "the new democracy that captured the country ... came from no theorist's dream of the German forest. It came, stark and strong and full of life from the American forest."[20] Nordholt further wrote that, for Turner, the metamorphosis of the European dressed in the "garments of civilization" into an American wearing moccasins, "was almost a religious experience."[21]

Thus, through the lines of this popular historian, one can perceive the bold assumptions he advocated concerning the magical effect of the frontier at the individual and social levels. Rooted at the core of the American collective imagination, this nationalistic feeling never completely faded. Whether Turner's assertions are well-founded or not is a question of personal interpretation. Historians' divergent viewpoints on the historical document prove that his arguments were not wholly convincing. If it contributed to the understanding of the American temper and laid the foundations of the democratic spirit, Turner's version of American democracy was certainly imbued with a romantic vein through the prism of his own inflamed imagination. However, his belief in America's exceptionalism and his conception of a Nature's God made of him the American historian *par excellence*.[22]

Serge Ricard also dealt with the theme of American exceptionalism in "The Exceptionalist Syndrome in U.S Continental and Overseas Expansionism." The French scholar focused on a similar paradox which highlighted the ambiguity of American political thinking as well: "The brand of republican messianism that was to be invoked to justify later territorial aggrandizements was derived from the above postulate of American uniqueness; but it rested on an irreducible contradiction that would for ever vitiate U.S. foreign policy: the basic incompatibility of the exceptionalist claim with political messianism."[23]

Indeed, for a foreign observer, American politics, fundamentally driven by a sense of moral responsibility often tinged with a messianic overtone, takes on a paradoxical turn when confronted with the notion of exceptionalism, understood as the acknowledgment of its superiority vis-à-vis other nations. Serge Ricard explained that "this antagonism could only be resolved through paternalism in the interest of peoples yet unready for democracy— in whom would be inculcated, as a preliminary step, those virtues that were intrinsically American."[24] In line with this reflection, he underlined another paradox relating to the discrepancy between the United States' expansionist policy and the principles of natural rights inscribed in the Declaration of Independence, thereby echoing John Jay, president of the Continental

Congress, who said that the cult of freedom was incompatible with "the passion for conquest."[25]

The notion of American exceptionalism did not only spring from ethical and intellectual considerations but from historical events themselves. Naturally, the unfolding of the territorial conquest disclosed many examples of this mental attitude. During every attempt at annexation, the U.S. used a "justificative rhetoric" which "throughout its continental expansion would be clothed in various garbs and invoke a diversity of principles, all tailored to meet the same end."[26]

Another element of justification that was often submitted by expansionists was scientific determinism. With the development of social sciences and research on biological factors liable to influence human behavior, the nineteenth century witnessed the emergence of new theories that legitimized expansionist goals: "nation-states, like all living organisms, needed to grow and fortify themselves; failure to respect that law of nature led to withering and death; America's exceptional vitality therefore demanded that full scope be given to it."[27] It is interesting to note that the idea of spiritual determinism that is attached to the notion of the providential God of the Puritans reappeared under the idea of biological determinism, linked with natural laws and Nature's God. Here again lies the profound dilemma inscribed at the core of American culture.

However, at the time of continental expansion, the greatest difficulty for the successive governments resided in combining the spirit of democracy with the resort to imperial tactics. Striving to reconcile their political ambition and the spread of republican ideas, they tried to avoid the harsh measures that characterized Empire, such as the presence of a military force and exploitation of the people of subdued states. Thomas R. Hietala wrote: "To justify the aggrandizement of the United States, expansionists had to convince themselves and, if possible, their adversaries, that their nation could expand indefinitely without resorting to undemocratic tactics characteristic of imperial rule."[28] For him, the crusaders of expansionism had elaborated an "ideology of republican empire," contending that territorial expansion would actually promote democracy within the nation.

According to Hietala, this "exceptional imperial ideology" had been nourished by two generations of American leaders, such as Benjamin Franklin, Thomas Jefferson, James Monroe, John Quincy Adams and Andrew Jackson. All contributed to this "evolving nationalistic ethos." As they were different from other empires, they could easily elude the failings and the "burden of colonialism and militarism." Moreover, to legitimize their acquisition of new lands, they undermined their adversaries' strength. They asserted that "the Anglo-Americans possessed an innate genius for self-rule" and they believed in the new technology that was bound to strengthen the country's cohesive union and propagate American values within the whole continent. Competing with the declining British Empire, the United States' technical advances could be made a "servant of empire." Astonishing progress in technology "gave Americans still another indication of their uniqueness and superiority."[29] In those days, western Democrats easily obtained financial aid from the federal government that was allocated to the construction of railroads, canals and steamboats which connected far-away regions and facilitated commercial exchanges, consolidating the empire.

The Republican senator Albert Beveridge, from Indiana, was one of the best representatives of the imperialistic ideology. In his speech before Congress (1900) "A Greater England with a Nobler Destiny," he gave a syncretic vision of America's glorious history and the superiority of the Anglo-Saxon race:

> It is a noble land that God has given us ... it is a mighty people that he has planted on this soil: a people sprung from the most masterful blood of history; a people perpetually revitalized by the virile man producing working folk of all the earth; a people imperial by virtue of their power, by right of their institutions, by authority of their heaven-directed purposes—the propagandists and not the misers of liberty.[30]

Beveridge also mentioned America's mission across the world on the economic, political and social levels. In the same article, he remarked: "Shall the Americans continue their march toward the commercial supremacy of the world? Shall free institutions broaden their blessed reign as the children of liberty wax in strength, until the empire of our principles is established over the hearts of all mankind ... have we no mission to perform, no duty to discharge to our fellow man?" The Anglo-Saxon race is thus privileged by God's wonder-working Providence: "Wonderfully has God guided us," claimed Beveridge. This sense of wonder expressed by the Pilgrim Fathers upon their arrival on the American soil belongs to the American consciousness. It constitutes a positive aspect of their character and nourishes a perpetual dynamism which makes them progress even though they make mistakes or fail. This capacity for wonder, of course, if used for wrong ends, brings them into the realm of utopia, as it seems to be the case in Beveridge's article.

America's noble destiny, according to Beveridge, entailed a messianic role over other nations: "It is ours to set the world its example of right and honor. We cannot fly from our world duties." Thus, Beveridge's ethnocentric vision of the Anglo-Saxons seems deeply rooted in the genesis of American culture. All these arguments belong to the dark face of the American dream when it reflects only a sense of earthly power and human glory, which led many Americans into disillusion. In his article, Beveridge gave a picture of America which was for a long time recognized and appreciated by

American citizens, although it sounded "unorthodox" to other nations, in particular to England itself. It must be remembered that the Anglo-Saxon League, created in 1898 to reinforce friendly bonds between the two countries ended in failure because Great Britain could not accept most of the American racial theories. This attitude seemed to have put an end to the Anglo-Saxon destiny.

Social Darwinism

The character of American exceptionalism, mainly advocated by Turner, was emphasized by the contributions from the evolutionary theories of Charles Darwin (1809–1882), the English naturalist whose work met with enormous success in the United States. American scientists promptly adopted the principle of natural selection and contributed significantly to the development of evolution in their country, in spite of violent protests from a large segment of the population who saw, in this approach, fundamental contradictions with Christianity.

Darwinian expressions such as "struggle for life" or "natural selection" applied to human life in society, suggested that in a competitive situation, it was natural for the strong to prevail over the weak. The idea of "the survival of the fittest" was not new to American economists, but Darwinism gave it the force of a natural law. Consequently, society could be regarded as an "organism," the needs and requirements of which were determined by the laws of Nature.

Social Darwinism rested on the idea that some people were fitter to compete than others. At the political level, this implied that governments should adopt a liberal economic system favoring free competition in business matters. Human society was considered a biological body similar to plants or animals: the weak and unfit people were bound to fail in their enterprises or die. British philosopher Herbert Spencer, the father of Social Determinism, based his theory of social evolution on individual competition which was the "law of life," his biological approach towards society relating to analogies between the natural and the human worlds.

Even though Social Darwinism was a secularist philosophy, Richard Hofstadter remarked, its main supporters were concerned with ethical issues and felt that "the Law of the Jungle" had to be canalized: "Theirs is a kind of naturalistic Calvinism in which man's relation to nature is as hard and demanding as man's relation to God under the Calvinist system. This secular piety found its practical expression in an economic ethic that seemed to be demanded with special urgency by a growing industrial society."[31]

This Darwinist theory was in line with the principles of Manifest Destiny, insofar as Americans knew how to adapt it to their ideological and transcendental vision. It was best exemplified by the historian and philosopher John Fiske (1842–1901), a Harvard graduate, a scientist and a convinced evolutionist who wrote many articles on the doctrine of evolution. Fiske declared that Anglo-Saxons, being a superior race, were destined to spread across the whole world and obtain sovereignty in all fields, on earth and over the sea, in order to take the world out of barbarism and make it truly Christian. This idea made Fiske extremely popular in America and in England; he gave some twenty lectures across America on Manifest Destiny, which were published in the prestigious magazine *Harper's* in 1885.

In one of his lectures, entitled "Manifest Destiny," Fiske developed his main ideas concerning the superiority of the Anglo-Saxon race. After a brief summary of world history, he applied himself to define the portentous role of the English race in American territorial expansion: "After the survey of universal history which we have now taken, I am fully prepared to show that the conquest of the North American continent by men of English race was unquestionably the most prodigious event in the political annals of mankind."[32] For him, not only is there a manifest destiny, but a racial destiny. He believed that the English race superseded all other races, although these rival powers were still unaware of this fact. Even people who founded the colonies could not foresee that they would become "imperial states." Only a few prescient thinkers at the time of the American Revolution were able to dimly sense the seeds of such destiny.

The prominent and much in vogue idea of total rupture with decadent Old Europe is put forward to illustrate the emergence of "ripest political ideas," mainly conceived by the British. It was high time for them to discard the defective monarchic systems. Fiske emphasized the failings and weaknesses of the civilization of "inferior type" (like the French), asserting that when these "began to become troublesome," they received a fatal blow from their English rivals. In his introduction, he pinpointed that the "bonds of feudalism were far looser" in England than in other parts of Europe, which explained why, on the political plan, the situation of the common people was more advantageous. Deeply influenced by the theory of Social Darwinism, Fiske envisioned the future of his nation according to a deterministic process:

> It is enough to point out to the general conclusion that the work which the English race began when it colonized North America is destined to go on until every land on the earth's surface that is not already the seat of an old civilization shall become English in its language, in its religion, in its political habits and traditions, and to a prominent extent in the blood of its people. The day is at hand when four-fifths of the human race will trace its pedigree to English forefathers, as four-fifths of the white people in the United States trace their pedigree to-day.[33]

At the time, Fiske's convictions were highly contagious and his Darwin-inclined and imperialistic rhetoric seduced many people. Social Darwinists often held such viewpoints because this theory sanctioned biological factors, such as race, as a fundamental element of progress. By progress, Fiske meant the end of barbarism that appeared as a "necessity" for inferior races, whereas, between civilized and Christian nations, it is an "absurdity." Fiske concluded his lecture by saying that American federalism, as the best political system to safeguard the citizens' interests, should be established in Europe, although the conditions of such an enterprise did not seem favorable at the time. Nevertheless, Fiske wrote, "the pacific pressure exerted upon Europe by America is becoming so great that it will doubtless before long overcome all these obstacles."[34]

Another figure, the Reverend Josiah Strong, also an advocate of Social Darwinism, influenced the American community at the turn of the nineteenth century. Strong, secretary of the Evangelical Alliance for the United States, published a book in 1885, *Our Country: Its Possible Future and Its Present Crisis*, which sold 175,000 copies, an impressive figure at the time. The Reverend Strong had written this work in order to raise funds for missionary communities. A proponent of the Darwinist theory, he announced that the "Anglo-Saxon race would extend beyond the world's frontiers, opening a new era in the history of humanity and witnessing a natural selection through competition between races."[35] Strong believed in universal progress and had hopes for the future of the Anglo-Saxon race. His religious rhetoric laid the emphasis on the divine mission allotted by God to the Anglo-Saxons:

> It is not necessary to argue to those to whom I write that the two great needs of mankind, so that all men may be lifted up into the light of the highest Christian civilization, are, at first a pure, spiritual Christianity, a second, civil liberty. Without controversy, these are the forces which, in the past, have contributed most to the elevation of the human race, and they must continue to be, in the future, the most efficient ministers to its progress. It follows then, that the Anglo-Saxon, as the great representative of these two ideas, the depository of these two great blessings, sustains peculiar relations to the world's future, is divinely commissioned to be, in a peculiar sense, his brother's keeper.[36]

The idea of progress is here underlain by the imperious necessity to resort to Christianity to uplift the human race. Serving as general secretary of the Evangelical Alliance for the United States (1886–1898), he pleaded for the application of religious principles in the industrial world and founded the Social Gospel movement. Striving against America's social ills, he contended that civilized countries had a moral responsibility. The reverend believed in an ideal society that would resemble God's kingdom on earth.

Given the rapid growth of their populations, the Anglo-Saxons had a prominent role to play: "The Anglo-Saxon people ... are multiplying more rapidly than any other European race. They already own one third of the earth, and will get more as it grows.... Since America is much bigger than the little English isle, it will be the seat of Anglo-Saxondom."[37] Strong also asserted that a new type of man was appearing, stronger and taller, as Darwin had predicted in *The Descent of Man*. According to Darwin, the progress made by the American people was true illustration of natural selection:

> There is apparently truth in the belief that the wonderful progress of the United States, as well as the character of the people, are the results of natural selection; for the most energetic, restless and courageous men from all parts of Europe have emigrated during the last ten or twelve generations to that great country, and have succeeded.[38]

As an overt proponent of Social Darwinism, Strong put forward his beliefs, based on the concept of natural law, stating: "From biological truths, the allied varieties of the Aryan race were destined to produce a more powerful type of man that had never existed before." Whatever difficulties or problems the Americans may encounter, they were to be part of a civilization "grander that any of the world has known." Their thirst for conquest would never end, explained Strong, quoting one of Dickens' remarks that "the typical American would hesitate to enter heaven unless assured he could go farther west!"

These examples illustrate how the idea of an inevitable destiny regarding the Anglo-Saxon race emerged in the expansionist theories of the time. They also demonstrate how and why the political and religious leaders evoked the law of progress and survival of the fittest, for example during the conflict with the Philippines. In 1899, Senator Albert Beveridge addressed the Senate as follows:

> God has not been preparing the English-speaking and Teutonic peoples for a thousand years for nothing but vain and idle admiration. No, no! He has made us the master organizers of the world to establish systems where chaos reigns.... He has made us adepts in government that we may administer government among savages and senile peoples.[39]

Thus, the progress and evolution of the world depended on the chosen race, the Anglo-Saxon race. Beveridge was not the only one to have such arguments. Even the anti-imperialist leaders held similar views, advocating a thesis of racial superiority as an argument against territorial annexations. Senator John Daniel, for example, declared in 1899: "There is one thing that neither time nor education can change. You may change the leopard's spots, but you will never change the different qualities of the races which God has created in order that they may fulfill separate and distinct missions in the cultivation and civilization of the world.[40]

Reflecting on the practical incidence of these talks, one notes that the expression "American exceptionalism" is not an abstract concept. It corresponds to diverse political and religious assumptions that wove the fabric of American national identity. Close to the idea of Manifest Destiny, the semantic content of the phrase can be traced back to Winthrop's idea of a "City upon a Hill," and can relate to the metaphoric representations of America as a "lighthouse of the world." Following the course of history, the term evolved, still retaining its religious overtone but interpreted according to biological principles founded on natural law. Considered as a positive expression by the nineteenth-century proponents of expansionism and Darwinism, today it tends to surprise the international community, which is not always convinced of the moral superiority of Americans.

Indeed, at present, these ideas appear somewhat arrogant and self-conceited, and obviously require being placed in their historical context in order to apprehend American history with its strengths and weaknesses. Although the flag of Manifest Destiny was unfurled during the march westward, it remains the spiritual cornerstone of a historical process conferring on the United States its unique identity. Nevertheless, at the turn of the nineteenth century, the awareness of this new identity, anchored in strong nationalism, led to American expansion beyond its borders. America's irresistible destiny has not only stamped its internal affairs but has also permeated its foreign policy.

Part III

The Foreign Policy of the United States

Part III

The Foreign Policy
of the United States

7

The Monroe Doctrine

Origin and Purpose of the Monroe Message

Having accomplished America's territorial unity according to the benevolent design of Divine Providence or the mysterious forces of biological determinism, the next question was to know whether one could avail oneself of this expansionist force to justify incursions into foreign territories. The Monroe Doctrine seemed to resolve such a fundamental dilemma. James Monroe,[1] then president of the United States, issued a special message in December 1823, presenting the main principles of his foreign policy. This message, delivered during his State of the Union speech and not until later called a "doctrine," fixed the limits on the intervention of European foreign powers in the Western Hemisphere on the American continents. As a counterpart, it guaranteed the nonintervention of the United States in European colonies.

When Monroe was first sworn in as president in 1817, his secretary of state, John Quincy Adams, had already implemented a foreign policy designed to protect and preserve America's national interests. This doctrine reasserted the separation between Europe and America, and presented the United States as solely responsible for the New World. As Bernard Vincent observed, "The unspoken idea that underlined the Monroe Doctrine was the consideration of the Western Hemisphere as the private territory of Manifest Destiny."[2]

The notion of "Western Hemisphere" is unusual in geography, since one traditionally uses the terms "northern" and "southern" hemispheres, but for the Americans of the time, the "Western Hemisphere" was differentiated from the "Eastern Hemisphere," which included Eurasia and Africa, parts of the Old World. The Monroe Doctrine designated the United States policy-makers as guarantors of half of the world, and gave Americans to understand that both Americas wished to put an end to any attempt at further colonization.

At that time, some sections of the American continent still felt threatened, especially Alaska, which feared Russia's territorial ambitions, and Oregon, to which Great Britain had staked solid claims. American political leaders implicitly informed the Europeans that they intended to remain guardians of the newfound continent, and that any European intervention against the new independent nations of Latin America would be regarded as an act of hostility. Moreover, at the time when Monroe set forth his doctrine in 1823, Europe was experiencing a conservative phase, as the powers of the Holy Alliance (Austria, Russia, Prussia, and France) intended to restore a monarchical order in Europe, as well as in the Spanish Empire in the New World. The American public was worried. Monroe, before his speech to Congress, had written to Jefferson to seek his advice on the subject. In a lengthy letter which clearly defined America's isolationist stance, Jefferson replied:

> Our first and fundamental maxim should be never to entangle ourselves in the broils of Europe. Our second, never to suffer Europe to intermeddle with these Atlantic affairs. America, North and South, has a set of interests distinct from those of Europe, and peculiarly her own. She should therefore have a system of her own, separate and apart from that of Europe. While the last is laboring to become the domicile of despotism, our endeavor should surely be to make our hemisphere that of freedom.[3]

These ideas were in line with most Americans' expectations and were accepted without the least objection. In his message, Monroe informed Congress that it was at the proposal of the Russian imperial government that an "amicable negotiation"[4] was arranged during which the United States took the occasion to assert its rights and interests. Reminding the audience that the American citizens wished to respect their European counterparts, Monroe's speech evoked the uniqueness of the American political system compared with that of the allied powers: "The political system of the allied powers is essentially different ... from that of America. This difference proceeds from that which exists in their respective governments; to the defense of our own, which has been achieved by the loss of so much blood and treasure, and mature by the wisdom of their most enlightened citizens, and under which we have enjoyed unexampled felicity, this whole nation is devoted."[5]

Regarding the nonintervention of European nations into American affairs, the message was clear: Monroe stipulated that "with existing colonies, or any dependencies of any European power," the United States had never interfered and did not intend to do so. But regarding governments which obtained their independence, Monroe went on, "We could not view any interposition for the purpose of oppressing them, or controlling in any other manner their destiny, by any European power in any other light than as the manifestation of an unfriendly disposition toward the United States."[6] At the time, the Europeans powers took little notice of this statement but it enclosed the main tenets of American foreign policy.

At first, the principles of the Monroe Doctrine were implicitly applied on the American continent during the territorial expansion, especially in 1848, when the U.S. government bought the Mexican territories through the treaty of Guadalupe Hidalgo. American policy makers resorted more to the moral doctrine of Manifest Destiny than to the principles of 1823 in the fulfillment of their expansionist ambitions. The lure of land and prosperity constituted a strong appeal as populations were pushed forward, driven by an irrepressible force. It was the time when politicians, journalists and writers united their voices to claim a God-given mission to "overspread the continent."

Gradually, the new settlers drove entire populations away from their homes, beginning with the Mexican community in Texas, then the British settlers in Oregon, and decimating the Native Americans on their way. They soon widely outnumbered their unfortunate predecessors, for it seemed to them a natural legitimacy to head for the Pacific Ocean and realize their "sea to sea" primary objective. Naturally, Polk's expansionist policy reinforced the already overwhelming western movement; economic interests were also a clear motivation, especially to open new markets, particularly with China. In his message to Congress, on December 2, 1845, President Polk alluded to the Monroe Doctrine and spoke in terms that conjured up the spirit of Manifest Destiny:

> The rapid extension of our settlements over our territories heretofore unoccupied, the addition of new states to our confederacy, the expansion of free principles, and our rising greatness as a nation are attracting the attention of the powers of Europe, and lately, the doctrine has been broached in some of them of a "balance power" on this continent to check our advancement. The United States, sincerely desirous of preserving relations of good understanding with all nations, cannot in silence permit any European interference on the North American continent, and should any interference be attempted, will be ready to resist at any and all hazards.[7]

In this speech, Polk also reasserted the United States' intention to remain master of its own ship: "We must ever maintain the principle that the people of that continent alone have the right to decide of their own destiny." In this perspective, he ended his address by stressing the key ideas of the Monroe message in strong and vigorous terms: "This principle will apply with greatly increased force should any European power attempt to establish any new colony in North America. In the existing circumstances of the world, the present is deemed a proper occasion to reiterate and reaffirm the principle avowed by Mr. Monroe and to state my cordial concurrence in its wisdom and sound policy."

The Monroe Doctrine, which was to be the cornerstone of American foreign policy, remained practically dormant until 1867, when the American government took the initiative to intervene in Mexican affairs. To safeguard French interests in Mexico, the French Emperor Napoleon III had contrived to place a Hapsburg on the Mexican throne. In 1864, the Austrian Prince Maximilian was established as the emperor of Mexico, on the grounds of overdue loans, which entailed warfare in the provinces where insurgents had formed armies. Despite the backing of conservative Mexicans, Maximilian did not succeed in containing the Republican forces to whom Americans supplied arms as soon as the Civil War ended. The U.S. regarded France's intervention in Mexican affairs as a threat and demanded that she withdraw her troops. French troops were soon defeated and Maximilian executed, to the satisfaction of President Andrew Johnson. For Johnson, the French presence in Mexico was a flagrant violation of the Monroe Doctrine, which forbade European powers to intervene in the western hemisphere.

Emergence of Ideological Principles in U.S. Foreign Policy

The Monroe Doctrine, closely linked to Manifest Destiny, included ideological principles that were reflected in the U.S. foreign policy in the 1890s, when the opportunity of overseas expansion arose. At the turn of the century, industrialization and urbanization developed as the two main agents of prosperity, and America began to explore new economic and financial outlets to expand its commercial trade. At that time, political crisis shook several colonies under Spanish rule, and insurgents frequently appealed to the Americans to sustain their causes and rebellions. It is interesting to note that, during the closing years of the nineteenth century which saw the rise of American imperialism, overseas expansionists borrowed the same ideas as those expressed by continental expansionists.

In *Ideology and U.S. Foreign Policy*, Michael H. Hunt rightly observed that "To establish a relationship between ideas and foreign policy is always a difficult task, and it is no accident that it attracted so few historians."[8] Nevertheless, Hunt mentioned that the subject should not be neglected, given its importance. American nationalism, he argued, is too often linked with an "assertive American foreign politics," which tends to lead to serious criticism within the national and international communities. Hunt questioned the objective integrity of American diplomacy:

Suppose, to begin with, that ideology is central, not incidental, to policymaking. Is it really possible to insulate or divorce one from the other? Suppose, moreover, that some of the central ideas in foreign policy are closely intertwined with domestic political values and arrangements, which continue to sustain them. Can those ideas be eradicated, and can fresh sources of inspiration and guidance appropriate to a policy of abnegation be found? Suppose finally that a major assault on those ideas proves successful but in the process shake national self-confidence and precipitates a prolonged and vituperative debate. How dangerous would such an outcome be, and how likely is it that we would find ourselves better off than we are now?"[9]

Hunt's reflection corroborated critics' main apprehensions regarding world affairs that, according to them, should be settled in the most objective and selflessness way. The author further noted that two "thoughtful interpreters" attempted to define the motives underlying the ideological principles of American foreign policy: George Kennan and William Appleman Williams. For Kennan, it was chiefly the ethical issue of moralism and the recourse to legalism which characterized the American relationship with international communities. Yet Hunt saw a negative attitude in Kennan's approach to American diplomacy and argued: "By moralism Kennan meant devotion to virtue without the power and will necessary to sustain it." As to the implication of legalism to deal with international affairs, it was "reflected in the application of domestic concepts of peacekeeping ... to an international sphere for which they were unsuited."[10]

William Appleman Williams, in Hunt's opinion, was inclined to focus on economic interest as the main driving force in American relationships with other nations. Author of *The Tragedy of American Diplomacy,* Williams believed that under the veil of ideological purposes lay the shadow of American capitalism, whose proponents were substantially interested in economic power. Nevertheless, Williams believed that it would be incumbent on Americans "to sustain democracy and prosperity without imperial expansion,"[11] which he called an open-door ideology. This reflection may explain why Williams contested the emergence of American imperialism in the 1890s: "Led by a shrewd, farsighted McKinley, the United States ended the old pattern of territorial expansion and took up the new one on informal open-door imperialism."[12] Indeed, it is currently acknowledged that the last decade of the nineteenth century was deeply marked by imperialist temptation, ideological assumptions remaining a strong incentive in the diplomatic arena.

To comprehend the ideological approach of such a foreign policy, Hunt believed that those interested in the subject should analyze and study American public rhetoric, fraught with rich symbolism and mythological overtones, in order to confront it with their personal statement. "Indeed," he added, "comparisons of public rhetoric with private statements, a sensitive test that cynics might justifiably insist on, suggests that the policy elite do recognize the cost of violations of these rules and do generally observe them."[13] Important political speeches and discourses reflect national identities in a given historical context, and constitute ample source in the understanding of ideological trends, but as Hunt rightly suggested, "it is important, to begin with, to accept the view that the relationship between ideas and action is not rigid."[14] In this perspective, the 1890s are a good illustration of the nascent American foreign policy, since public rhetoric revealed the main ideological characteristics of this transitional decade, which challenged the main tenets of the Monroe Doctrine.

McKinley's Foreign Policy in the 1890s and the Monroe Doctrine

When McKinley arrived on the political scene in 1897, a spirit of staunch nationalism had already suffused American public opinion. The financial crisis of 1893 was resolved, and the twenty-fifth President of the United States intended to promote economic prosperity, focusing his energies on the development of industry and banking. He was soon recognized as the "advance agent of prosperity," thanks to the various economic improvements that occurred after his election. Yet, to sustain his trade policy, McKinley needed to open new foreign markets. The opportunity was provided when American businessmen who had interests in the islands of Cuba, Hawaii and the Philippines began to be harassed by local authorities. McKinley's administration then did not hesitate to extend aid and hasten to the rescue of the natives who initiated rebellions against Spanish rule.

Although McKinley preached a pacific approach towards the issues raised by Spanish colonialism, he was often influenced by American public opinion: "Of all the presidents of the United States, indeed, there could have been none less bellicose by instinct than William McKinley; his whole habit of mind was pacific; his mode of action essentially emollient; his instinct not for the forceful leadership, but for discreet interpretation of the popular will."[15] Hence, despite his reluctance towards war or any form of aggression, President McKinley found himself surreptitiously involved in military conflicts with the Spanish government. The Monroe Doctrine was thus challenged through this intervention of the United States in European affairs, but expansionists frequently justified its principles, claiming that American interests had to be safeguarded. This is well exemplified in Perkins' remark: "Implicit in the language of President Monroe had been the idea of America for Americans; implicit in it also had been a sympathy with republics struggling to be free; and in addition to all this there was always the possibility of alleging that unsettled conditions in any American colony might afford the excuse for the wicked intervention of the unscrupulous powers of the Old World."[16]

Moreover, in 1823, Secretary of State John Quincy Adams, reflecting the expansionist spirit, had already defined Cuba and the other West Indian islands as "natural appendages" to North America. With some irony, David Healy observed "to President James Monroe, Cuba formed a part of the mouth of the Mississippi. Not only was the United States destined to include all of North America, according to these expansionists, but by a sort of geographical affinity, the nearby islands ought naturally to come with the rest. Ultimately the principle was extended all the way to Hawaii, now regarded as the natural outpost of the continent."

Thus, it was mainly under McKinley's presidency, 1887 through 1890, that the Monroe Doctrine was often invoked, since the president's claims on Cuba, Hawaii, and the Philippines seemed to contradict some of its principles. As already mentioned, Monroe's message in 1823 had stipulated that the United States would not intervene in already existing European colonies or in any other territories situated outside the continents of North and South America.

Cuba: "The Splendid Little War"

In the 1890s, the Cuban crisis equally led to a revival of 1823 principles to sanction or criticize American intervention. The economic situation of the island had declined during the "Ten Years War" and the Cuban rebels were in a drastic situation, calling the Americans to their rescue against the Spanish rulers. H. W. Morgan notes that Americans "could not fail to heed the cry of oppressed Cubans, who wove into their appeals subtle reminders of special American responsibilities and interests in the hemisphere. Did the Monroe Doctrine selfishly protect some and oppress others?"[17] Like the American investors who had settled on their soil, the Cubans were disturbed by Cuba's slow agony and deterioration, the island's exports to the United States falling drastically. Moreover, as the "yellow press," prodded by the well-known William Randolph Hearst, began to relate atrocities committed by Spanish officials, and a deep concern began to develop in American public opinion. It was revealed that members of the Spanish administration mistreated American nationals.

In addition, when McKinley took office, he was backed by "a small but potent group of intellectuals who preached the new doctrine of expansion, playing on national pride by linking it with slogans of 'manifest destiny' and the prospect of acquiring foreign markets."[18] Finally, after careful consideration, McKinley's decision to intervene in Cuba rested on his promise to restore prosperity by supporting the businessmen's interests. In the same line of ideas, a patriotic publicist wrote that America's dogma could not be applied literally, observing that "it may be urged with some degree of plausibility by those who cling to its letter rather than to its spirit, that the Monroe Doctrine, if it applies to Cuba, commits us to a policy of non-intervention with regard to this island," but "surely the *spirit* of the Monroe Doctrine, which was specially launched against the oppressive and despotic government on this hemisphere, may be invoked to justify intervention against Spain in behalf of Cuba by the recognition of her independence."[19]

In Europe, critics who felt the Principles of 1823 were going unheeded began to express themselves. The Frenchman Maurice de Beaumarchais drew people's attention by pointing out that the Monroe Doctrine "has in the Cuban business, been once more openly violated both in its text and its spirit."[20] Other European countries agreed with Beaumarchais and made it clear that the U.S. actions were an overt and drastic repudiation of the 1823 principles insofar as the doctrine included a clear principle of reciprocity — the United States claiming the right to block Europe from intervening in their affairs, in return for America's noninterference in European affairs.

In the United States, dissenting voices were more discreet than in Europe. In defense of the American posture, Perkins noted that judgmental reflections emanating from irritated Europeans may have been the result of some "dislike of the United States so common in continental Europe." However, fifteen years later, an eminent German scholar, Herbert Kraus, who was invited to speak at summer schools in the universities of Chicago and Philadelphia in 1924, published a serious work on the language of the doctrine, and drew the conclusion that "the conduct of the United States with regard to Spain in this instance was an extraordinary drastic and obvious repudiation of the principles" of this American iconic message. With the intention of unifying these diverse and antagonistic interpretations, Perkins tried to find an intermediate and comprehensible synthesis:

> But if, on the one hand, we must repudiate the view that the Monroe Doctrine forbade interposition in the affairs of Cuba, we must also repudiate with equal definiteness the notion that it justified such intervention. As we have seen, the administration itself made no such claim. The Senate Foreign Relations Committee attempted a specious justification based upon the non-colonization principle, and upon a general right of intervention of which the doctrine was claimed to be an American expression, but neither of these appears to me convincing. The first is decidedly strained, the second a departure from the language of the original message. In attempting, indeed, to justify the intervention by the principles of 1823, Senator Foraker for example, or Professor Hershey, those who cited the

Monroe Message, were giving it a tremendous extension. They appealed to the general idea of "America for Americans," but the idea "America for Americans" is not the Monroe Doctrine, any more than Pan-Americanism is the Monroe Doctrine, or the rule of non-participation in European affairs the Monroe Doctrine. These ideas are related to one another, of course; but there can be no clear thinking about the doctrine itself as long as they are confused with one another. Confused they have often been, and the historian must note the confusion; but they are not identical. It was a prudent sense of value which led the McKinley administration to make no allusion at any time in its Cuban policy to the policy of the principles of 1823.[21]

Hawaii: The Rise of Economic Imperialism

During the debate over the annexation of Hawaii that followed an internal insurrection, the supporters of the Monroe Doctrine refrained from mentioning it; nonetheless, the message was revived when the issue of annexing the islands in June and July 1898 generated heated polemics. The Hawaiian Islands, discovered by the British explorer James Cook in 1778, were later visited by many Europeans for trade purposes. During the 1780s and 1790s, after tribal warfare, a charismatic ruler was named King Kamehameha the Great. His dynasty ruled the country until 1872 when, the last descendant having no heir, power shifted to another house, bringing internal clashes. In 1887, a group of American and European businessmen, together with Hawaiian officials, forced the new head of state, King Kalakaua, to sign the "Bayonet Constitution," which undermined the king's authority and favored the wealthy elite, made up of natives and foreigners. After his death, in 1891, his sister Liliuokalani ascended the throne. In 1893, a white citizens' revolt overthrew the reigning queen, who had claimed "Hawaii for the Hawaiians!" The rebels then asked for an annexation treaty by the United States, but President Grover Cleveland was unwilling to resort to force, and even endeavored to restore the queen's throne.

When McKinley took office in 1897, the previous administration had already issued a long series of declarations stipulating that the United States would not remain indifferent to the transfer of these islands to any foreign power, thereby confirming the previous statements made, in 1842, by President Tyler and the Secretary of State Daniel Webster, who recognized the importance of Hawaii for the United States and rejected the idea of any foreign influence. They sought to extend the Monroe Doctrine by bringing the Hawaiian Islands under American control, thus opening the way for trade with China.

Regarding the European views on Cuba at the time, a British navy officer had suggested the transfer of the Hawaiian Islands to the British Empire. The U.S. promptly reacted, stating that, if necessary, it would resort to force to prevent the islands from falling into the hands of one of the European great powers. Indeed, England, France and the new German empire had divergent interests in the Pacific Ocean, and were actually looking for new territories on which to fly their flags. France had already begun eyeing the islands in 1850 and 1851, leading Webster to issue the same message with the same firmness, as he had done previously.

Strong links between the U.S. and Hawaii dated back to 1820 when Americans businessmen sought to settle on the island and establish economic ties with their mother country. A group of American Presbyterian missionaries had also landed in Hawaii to convert the natives at around the same time. In the 1850s, sixteen Congregationalist missionaries occupied large tracts of land. The U.S. consul called them "bloodsuckers of the community" and accused them of "living like lords" and "disturbing the minds of these children of nature."[22] However, no political leader, including Secretary of State Webster, mentioned either the spirit or the letter of the Monroe Doctrine.

On the other hand, in 1898, the opponents of expansionism started to react. Resorting to extensive propaganda through the press or printed leaflets, they intended to have their protests heard. Regarding Hawaii, the protesters were bold enough to affirm that the annexation of territories located outside the American continent was a violation of the 1823 principles. This is what Senator William V. Allen, from Nebraska, pointed out on the Senate floor:

> Mr. President, the plain and comprehensive question before the Senate is this: Shall the United States abandon the well-defined and universally accepted Monroe Doctrine and her traditional domestic policy, and at this time enter on the dangerous career of colonial expansion and European imperialism? ... If anything can be said to be completely settled in our country, it is the Monroe Doctrine, which declares that, while we will not ourselves engage in a career of imperialism and colonial acquisition, no other nation shall invade or extend her dominion on this continent to the detriment or injury of the United States, and if we hold to this doctrine, we must also be bound by its terms.[23]

Senator Bate added: "What is to become of our most cherished principle, the Monroe Doctrine, when once this country has adopted the policy of expansion to the isles of the Pacific Ocean?" Under the Monroe Doctrine, the United States denied European powers all colonial rights on the American continent. Pursuing his point vehemently, he asked, "Can this country at the same time assert and exercise the right to extend its system to the archipelagos of the Pacific?" Finally, Bate concluded with bitter disappointment: "This would be glaring inconsistency, piracy in violation of the principles of 1823..., the rifting of our hitherto gnarled and unwedgeable oak, the declaration of President Monroe."[24]

Several people used irony to argue that the Monroe Doctrine was a very "elastic" doctrine, since it could be extended two thousand miles into the Pacific Ocean. Although confronted by these attacks and allusions to the 1823 principles, those advocating annexation remained silent. However, in Europe, a British newspaper, *The St. James Gazette*, published a sarcastic article on the Monroe Doctrine and the annexation of Hawaii:

> Monroeism ... cannot tolerate a foreign flag in the Pacific, 2.000 miles from the nearest American port; and therefore, so that the bones of Monroe may rest in peace, the American coastline is to be pushed 2.000 miles west. To an English reader this may sound absurd ... I am indulging in no levity.... The Monroe Doctrine can be stretched so as to cover everything; and when the Monroe Doctrine is preached, it is a jihad to which all the faithful must give heed.[25]

The Hawaiian issue was resolved through McKinley's negotiations for an annexation treaty. In May 1898, he asked Congress to pass a joint resolution in order to annex the island. This decision was motivated by economic and political interests since Hawaii had been managed by white planters "who used the island as the extension of the frontier in Oregon and California."[26] From the economic viewpoint, sugar plantations produced a substantial output and served a large part of the U.S. markets. Politically, McKinley needed Hawaii, as it was an important military base and outpost to reach Chinese ports. As for the missionaries, they favored the annexation on the grounds that it could become "a base of operations for the enterprise of universal evangelization."[27] Due to the strong opposition of the anti-expansionists, it took four days of discussions before reaching an agreement. Resolute opponents contended that the annexation was liable to open "a second avenue of conquest" leading to "the Philippines next."[28]

The Philippine Issue: A Heated Debate

Indeed, the Philippines were invaded by the U.S troops, and this question raised similar controversy and polemics in the American community. A brief overview of the history of the Philippines may shed some light on the causes of its invasion by the McKinley administration which aroused many impassioned debates and harsh contestation. After their discovery by Ferdinand Magellan in 1521, the Philippines were placed under Spanish rule. The first Spanish settlement was not established until 1565, but it led to the social, economic and political development of Manila, capital of the largest island, Luzon. The Filipinos, led by Emilio Aguinaldo, began to revolt against the colonizers in 1896. From the very beginning of the conflict, Americans (economically interested in the acquisition of the islands) and Filipinos had been allies against Spain. Aguinaldo and his supporters conquered nearly all of the Spanish-held ground except Manila. On June 12, Aguinaldo declared independence and in August, American forces captured the city of Manila from the Spaniards. From then on, and to the great disappointment of the rebellious Filipinos, the U.S. army was in control of the insurrection. The Declaration on Independence was not recognized, and the Spanish government ceded the Philippines to the United States on December 10, 1898 by the Treaty of Paris. Yet Aguinaldo was declared president of the Philippines on January 1, 1899.

However, during the conflict, after ordering a commission to investigate internal affairs on the islands, McKinley had declared that the Filipinos were not ready for independence. The report from Dr. Shurman, who headed the commission, read as follows:

> Should our power by any fatality be withdrawn, the commission believe that the government of the Philippines would speedily lapse into anarchy, which would excuse, if it did not necessitate, the intervention of other powers and the eventual division of the islands among them. Only through American occupation, therefore, is the idea of a free, self-governing, and united Philippine commonwealth at all conceivable. And the indispensable need from the Filipino point of view of maintaining American sovereignty over the archipelago is recognized by all intelligent Filipinos and even by those insurgents who desire an American protectorate. The latter, it is true, would take the revenues and leave us the responsibilities. Nevertheless, they recognize the indubitable fact that the Filipinos cannot stand alone. Thus the welfare of the Filipinos coincides with the dictates of national honor in forbidding our abandonment of the archipelago. We cannot from any point of view escape the responsibilities of government which our sovereignty entails; and the commission is strongly persuaded that the performance of our national duty will prove the greatest blessing to the peoples of the Philippine Islands.[29]

Conditions deteriorated when an American soldier shot a Filipino, which led to major riots in Manila. The situation worsened when the American government sent troops, causing many casualties among the natives. Aguilnaldo's answer was quick:

> I order and command 1.— that peace and friendly relations with the Americans be broken and that the latter be treated as enemies, within the limits prescribed by the laws of war. 2.— that the Americans captured be held as prisoners of war. 3.— that this proclamation be communicated to the consuls and that Congress order and accord a suspension of the constitutional guarantee, resulting from the declaration of war.[30]

To justify war on the Philippines, it was reported that President William McKinley had declared "that the insurgents had attacked Manila." Aguinaldo was treated as an "outlaw bandit" by the McKinley administration, but no official declaration of war was proclaimed. Then McKinley ordered a second Philippine Commission, and more troops were sent to the islands. By the end of 1899, the Philippine Army was defeated. Guerrilla warfare ensued, and the Americans responded with ruthlessness, burning villages, shooting surrendering soldiers and putting civilians in concentration camps. On March 23, 1901, Aguinaldo was captured by General Frederick Funston and his troops and, laying down his arms, had to swear an oath to accept the authority of the United States.

During the heated debates that took place at the time of the conflict, the advocates of overseas expansionism, such as Theodore Roosevelt, Senator Henry Cabot Lodge and Captain Alfred Mahan, justified their arguments using the formula Manifest Destiny and "national duty."[31] To uphold its world power, they contended, the United Sates had to protect itself against its enemies. The slogan "America's Manifest Destiny" reappeared, and McKinley himself later told some clergymen that God had asked him to annex the islands and "do the best we could for them."[32]

The anti-imperialist movement also voiced its protest on the Philippine issue. Its mentor, U.S. Senator George Frisbie Hoar, declared, "The Monroe Doctrine is dead.... Every European nation, every European alliance has the right to acquire dominion in this hemisphere when we acquire it in the other."[33] U.S. senator from 1877 until his death, Hoar issued a severe and condemning statement before the Senate in May 1902:

> You have wasted nearly six hundred millions of treasure. You have sacrificed nearly ten thousand American lives—the flower of our youth. You have devastated provinces. You have slain uncounted thousands of the people you desire to benefit. You have established concentration camps.... You make the American flag in the eyes of a numerous people the emblem of sacrilege in Christian churches, and of the burning of human dwellings, and of the horror of water torture.... Mr. President, this is the eternal law of human nature. You may struggle against it, you may try to escape it, you may persuade yourself that your intentions are benevolent, that your yoke will be easy and your burden will be light, but it will assert itself again. Government without the consent of the government—an authority which heaven never gave—can only be supported by means which heaven never can sanction.
>
> The American people have got this one question to answer ... John Quincy Adams and James Monroe answered it again in the Monroe Doctrine, which John Quincy Adams declared was only the doctrine of the consent of the government.
>
> The question will be answered again hereafter. ... it will be answered in the churches and in the schools and in colleges. It will be answered right.[34]

The Monroe Doctrine was mentioned not only in the political arena but also in public opinion, which became wary of politicians advocating the principles of nonintervention without applying them. The press took up the same arguments. *The Springfield Republican* reported "the smashing of the Monroe Doctrine."[35] *The Boston Herald* stated that the takeover of the

Philippines was an act so contrary to the traditional policy of the United States that "it would tear the Monroe Doctrine from top to bottom." As for *The Chicago Chronicle,* it observed that the invasion of the Philippines would mean "cutting loose from the Monroe Doctrine and following the precepts of Napoleon and Frederick the Great."[36]

In the United States, while the discussion on the annexation of the Philippines seemed to toll an end to the Monroe Doctrine, in Europe protests took place denouncing American policy. British politicians loudly proclaimed that the Monroe Doctrine had died. An anecdote on the subject was published in *Punch* in the form of a humorous dialogue between America and Europe:

"Who are you?" says Dame Europe to a figure of Uncle Sam.
"Uncle Sam" is the answer.
"Ah! Any relation to the late colonel Monroe?"[37]

American people started to react against these insidious European attacks, *The American Nation* claiming that a new debate had surfaced over the doctrine in order to quiet the rumors, especially since a book on the Monroe Doctrine had been published in France in 1900 by Hector Pétin, who observed:

> The whole pre-doctrine of Monroe imposes on the United States a complete abstention from non–American affairs; in every application which they have made of the message of 1823, the presidents have set forth, in deference to the prescriptions which they impose, their perpetual disinterestedness in extra-American affairs. Today, it is no longer so; retaining from the Monroe Doctrine the prohibition made to Europe, they repudiate the obligations which flow from it, detach the anti–European part of the message, and declare that only this part is applicable. Even more, certain advanced imperialists do not hesitate to declare that Monroeism has run its course, and that it is no longer to be applied.[38]

However, the McKinley administration did not respond to these charges, and when the Russian czar issued invitations on August 24, of the same year, for the first Hague Peace Conference, the American government was surprised to be invited, and welcomed the invitation with enthusiasm and gratitude. In the course of this international conference, the American delegation was in charge of establishing an international tribunal, the statutes of which were to stipulate that: "The contracting nations will mutually agree to submit to the international tribunal all questions of disagreement between them, excepting such as may relate to or involve their political independence or territorial integrity."[39]

John Hay, American Secretary of State at the time, signed the agreement. Conflicts relating to territorial questions or problems concerning intervention in the affairs of independent states were not subject to this international tribunal, which allowed the Monroe Doctrine to enlarge its scope of action and for Manifest Destiny to continue "running loose." Since "Monroeism" had no clear borders, the principles of an ideological diplomacy were implicitly adopted to guide American foreign policy and opened the way to various claims relating to the spread of democracy throughout the world.

The Anti-Imperialist Movement

As already indicated, hidden within the Monroe message lay deep conceptual confusion that surfaced in different ways, depending on each individual's or group's ideological viewpoints. Many of its propagandists, convinced of the validity of its principles, sought to interpret it in a convenient manner to justify multifarious American interests. Yet by and large the message was clear for most anti-imperialists who firmly opposed the bold undertakings of the McKinley administration. The nonconforming voices came from diverse origins, unfortunately failing to form a coherent and united opposition; but they cannot be neglected as they included major political and intellectual figures. Their arguments, however, were not always based on sound and orthodox premises. Several were tinted with racial overtones, others involved personal interests or fears regarding problems that expansionist move would create; few of them reacted with moral integrity or true perspicacity. However, the temptation to legitimize the imperialist urge was great, inasmuch as most of the overseas colonies under the Spanish rule suffered from political disorder and social instability.

One of the strongest opponents was Carl Schurz, a senator from Missouri. Born in Germany, he came to the United States in 1852 as a political émigré after the 1848 German revolution and settled in Philadelphia. After studying law, he actively participated in American political life and was soon acknowledged as a prominent public figure. Embracing the Union cause, he was made a diplomat and a general by Abraham Lincoln, and in the 1870s, became Secretary of the Interior under Hayes. After his retirement, he moved to New York and devoted himself to journalism and lecturing.

Schurz's theory against expansionism was founded on beliefs in racial differences. He considered tropical populations as a threat to the American democracy for, he argued, these populations, living in hot climates, were inclined to lethargy. Consequently, Schurz deplored the spirit of Manifest Destiny that underlay the expansionist rhetoric. In an article published by *Harper's Magazine* in 1893, he stated:

> Whenever there is a project on foot to annex foreign territory to this republic, the cry of "manifest destiny" is raised to produce the impression that all opposi-

tion to such a project is a struggle against fate. Forty years ago this cry had a peculiar significance. The slaveholders saw in this rapid growth of the free States a menace to the existence of slavery. In order to strengthen themselves in Congress, they needed most slave States, and looked therefore to the acquisition of foreign territory on which slavery existed — in the first place, the island of Cuba. Thus to the pro-slavery man, "manifest destiny" meant an increase of the number of slave States by annexation. There was still another force behind the demand for territorial expansion. It consisted in the youthful optimism at that time still inspiring the minds of many Americans with the idea that this republic, being charged with the mission of bearing the banner of freedom over the whole civilized world, could transform any country, inhabited by any kind of population, into something like itself simply by extending over it the magic charm of its political institutions.... It was, however, the Southern "manifest destiny" movement, with a strong organized interest behind it and well-defined purposes in view, that exercised the greater influence upon the policy of this country.[40]

However, if Manifest Destiny was, for Carl Schurz, at the root of the slavery cause or the expression of a romantic emotion, the focal point of his article concentrated on the fact that people born in the tropics were prone to laziness. When President Harrison attempted to annex Hawaii in 1893, Schurz took the opportunity to remind the Americans that overseas annexation would certainly drive them into "reckless enterprises." It was unwise, he said, to incorporate these tropical natives into the American community, as they would have to be admitted as "fellow-citizens on a footing of equality." Such a situation would weaken and degrade the American institutions as it was "a matter of universal experience that democratic institutions have never on a large scale prospered in tropical latitudes."[41]

Senator Richard Franklin Pettigrew from South Dakota, who participated in the various debates on the Hawaiian issue, was also a severe critic of the destinarian concept. Resorting to harsh language and using strong and evocative terms, he did not hesitate to fustigate the religiously inclined notion, claiming that from its inception, Manifest Destiny had been "the murderer of men," having committed "more crimes, done more to oppress and wrong the inhabitants of the world than any other tribute to which mankind has fallen heir." Suggesting the often-quoted criticism relating to old Europe and the absolutist principles of its monarchical systems, he reminded the Senate that "manifest destiny built the feudal castle and supplied the castle with its serfs."[42] In subduing weak people, republics had ruined themselves and perished. For him, Manifest Destiny was simply the expression of an injustice, the strong wishing to prevail over the weak.

E. L. Godkin was another architect of the anti-imperialist movement. Born in Ireland, he graduated from Queen's College, Belfast, and studied law in London. He traveled in Europe, and in 1856 arrived in New York where he founded *The Nation*, a leading liberal weekly magazine, which attracted intellectual and influential readers. In one of his articles, published on August 9, 1900, he denounced the United States' political ideals, reminding his readership that the world had already suffered from the results of "dynastic ambitions," that whole populations were burdened by the exactions of the "superior classes" which led to a universal revulsion against autocratic systems. But despite the eighteenth-century enlightened philosophers' ideas, which were "the soil in which modern liberalism flourished," the new generation had been blinded by the lure of material comfort. The United States has thus regressed and lost ground, he argued, disfigured and distorted the true sense of the Declaration of Independence. Similarly, the Constitution was said to be "outgrown." Pursuing his analysis, Godkin tackled the religious implications of such political posture vis-à-vis territorial expansion:

> Nationalism in the sense of national greed has supplanted Liberalism. It is an old foe under a new name. By making the aggrandizement of a particular nation a higher end than the welfare of mankind, it has sophisticated the moral sense of Christendom. Aristotle justified slavery, because Barbarians were "naturally" inferior to Greeks, and we have gone back to his philosophy. We hear no more of natural rights, but of inferior races, whose part it is to submit to the government of those whom God has made their superiors.

The socialist Morrison I. Swift, in *Imperialism and Liberty*, did not mince his words either, while harshly criticizing the McKinley administration for its involvement in the Philippines issue. His long diatribe thrashed every military and political enterprise and focused on wrongdoings and misdeeds of the American army. The vehement and incisive tone of his arguments shocked certain advocates of the anti-imperialist movement. The concluding lines of his work, fraught with cynical irony, referred to the oft-quoted identification of the American people with the Hebrews:

> Our light and civilization and science, our annexations of Jesus and the Holy Ghost with the pirate God of Moses, have not carried us beyond that guerilla one inch. Thou shall not kill any but outsiders who have desirable land and property, engage the Lord to kill them with thy aid, and beware lest thou forget the Lord when thy barns and thy temple and thy stomach groan with the fullness of stolen things.[43]

Another well-known socialist, Samuel Gompers, equally belonged to the anti-imperialist movement. For a long period regarded as the nation's leading trade unionist, and head of the American Federation of Labor, Gompers was genuinely concerned about the annexations of Hawaii and the Philippines as he feared that problems inherent to the different labor systems would jeopardize the American markets.

Andrew Carnegie, an icon of American capitalism and a major philanthropist who had made a fortune in the steel industry, also greatly contributed to the cause of anti-imperialism through his financial aid. In a letter tinted with a certain sense of humor, Carnegie wrote to Carl Schurz: "You have brains and I have dollars.... I can devote some of my dollars to spreading your brains," which he graciously did.

The statesman William Jennings Bryan, democratic candidate in the presidential elections of 1896 and 1900, also stood as a foe to the movement. A devout Presbyterian and a popular speaker, Bryan was called "the Great Commoner." Twice defeated by McKinley, he remained for a long time head of the Democratic Party, widely embracing populist ideas. In "The Paralyzing Influence of Imperialism," Bryan, referring to the Philippine issue, argued that those who wished to adhere to imperialism had to consider not only the effect of this policy on the Filipinos but also on the American nation. He summarized the imperialists' principal arguments concerning overseas expansion: America's ambition to become a world power; the lure of commercial interests; the spread of the Christian religion; impossibility of an honorable retreat for the United States when already engaged. Regarding the spread of Christianity, he further noted:

> "The religious argument varies in positiveness from a passive belief that Providence delivered the Filipinos into our hands for their good and our glory to the exultation of the minister who said that we ought to "thrash the native Filipinos until they understand who we are," and that "every bullet sent, every cannon shot, and every flag waved means righteousness."[44]

In the literary realm, Mark Twain was the most prominent writer to condemn the Spanish-American War. He delivered many statements, speeches and interviews on the subject that revealed his indignation, using at times caustic sarcasm: "I have read carefully the treaty of Paris, and I have seen that we do not intend to free, but to subjugate the people of the Philippines. We have gone there to conquer, not to redeem. It should, it seems to me, be our pleasure and duty to make those people free, and let them deal with their own domestic questions in their own way. And so I am anti-imperialist. I am opposed to having the eagle put its talons on any other land."[45]

In June 1898, such distinguished figures in politics, business, journalism and education organized the Anti-Imperialist League to oppose U.S. annexation of the Philippines. Mark Twain himself was vice president of the league from 1901 until his death in 1910. The original organization was founded in New England but the movement soon developed westward. The subject of colonial expansion was discussed in numerous conferences, and propaganda flooded the country. However, the league mainly gathered members from the intellectual elite and vainly strove to attract popular support. Moreover, dissensions within the group arose as the members had divergent viewpoints on home policy and could not agree on a common strategy, which led to its final breakup. One of its members said with bitterness:

We are the most impracticable set of cranks probably to be found on the face of the earth. By "we" I refer to our [anti] imperialist crowd. We cannot agree on anything: and the standards we set up are so exalted and all embracing, and any infringements upon them are so objectionable, that to reach an agreement is impossible, and our influence is, therefore, wasted.[46]

8

Racism and the Ethnocentric Debate

One of the consequences of territorial expansion was the emergence of several racial theories, resulting from numerous problems associated with the integration of people of diverse origins. Originally peopled by Native Americans, America had to find a way to deal with these local populations, particularly since slavery had already fueled countless controversies. The problem of race relations had to be considered by the entire American community, given that "those who opposed expansion and those who supported expansion agreed that the peoples of the newly acquired territory were incapable of self-government. Race was the common denominator."[1]

The origins of racism are difficult to determine and are often based on irrational behavior and fears due to complex psychological factors. From time immemorial in the Western psyche, racism is often associated with dark skin color evoking "filth, death and radical evil generally." Richard Drinnon notes that, in the United States, "the *consequences* of racism are more tangible. Anchored however obscurely in the unconscious, it became a key component of the national theology, from the Bay Colonys' New Israel to the republic's Manifest Destiny and white man's burden and New Frontier."[2] Given the religious and ideological orientation of this study, the racial questions and theories are generally sustained by such argumentation.

In this perspective, the issue of the Philippines raised impassionate debates, epitomizing racial dilemma and entailing deep moral reflection, even though the defenders or opponents of expansionism frequently agreed on the inferiority of "colored" people. Representative Weston, evoking the tense atmosphere in Congress at the time of the Philippines acquisition, stated:

> We are asked to annex to the United States a witch's caldron.... We are not only asked to annex the caldron and make it a part of our great, broad, Christian, Anglo-Saxon, American land, but we are asked also to annex the contents and take this brew-mixed races ... anybody who has come along in three hundred

years, in all of their concatenations and colors.... There has never been such condescension from a high ideal and from a noble and manifest destiny. Not only is it a degradation of this American land and of this American race, but of the scholars and thinkers of this country.... I am startled, I am thrown away from my ordinary bearings and conception of things to think that such gentlemen and such a body should contemplate the adoption of a treaty that utterly scorns and repudiates our position; that is essentially at war with our institutions; that embodies a country which is not part of the American continent and can not be made so, and that must inevitably take up and work into the destiny of the American people these alien races, or must make us get down from the throne of freedom."[3]

Such arguments were very common in political circles, whose members frequently disregarded the provisions of the American Constitution. Many Republicans and Democrats coalesced to voice the same political conception of the racial issue. Through policy makers' biased position, the colored man often realized the discrepancy between the egalitarian principles inscribed in the American institutions and their implementation as to their own rights. After the annexations of new territories, the American government treated native peoples, in the same manner as they did black people. Weston observed: "From his own experience, the black man learns to penetrate the white man's hypocrisies—to see how his appeals to God, the flag, and the Constitution often serve as a cloak for racial prejudice and self-righteousness."[4]

In an attempt to justify racial discrimination, when the issue of citizenship rights was raised, most imperialists did not hesitate to promote the white man's ethnological features. Dark-skinned people were often likened to blacks, who were all classified as an inferior race, bereft of intellectual and rational abilities. After his visit in 1899 to American troops based in the Philippines, Senator Albert Beveridge was interviewed by the *Saturday Evening Post* which reported his comments on the exceptional ethnological traits of the Anglo-Saxon type. Beveridge had been struck by the soldiers' physical appearances: "Everywhere the pale blue or grey eye, everywhere the fair skin, everywhere the tawny hair and beard.... The whole face and figure is the face and figure of the thoroughbred fighter, who has always been the fine-creature, delicate-nostril, thin-eared, and generally clean-cut featured man."[5] One finds in this reflection a reminder of the Teutonic theory, advocated by the Hopkins historians, who portrayed the typical Teuton as a blue-eyed and blond-haired individual.

These ideas, shared to a large extent by ardent imperialists who believed in white supremacy, clearly contrasted with the often-quoted portrayal of the Filipinos who were described as a debilitated race, having bulldog jaws and living in slyness and sloth. Dirtiness was, in the popular mind, a backward and devilish attribute to human beings, as people often quoted the well-known saying "Cleanliness is near to Godliness." The adage is exemplified in the following anecdote: "On the inside cover of *McClure's Magazine* in October 1899, there was an advertisement for Pears' Soap featuring a resplendently uniformed Admiral George Dewey bending over a washbowl. His attitude was to be associated with the civilizing duty of advance nations: 'The first step towards lightening The White Man's Burden is through teaching the virtues of cleanliness. Pears' Soap is a potent factor in brightening the dark corners of the earth, as civilization advances, while among the cultured of all nations it holds the highest place.'"[6]

However, the expansionists, proponents of Darwinism, did not specifically lay emphasis on color, as noted Welch, but on the notion of the "superior fitness of certain peoples." Superior races were endowed with superior physical and intellectual qualities and were more apt to rule than others because they enjoyed more favorable conditions of life, for instance a temperate climate. Henry Adams, American novelist, journalist and historian, evoked, not without a certain humor, the fate of a European who is compelled to go and work in the tropics: "The European in face of the tropic is a sweet study," he wrote to Henry Cabot Lodge in 1891. "He admits himself to be an abject failure there; he can make nothing of it; he can't work; he can't digest; he can't sleep; he gets disease, and he grumbles without ceasing; but he won't let anyone else go there. ..I find no fault with him; but what the deuce he can make of it?"[7]

Racial Theories and Social Darwinism

In the mid–nineteenth century, these strands of belief on racial particularities were extensively nourished by the development of social sciences, widely related to the evolutionary process. The new findings rested on experimental discoveries that connected the nature of biological man with that of the organic and animal world. At the turn of the century, these ideas gave rise to what was called behaviorism, a social theory developed by John B. Watson, often referred to as the "father of behaviorism," who graduated from the University of Chicago in 1903. The psychologist explained that the "subject matter of human psychology" was the "behavior of a human being" which followed the pattern of animal conduct. According to him, consciousness was no more a "usable concept" and belonged to the "ancient days of superstition and magic…. Christ had his magic: he turned water into wine and raised the dead to life."[8]

This scientific approach was greatly influenced by Darwinism, and led many social theorists and Social Darwinists to adopt a secular turn of mind, which tended to disregard religious motives in the elaboration of the world.

Yet, in *Social Darwinism in American Thought*, Richard Hofstadter observed that the influential American social thinker William Graham Sumner and his followers professed a kind of "naturalistic Calvinism in which man's relation to nature is as hard and demanding as man's relation to God under the Calvinistic system."[9] He thus sought to link deterministic arguments to moral injunction, in the sense that the efforts of the virtuous man were bound to be rewarded.

For many American believers, Darwinism developed principles of racial superiority contravening the spirit of the Holy Scriptures and thus shaking the foundation of the Christian faith. Indeed, the new Darwinist theory threw the traditional ideas on the origin of mankind into disarray, and the belief in natural selection itself challenged the prevailing religious and theological foundations. Indeed, the concept of "natural selection" implied the notion of struggle among members of the same society or among different nations and races as a natural and necessary behavior. Racial conflicts, far from being an evil, could be considered as a natural process indispensable and essential to the evolution of society. As Weston reported, citing Blake and Bark in *United States in Its World Relations*: "There was in the United States a climate of opinion, a mystique, of white supremacy supported by the Darwinian concept of the survival of the fittest, which led racial theorists to be confident that the white man was superior."[10] These sociologists argued that heredity was a determining factor in the development of society, and led many people to think that the notions of race and heredity were one and could be combined.

One of them, Herbert Spencer (1820–1903), a sociologist and philosopher, gave form to Social Darwinism by putting forth his own theories.[11] Spencer was born in Derby, England, on April 27, 1820. Raised in the Quaker religion, he received a thorough education including subjects such as mathematics, physics and Latin. The young man later worked as a civil engineer, journalist and writer. From then on, Spencer devoted his life to the study of evolution in the social and political fields and became more popular in the United States than he was in his own country. In *Principles of Psychology* (1855), he focused on the important role and effects of biology on the human mind.

It is generally acknowledged that the terms "struggle for life" and "survival of the fittest" were actually coined by him in his *Principles of Biology*.[12] Spencer extended the notion of evolutionism to the domain of sociology, which gave rise to the theory of Social Darwinism. His main goal was to prove, scientifically, that the mental faculties of human beings were submitted to natural laws and that thoughts were the products of a certain disposition of the brain cells. People were then somewhat governed or conditioned by their past or their environment, which had been irremediably registered in their brain tissue. This scientific posture met with severe criticism among theologians as it implied the negation of free will and challenged the existence of the human soul.

Spencer endeavored to further explain his main theory by drawing analogies between the biological determinism of natural laws that control man's behavior and the evolution of societies. Societies evolved under the implacable force of evolution, inscribed in immutable biological and physical principles that conditioned the individual. Nothing could intervene in this progressive and slow mutation. Spencer illustrated this idea of the evolution of men in society by going back to the origin of man.

Spencer viewed man in his primitive state as being conditioned by violence and warfare. These radical actions were an implicit method for eliminating inferior races, as warfare had a "eugenic" effect by "killing off the inferior races."[13] Throughout the evolution of humanity, armed conflicts would be transformed into economic conflicts, and ultimately war would disappear. From Spencer's point of view, this process of natural selection would encourage the development of industrial societies as a factor of civilization. This social theory would have social consequences, since primitive peoples, being by definition less advanced, would find themselves in a state of inferiority vis-à-vis the developed nations in their "struggle for life." Spencer illustrated his ideas by means of an analogy: "The mind of a child recapitulates the history of the human race in a development from savagery to civilization. To understand the mind of primitive races, the civilized races should examine the character of the minds of their own children."[14]

In Spencer's opinion, the minds of inferior races did not evolve during their lifetime and remained similar to children's minds. Moreover, he proposed the idea that superior races surpassed inferior races "by virtue of the great quantity of energy in which this greater mental mass shows itself." By "mental mass," Spencer meant several factors, such as body size, brain size and the "richness" of blood. For example, in a letter he wrote to a friend, Spencer stated that the origin of France's defeat in 1870 had to be found in certain causes difficult to define such as "race or the particular mixes being at the root."[15] Spencer concluded by asserting that a regenerative process was most improbable after such a decline of French power. On the other hand, during a visit to the United States, he convinced the Americans that, with regard to their own population, the racial mixture had produced a beneficial effect: "From biological truths it is inferred that the eventual mixture of all allied varieties of the Aryan race ... will produce a more powerful type of man than has hitherto existed ... I think ... the Americans may reasonably look forward to a time when they will have produced a civilization grander than any the world has known."[16]

Spencer had an optimistic and utilitarian view of the impact of evolutionism on societies, as he believed that, in spite of all the hardships and grievances met by populations over the ages, social evolution was bound to ensure happiness through the comforts of progress, bringing about the final stage of human perfection:

> Whereas the actual progress consists in the produce of a greater quantity and variety of articles for the satisfaction of men's wants; in the increasing security of person and property; in the widening freedom of action enjoyed whereas, rightly understood, social progress consists in those changes of structure in the social organism which have entailed these consequences. The current conception is a teleological one. The phenomena are contemplated solely as bearing on human happiness. Only those changes are held to constitute progress which directly or indirectly tends to heighten human happiness. And they are thought to constitute progress simply because they tend to heighten human happiness.[17]

In those days, such ideas produced a very favorable echo in the United States and abroad, attracting many followers. One of them, William Graham Sumner, a professor of political science and founder of American sociology, did not believe in the equality of the races either. Born in Paterson, New Jersey in 1840, and raised by a hard-working father who taught him Protestant values, he was for several years an Episcopalian clergyman before entering an academic career. As a professor at Yale University, he wrote many essays on social and political subjects, praising the *laissez-faire* theory that he justified through Darwin's law of evolution.

On the social level, Sumner had his own conception regarding man's involvement in economic activity. Influenced by his stern religious upbringing, he believed that men of good character tended to succeed whereas the "negligent, shiftless, inefficient, silly and imprudent" were doomed to failure and punished."[18] The notion of punishment and reward were thus at the core of every human experience and could be checked in all fields of activity. Retribution and reward were the natural consequences of the practice of vices and virtues: "Nature's remedies against vices are terrible. She removes the victims without pity. A drunkard in the gutter is just where he ought to be, according to the fitness and tendency of things. Nature has set upon him the process of decline and dissolution by which she removes things which have survived their usefulness.[19] Sumner boldly asserted that if Jefferson had been asked whether the statement "All men were created equal" included blacks, he would have answered that "he was not talking about Negroes." He further declared: "A man may curse his fate because he is born of an inferior race, but he will get no answer from heaven for his imprecations."[20]

Spencer had another follower, Granville Stanley Hall (1844–1924), born of Puritan ancestry in Ashfield, Massachusetts. His parents were hardworking and pious teachers who had gone back to school while farming. Hall studied at Williams College, where he learned the theory of evolution and prepared for the ministry. Not particularly interested in theology (although he had been a preacher for a short time), he traveled to Europe, settling in Berlin where he focused his interest on physiology and physics. On his return from Berlin, Hall was admitted to Harvard, where he was the first to obtain a Ph.D. in psychology. In 1892, he founded the American Psychological Association, a scientific and professional organization which still exists today.

A specialist in child psychology, Hall agreed with Spencer that a child's mind recapitulated the history of the human race during its evolution. Although he felt that civilized peoples should treat inferior races with benevolence and avoid warfare, he tended to privilege the standards of white culture, denying any form of improvement to "backward" peoples. Supporters of American expansionism took up this idea when they spoke about the Filipinos, calling them "little brown brothers." Hall was also pessimistic as to the possibilities of assimilation and education of immigrants coming from southern and eastern Europe.

These racial issues raised many debates among sociologists, especially at a time when the eugenics movement[21] began to emerge. Daniel Kelves in *In the Name of Eugenics* informs us on the origin of eugenics:

> Eugenics was rooted in the social Darwinism of the late nineteenth century, a period in which notions of fitness, competition and biological rationalizations of inequality were popular. At the time, a growing number of theorists introduced Darwinian analogies of "survival of the fittest" into social argument. Many social Darwinists insisted that biology was destiny, at least for the unfit, and that a broad spectrum of socially deleterious traits, ranging from "pauperism to mental illness," resulted from heredity.[22]

The eugenicists tried to prove that the brilliant minds came from superior races and that, for genetic reasons, feeblemindedness and poverty were the fate of inferior races. Francis Galton, Charles Darwin's cousin, was one of their mentors, heading the eugenic movement that was formed in Great Britain. Born in Birmingham, England in 1822, into a wealthy family of Quaker gun-manufacturers and bankers, Galton was extremely gifted, reading literature at a very early age. After studying medicine in Birmingham, he traveled around the world. Impressed by Charles Darwin's *The Origin of Species*, published in 1859, he devoted much of his time to the study of the implications of evolutionism in human populations.

In *Hereditary Genius* (1869), he focused his attention on the links between hereditary characteristics and human ability, attempting to prove, for instance, that most brilliant men often belonged to a small number of families whose members were all more or less related. He wrote in his introductory chapter:

8—Racism and the Ethnocentric Debate 141

I propose to show in this book that a man's natural abilities are derived by inheritance, under exactly the same limitations as are the form and physical features of the whole organic world. Consequently as it is easy, notwithstanding those limitations, to obtain by careful selection a permanent breed of dogs or horses gifted with peculiar powers of running, or of doing anything else, so it would be quite practicable to produce a highly gifted race of men by judicious marriages during several consecutive generations. I shall show that social agencies of an ordinary character, whose influences are little suspected, are at this moment working towards the degradation of human nature, and that others are working towards its improvement. I conclude that each generation has enormous power over the natural gifts of those that follow, and maintain that it is a duty we owe to humanity to investigate the range of that power, and exercise it in a way that, without being unwise towards ourselves, shall be the most advantageous to future inhabitants of the earth.[23]

These ideas were in line with the development of scientific research in agronomics. Farmers began to use artificial selection to improve the quality of plants and animals and obtain better breeds. By sorting out the "better" or "worse" components of human species, eugenics could ameliorate racial qualities. The "cult of the elite" is well expressed in Galton's remark: "I am sure that no one who has had the privilege of mixing in the society of the abler man of any great capital, or who is acquainted with the biographies of the heroes of history, can doubt the existence of grand human animals, of natures pre-eminently noble, of individuals born to be kings of men."[24] Eugenicists differed from Darwinian theorists in the sense that they suggested intervening scientifically in the natural course of events.

Galton acknowledged differences among the races themselves when he submitted the idea that beyond the English Channel, the white race was somewhat defective because people had been victims of governments or repressive churches. He affirmed, for instance, that the celibacy of French Catholic priests had deprived mankind of offspring of quality. Similarly, the persecution of heretics had decimated many of the most courageous and intelligent population. In France, this catastrophe had found its illustration in the French Revolution, since the "guillotine made sad havoc among the progeny of her abler race."[25] As for the decline of the Italian civilization, it was due to the different revolutions which had resulted in many victims among the elites. It was, thus, not surprising that the blood of Europeans had weakened and contributed to undermining their level of competence. Nowadays, these notions seem so outlandish that one wonders how they could have germinated in these so-called scientific minds!

The supporters of the eugenic movement were convinced that the "vigorous" class, as the embodiment of future progress, had not produced enough children compared to the underprivileged, poor, and unskilled classes. It was thus necessary to develop a policy that would encourage and support a rising birth rate, as only members of the elite could contribute to the evolution of mankind. This partly explains the new and enthusiastic vogue for genealogy that emerged at that time; people became interested in their ancestral origin. John Graham Brooks, a distinguished American pastor, noted in 1903: "Heraldry now is a charmed word for multitudes of very humble people. Librarians are suddenly plagued by the importunity for genealogical evidence of distinguished ancestry. Daughters of this and daughters of that; clubs, coteries, everywhere springing into life, bound to discover proof that they are not quite like other people."[26] Senator Henry Cabot Lodge participated in this new impetus for genealogy, pointing out, "The waves of democracy have submerged the old and narrow lines within which the few sat apart and definition of a man's birth and ancestry has become more necessary."[27]

However, a movement of opposition to these pseudo-theories began to emerge. Headed by Lester F. Ward, one of its main protagonists, it was hostile to the deterministic views of the eugenicists. American botanist, paleontologist, and sociologist, he was among the most prominent dissenters who believed that the political, social and economic implications of Social Darwinism would raise philosophical problems in underestimating the fundamental driving force of the human mind: willpower. In *The Psychic Factors of Civilization*, Ward presented his theory, insisting on the power of the mental faculties and psychic emotions over the natural biological factors, at the same time acknowledging that both forces were inextricably intermingled:

> Mind only becomes a science when grasped in its entirety. The dynamic agent resides in the feelings. The mind-force is the soul. The psychic power inheres in the emotions. The propelling energy of the world is the "Will" of Schopenhauer. The active principle of sentient nature is desire. In the language of romance and of popular speech the emotional side of life is called the *heart*. Some physiologists have been disposed to attribute this to ignorance, but there is a sense in which it is more than half-true, even from the standpoint of physiology. It is not supposed to refer to blood-currents, but to nerve-currents, and if there is any nerve center that is entitled to be called the seat of the emotions, it is the great cardiac plexus of the sympathetic system, and the strongest emotions can be definitely located in that region of the body.... The physiological heart is more than any organ, the engine of the living body the force-pump of the life-current, and the seat of vital power. Behind it and impelling, it is the system of nerve fibers, plexuses, and ganglia storing and transmitting the nerve-current that constitutes the power itself. But it is the same power, only ramifying throughout the system and controlling every organ of the body that impels, by its rhythmic pulsations, every bodily movement and every act of life, the conscious and rational actions, as well as the involuntary and vegetative functions.[28]

Ward equally insisted on the intervention of human intelligence in the evolutionary process, asserting that the role of education was to develop the latent intellectual abilities of inferior classes and that the intellectual or physical superiority of races mainly depended on their environment. The mental abilities of poor people, therefore, were not necessarily inferior to those of the wealthy: "So far as the native capacity, the potential quality, the 'promise and potency,' of a higher life are concerned, these swarming, spawning millions, the bottom layer of society, the proletariat, the working class, the 'hewers of wood and drawers of water,' are by nature the peers of the boasted 'aristocracy of brains' that now dominates society and looks down upon them, and the equals in all but privilege of the most enlightened teachers of Eugenics."[29]

In *Human Nature and the Social Order* (1902), the American sociologist Charles H. Cooley (1864–1929) also strongly opposed the social theories of Social Darwinism. Like Ward, he emphasized the role of the individual's mental process in the evolution of society. Individuals, he argued, could not be regarded as forming a whole entity unless they were bereft of their own identities. Society must be considered as an aggregate of human beings, "members of a group" or as a "group," but the meaning of these designations was different: "When we speak of society, or use any other collective term, we fix our minds upon some general view of the people concerned, while when we speak of individuals we disregard the general aspect and think of them as if they were separate. Thus, the 'Cabinet' may consist of President Lincoln, Secretary Stanton, Secretary Seward, and so on; but when I say 'the Cabinet' I do not suggest the same idea as when I enumerate these gentlemen separately. Society, or any complex group, may, to ordinary observation, be a very different thing from all of its members viewed one by one."[30] After carrying out research on sociology at the beginning of the twentieth century, Cooley showed that the evolution of man depended more on his social environment than on competitive struggle.

Professor E. A. Ross, an American sociologist who taught economics at Stanford University and sociology at the University of Wisconsin, also disputed these racial theories. In an article published in 1901, he declared that the "race" factor based on hereditary determinism was an error and that the emphasis on such a factor had gained too much publicity. Although he had shown some interest in racial theories, he noted in his autobiography that he had gradually lost faith "in race as a key of social interpretation."[31] Ross argued that the primary concern of sociology was to cure the ills of society. In his popular essay *Sin and Society: An Analysis of Latter-Day Iniquity* (1907), Ross observed that as societies grew, the propensity to sin was greater, as interests of the individuals were more and more threatened and led to individualist values.

As a whole, these liberal thinkers defended their viewpoints on sociological issues in different ways, but the common denominator was that they did not accept the principles of Social Darwinism which, in their opinion, stood as a check to the free expression of the human will. If, at the time, the overwhelming wave of evolutionism stifled their dissenting voices, it may be because of their racial prejudices, which prevented them from rising above the mass of peoples. They believed that cooperation between men prevailed over the natural law of competition, but, as far as races were concerned, they the supported their fellow men's racial conceptions.

The American Indian Question

The problems raised by the indigenous population in the United States were obviously related to the racial question, and government officials in charge of Indian policy faced a great dilemma regarding assimilation. The official policy during the American territorial conquest was to subdue the Indians and then grant them unoccupied lands. But this governmental project failed, leading to hostilities and permanent conflicts. Despite good intentions, promises were not kept, aggravating relations on both sides to such an extent that settlers and farmers were encouraged to exterminate the Indians so that governments would not have to pay their troops, hence the well-remembered slogan "A good Indian is a dead Indian."

This encouragement to the progressive extermination of the Indians found its origin in statements issued by Cotton Mather (1663–1728), a Protestant pastor and author of the noted work *Magnalia Christi Americana* (1702), who regarded the Indians as adepts of the Devil, damned by God at birth and consequently unable to be saved. After the American community as a whole acknowledged these Puritan assumptions in the sixteenth and seventeenth centuries, the pseudoscientific theorists of the nineteenth century strengthened this idea, stating that, from a biological point of view, the Indians were an impossible race to civilize.[32]

In 1800, President John Quincy Adams became the spokesman of an entire generation when he expressed his views concerning the Indian question. According to him, the generous bosom of Mother Nature was to provide for a multitude of people rather than for a small minority of hunters, scattered by accident over the gigantic forests: "But what is the right of a huntsman of the forest of a thousand miles, over which he has accidentally ranged in quest of prey? ... Shall the exuberant bosom of the common mother, amply adequate to the nourishment of millions, be claimed exclusively by a few hundreds of her offspring?"[33]

Adams asserted that only the Indians who cultivated the soil would become owners of their lands. This policy, which consisted of allotting land to Indians and of transporting them to selected reservations, was modified from 1825 onward, notably because of increasing conflicts. While the settlers gradually took over western territories, the American government decided to transfer the Indians west of the Mississippi River. This decision led to serious tensions, many tribes being decimated in the process and several tribes in the Midwest preferring to abandon their lands rather than be exterminated.

Unique among the many tribes, the Cherokees had started to cultivate their land, to open schools, and even to draft a constitution similar to the U.S. Constitution. They even had their own alphabet and newspaper. Despite these initiatives, the tribe was not spared. In 1830, Congress passed the Indian Removal Bill, allowing the president of the United States to remove all Indian tribes settled on the eastern side of the Mississippi River, disregarding the previously signed treaties. In 1834, General Winfield Scott invaded the Cherokee territory with a large troop of soldiers who seized the natives' goods and belongings. Approximately fourteen thousand Indians were sent into exile, traveling the notorious Trail of Tears during which many of them perished.

After the Mexican War, the Texan, General Sam Houston made the decision to apply the same policy in his region, contending that the if government could inflict the fate of the Indians on the Mexicans, "I can see no reason why we should not go on the same course now and take their lands."[34] This was not very shocking to the Americans, as, in those days, killing an Indian was not considered a crime.

However, a great number of authors acknowledged and condemned these dramatic events of American history, among them James Fenimore Cooper (1789–1851), in *The Last of the Mohicans* (1826). Generally, Cooper painted his Indian protagonists as outstanding and honest characters, worthy of trust. One of them in *Redskins* (1846) has the "nobility of a great soul." In *The Pioneers*, another character meditates on the inequality of the races and concludes, "There is One greater than all, who will bring the just together at his own time ... and place him on a footing with princes."[35] Helen Hunt Jackson (1830–1885), who wrote historical novels and became a famous advocate of the Indian cause, noted in 1881, in *A Century of Dishonor*:

> It makes little difference ... where one opens the record of the history of the Indians; every page and every year has its dark stain. The story of one tribe is the story of all, varied only by differences of time and place; but neither time nor place makes any difference in the main facts. Colorado is as greedy and unjust in 1880 as was Georgia in 1830, and Ohio in 1795; and the United States Government breaks promises now as deftly as then, and with an added ingenuity from long practice.[36]

Helen Jackson sent a copy of her book to the members of Congress, but it did not meet with the success she believed it deserved.

The Reverend Jedidiah Morse (1751–1826), a minister and geographer, created another opposition movement in support of the Native Americans. Asked by the Department of War to write a report on the Indian question in 1820, he studied many Indian tribes and discovered that the Indian temper was "mild and obliging, with a strong sense of honor, justice and fair dealing, and great sensibility."[37] Morse, overtly cautious in his speeches, denounced the settlers' attitude as he had already caught a glimpse of the fate awaiting the Indian race. He proposed that the government take the Indians under its wing, declaring that they formed a race worthy to be saved: "The Indians are a race, which on every correct principle ought to be saved from extinction, if it were possible to save them."[38]

As a rule, Americans recognized some virtues in the Indian race, but could not prevent themselves from thinking that the Indians were destined to be erased from the American continent, either by a decision from the Almighty or according to the inexorable process of natural laws. In the nineteenth century, American theorists, as mentioned above, were convinced that the Indians could not be educated. Yet, on the other side of the border, the Canadians, scrupulous and anxious to respect treaties, did not share this idea. In Canada, the Indian population was gradually assimilated and the situation was less painful.

In the United States, the Indian wars came to a tragic end in 1890 during an episode that marked the American collective conscience — the massacre at Wounded Knee, related by Dee Brown in *Bury My Heart at Wounded Knee* (1970). While the Sioux were performing traditional religious dances, American forces, which were not accustomed to such rituals, took them for war threats and killed more than 200 unarmed men, women, and children. After this massacre, which provoked a strong reaction among American citizens, humanitarian organizations replaced armed troops. Missionaries were entrusted with educating the seriously diminished number of Indians and teaching them English. As time went on, attempts to assimilate them into the American population multiplied. Some Indians participated in the First World War before obtaining their citizenship in 1924. Yet, the problem of their assimilation always remained a delicate issue.

The Race Issue and the Black Community from the 1890s to the 1920s

In the United States, the Indian and the Negro problems entailed consequences of crucial importance, as they were both inherent to the development of American culture. History and social theories contributed to the fact the blacks were identified with inferior races. Since the abolition of slavery, the blacks had been regarded as second-class citizens. For instance, a spokesman of McKinley's administration, Representative Grosvenor of Ohio, contested their involvement in political life: "In physical, mental, social, inventive, religious, and ruling power, the African race holds the lowest place.... To force this lowest stratum into a position of political equality with the highest is only to clog the progress of all mankind in its march, ever strenuous and in proper order, toward the highest planes of human aspiration."[39]

In addition, most of the anti-imperialists, generally Democrats, had advocated white supremacy in their arguments on overseas expansion. Given the national consensus, practically all Americans held a similar position towards the native Caribbean and Pacific people as towards the blacks. However, during the Philippine issue, as several Democrats had expressed their resentment on the annexation on the islands, *The Nation* observed with irony: "How hollow will ring Democratic protest against the oppression of the Filipinos while there is Democratic acquiescence in injustice to the negro.... The campaign of the Democrats would be, in that respect, one of overflowing love for the brown brother whom they cannot see, but of callous disregard of the black brother whom they can see."[40]

At the turn of the century, due to the general situation, black people's civil rights were even more threatened than they had been just after the Civil War. Moreover, the rise of Anglo-Saxonism reinforced racial prejudices amid the intellectual elite. During the last decade of the nineteenth century, many black citizens became victims of social injustice, and the tendency was to proclaim that the principles of the Constitution did not apply to them. As a consequence, black people underwent even further discrimination by opponents or defenders of expansion, finding little support to sustain their cause.

However, several anti-imperialists, including George F. Hoar, expressed their concerns and feared that "tyranny over colored peoples abroad would increase racial animosities at home and lead to the further subjugation of the American Negro."[41] Indeed, at the time, there was a revival of racial segregation, in spite of the rights granted to the African-

Americans by the new amendments added to the Constitution during the Reconstruction. The 1890s saw a revival of harsh discrimination by the white population, especially in the South where a wave of terrorism and lynching surfaced through the actions of the Ku Klux Klan.

Three African-American leaders now appeared on the political scene: Booker T. Washington, W. E. B. Du Bois, and Marcus Garvey. Booker T. Washington, born in Virginia in 1856 into a slave family, attended Hampton Institute, one of the very few black high schools in the South. After further schooling, he was appointed head of the Tuskegee Institute to train black teachers, skilled workers and farmers. For Washington, the first priority was education. Believing that educating the blacks was of prime importance for the future of the country, he once said to a white audience, "In all things social we can be as separate as the fingers, yet one as the hand in all things essential to mutual progress."[42] He was convinced that political equality with the white community could be achieved through learning and that racial segregation should be put aside until the African-American proved he was able to assume the same responsibilities as the whites, especially in the economic field. In his address before the Institute of Arts and Sciences, Brooklyn, New York, on September 30, 1896, he insisted on the strong link that bound both communities:

> My friends, we are one in this country. The question of the highest citizenship and the complete education of all concerns nearly ten millions of my own people and over sixty million of yours. We rise as you rise; when we fall you fall. When you are strong we are strong; when we are weak you are weak. There is no power that can separate our destiny. The Negro can afford to be wronged; the white man cannot afford to wrong him.... If a white man steals a Negro's ballot it is the white man who is permanently injured. Physical death comes to the one Negro lynched in a country, but death of the morals—death of the soul—comes to the thousands responsible for lynching.[43]

W. E. B. Du Bois was a scholar and political activist who became the first African-American to receive a Ph.D. from Harvard University. Du Bois disagreed with Booker T. Washington about putting segregation aside; he stood for African unity. In 1909, he helped to found the National Association for the Advancement of Colored People (NAACP), to combat segregation laws, racial discrimination and the lynching of blacks. A prolific writer, he wrote many novels and essays covering a large range of subjects in sociology, history and journalism. In *The Souls of Black Folk*, he raised the issue of black identity: "It is a peculiar sensation, this sense of always looking at oneself through the eyes of others, of measuring one's soul by the tape of a world that looks on in amused contempt and pity. One ever feels his twoness,—an American, a Negro, two unreconciled strivings; two warring ideals in one dark body, whose dogged strength alone keeps it from being torn asunder."[44]

8—Racism and the Ethnocentric Debate 149

Du Bois had a pessimistic vision of the Americanization of blacks. He felt that even through a sincere relationship with the white American community, the black man's "double self" could never completely merge into a "truer self." But his dearest wish was not to be despised by his American fellowmen. He further stated that even African-Americans who were learned or became artists would not better their fate in trying to "reconcile ideals, which only resulted in "sad havoc." In his view, the only hope that ever existed for blacks, since their days of slavery, resided in religious experience:

> Away back in the days of bondage they thought to see, in one divine event, the end of all doubt and disappointment; few men ever worshipped Freedom with half such unquestioning faith as did the American Negro for two centuries. To him, so far as he thought and dreamed, slavery was indeed the sum of villainies, the cause of all sorrow, the root of all prejudice; Emancipation was the key to the Promised Land of sweeter beauty than ever stretched before the eyes of wearied Israelites. In songs and exhortation swelled one refrain—Liberty; in his tears and curses the god he implored had Freedom in his right hand. At last, it came—suddenly, fearfully, like a dream. With one wild carnival of blood and passion came the message in his plaintive cadences:
> "Shout, O children!
> Shout, you are free!
> For God has bought your liberty!"
> Years have passed away since then—ten twenty, forty years of national life, forty years of renewal and development, and yet the swarthy specter sits in its accustomed seat at the Nation's feast.[45]

As a consequence, a vain and sterile search for freedom, the terrorism of the Ku Klux Klan, and the contradictory position of American officials left "the serf bewildered." As a cure to compensate for such a misunderstanding of the two cultures, Du Bois focused his attention on the condition of African-Americans. In 1900, he attended the First Pan-African Conference, held in London, to deliberate on the current situation of men and women of African descent. In his "Address to the Nations of the World," Du Bois reminded the audience that if the darker races were the least advanced in modern civilization, they would in the future have a great influence, "by reason of sheer numbers and physical contact." Consequently, if these were given the opportunity to educate themselves, this would hasten human progress. However, if discrimination in all its forms were to persist, the results would be deplorable for the high ideals of the Christian civilization.[46]

Marcus Garvey, another black American visionary, was born in Jamaica in 1887. After traveling around the world as a journalist, he settled in America and founded the Universal Negro Improvement Association (UNIA) in 1914. Like Du Bois, he believed that black Americans would never merge with white society and contemplated the idea of an African world within the American world, especially in the economic sphere. His slogan "Africa for

Africans" expressed his profound wish and beliefs regarding the two communities which could live side by side and in good intelligence. At one point, he encouraged all African-Americans to return to Africa and free the continent from colonialism. In keeping with this idea, Garvey did not oppose segregation laws.

At the first UNIA convention in New York, in 1920, a "Declaration of Negro Rights" was issued, condemning racial discrimination, and Garvey was appointed "Provisional President of Africa." The text of the declaration comprised a series of principles with a preamble. The introduction to the first principle read:

> In order to encourage our race all over the world and to stimulate it to overcome the handicaps and difficulties surrounding it, and to push forward to a higher and grander destiny, we demand and insist on the following Declaration of Rights:
> Be it known to all men that whereas all men are created equal and entitled to the rights of life, liberty and the pursuit of happiness, and because of this we, the duly elected representatives of the Negro peoples of the world, invoking the aide of the Just and Almighty God, do declare all men, women and children of our blood throughout the world free denizens, and do claim them as free citizens, the Motherland of all Negroes.[47]

Unfortunately, great social changes did not follow the forethought of these three leading African-Americans. Racial discrimination remained deeply rooted in American consciousness until the mid–1950s, when Martin Luther King's civil rights movement and his tragic fate in 1968 led to an acute mainstream awareness of the African-Americans' plight.

Imperialism and Anglo-Saxons

The focal point of the racial issue in the United States derived not only from controversies on the mental inferiority of alien and colored peoples, but also from the imperialist spirit which dominated the last decades of the nineteenth century. The term "imperialism" has a negative connotation, and Americans have always been reluctant to use it, as it evokes the fight against the British Empire in 1775. The term "imperialism" presupposes the intention and desire to master a nation, imposing on it one's own laws and customs. The conquest of the West revealed aspects of American imperialism inasmuch as the annexed territories were often occupied by native peoples who were obliged to comply with new rules or cultural habits. Until 1890, Americans had concentrated their energy on developing the wealth of their own continent, but with the closure of the frontier, new economic and political stakes induced them to cross other borders.

American imperialism, contrary to English mercantilism, was often based on religious grounds, still deeply bound to the Puritan theology. During the period of the territorial conquest, the Reverend Oliver C. Miller, of San Francisco, noted: "Bloodletting is still good for all nations.... For nation and individual the law of cleansing is the same.... Without the shedding of blood there is no remission of sins."[48]

However, it was the Reverend Josiah Strong who most clearly saw the relationship between war and God's "plan." "The Anglo-Saxon expansion," he said in 1900, "was God's alphabet with which He spells for man His providential purposes."[49] From his point of view, those who opposed expansion opposed Divine will. Their resistance to national destiny, and especially to Divine providence, blinded them.

Several politicians offered moral arguments and pretended to be liberators of oppressed races and slaves, especially when it came to the issues of Cuba and the Philippines. Senator Beveridge, a Republican from Indiana, even said that it was immoral to dispute the acquisition of foreign territories. He maintained that the role of the American Republic was to master racial evolution, which did not depend on man's goodwill but proceeded from a Divine order:

> The American Republic is a part of the movement of a race, — the most masterful race of history, — and race movements are not to be stayed by the hand of man. They are mighty answers to Divine commands. Their leaders are not only statesmen of peoples— they are prophets of God. The inherent tendencies of a race are its highest law. They precede and survive all statutes, all constitutions.... The sovereign tendencies of our race are organization and government.[50]

During periods of crisis, the theory of Anglo-Saxon racial superiority was called upon to strengthen the bonds between Great Britain and the United States. In 1839, the Englishman Thomas Carlyle had suggested the idea of a union between these two countries when he asked Emerson to organize a meeting every year in London, Boston or New York. In 1852, the English poet Tennyson published a poem "Hands All Round" that encouraged a mother-daughter relationship between the two countries:

> Gigantic daughter of the West
> We drink to thee across the flood,
> We know thee most, we love thee best,
> For art thou not British Blood?
> Should war's mad blast again be blown,
> Permit not thou the tyrant powers
> To fight thy mother here alone,
> But let thy broadsides roar with ours.
> Hands all round![51]

Few Americans answered the call for an Anglo-American "sacred union," but among those who did, John Fiske strongly incited English-speaking countries to unite in order to undertake the regeneration of the world. However, the anti–British feeling, inherited from the revolution, and the British government's attachment to the institution of slavery discouraged such an initiative. Yet, at the time of the Spanish-American War, the United States needed to form an alliance with the British, because its military power was feared to be inferior to Spain's. John Hay, American ambassador to London in 1897, was in favor of such a union: "Shoulder to shoulder, we could command peace the world over."[52] Some weeks later, Joseph Chamberlain, British Colonial Secretary, declared, "Our first duty is to draw all parts of the empire into close unity and our next to maintain the bonds of permanent unity with our kinsmen across the Atlantic."[53] If national patriotism was alive, there also existed a "patriotism of race" freed from religious and transcendental concerns.

Despite the lack of enthusiasm on behalf of the British, a number of leading figures met in London, in July 1898 to organize an Anglo-American league which acknowledged blood ties between the British Empire and the United States: "Considering that the people of the British Empire and the United States are closely allied by blood, inherit the same literature and laws, hold the same principles of self-government, recognize the same ideas of freedom and humanity in the guidance of their National policy and are drawn together by strong common interests in many parts of the world."[54]

The Anglo-American League was organized under the leadership of Whitelaw Reid, but it was gradually dissolved after the war against Spain, as the Americans no longer needed the support of a British alliance. As for Great Britain, she moved away from America because the country was quite skeptical of the new racial theories which were in vogue in America. Indeed, when the issue concerning citizenship for the Filipinos was raised, the imperialists' arguments made it clear that national institutions had been established only for superior races. Theodore Roosevelt declared that "fitness for self-government" was not a "God-given, natural right," but it had to be acquired through the years, and was only given to races which possessed "common sense and morality."[55] Senator Beveridge added that Filipinos did not belong to a governing race. And assuming they were not able to take care of themselves, he observed:

> Shall we leave them to themselves? Shall tribal wars scourge them, disease them, waste them, and savagery brutalize them more and more? Shall their fields lie fallow, their forests rot, their mines remain sealed, and all the purposes and possibilities of nature be nullified? If not, who shall govern them rather than the kindest and most merciful of the world's great race of administrators, the people of the American Republic?[56]

To counterbalance this overt imperialist vision, English and American writers used their talents to express their opinions. Mark Twain (1835–1910) wrote a satire of the American civilization in his poem "To a Person

Sitting in Darkness." Rudyard Kipling published his well-known poem "The White Man's Burden" in *McClure's Magazine,* in which he insinuated that the white race had a heavy task to assume. Yet, it is difficult to evaluate the impact of such publications. Despite their extreme popularity, American public opinion was little influenced by the writers' and poets' anti-imperialist stance. On the other hand, William Dean Howells, vice president of the Anti-Imperialist League, never wrote an article or a document likely to publicize his ideas, and nobody truly understood why he and his colleagues remained silent. Some thought that the imperialist wave was so strong that it overwhelmed all attempts to react against it.

9

Civil Religion and American Messianism

The Concept of Civil Religion According to Rousseau

The idea of a civil religion has become widespread in the United States thanks to Robert Neelly Bellah, an American sociologist who wrote an article entitled "American Civil Religion" in 1967. Bellah defined it as a "genuine apprehension of universal and transcendent religious reality as seen in or as, one could almost say, revealed through the experience of the American people."[1] Nevertheless, the French philosopher Jean-Jacques Rousseau was the first to coin this expression in one of his major works, *The Social Contract*, and it is interesting to understand what he meant when referring to this concept.

As an advocate of the theory of Natural Man, Rousseau believed that man in his state of nature was good, that it was life in society which corrupted him. Hence his idea of the Good Savage who mirrored the natural goodness of humanity. In *The Social Contract*, Rousseau resorted to the expression "civil religion" with the intention of reconciling man with the vices of political society through the practice of religion, noting that it mattered to the community that citizens should have a religion. He based his theory on universal religious beliefs which could be adopted by all governments and liable to form a strong bond between the men and the body politic, namely, belief in an afterlife, in which virtue was rewarded and vice punished, happiness being the reward of the just and moral distress being the punishment of the wicked. He adhered to his predecessor John Locke's belief in religious toleration, as intolerance belongs to the "negative dogmas" of religion. But foremost, he stressed the religion of the citizen, asserting that "it was good in that it unites worship with love of the laws, and in making the homeland the object of citizens' adoration, it teaches them that to serve the State is to serve its tutelary God."[2]

Published in 1762, *The Social Contract* had an important impact on political philosophy. Its opening and well-known lines embodied Rousseau's bitter reflection concerning the role of society on human beings: "Man is born free, and everywhere he is in chains. One man thinks himself a master of others, but remains more of a slave than they." Rousseau referred to the development of society which requires cooperation and understanding between men, but which is often marred by mutual competition and conflicting attitudes. A transcendental and universal law is thus necessary to favor good relationships and prevent individuals from depending on others or having to submit to their will. This universal law should take the form of a "purely civil profession of faith, whose articles are for the Sovereign to establish, not exactly as dogmas of Religion, but as feelings of sociability without which it is impossible be a good citizen or a faithful subject."[3]

As to civil religion, Rousseau's ideas were in agreement with the philosophy of the Enlightenment in that he rose against the oppressive bonds and prejudices of society. However, he did not have a genuine impact on American thought, as his political and religious arguments, imbued with Romanticism, seemed to contravene the American pragmatic and down-to-earth mind. On the other hand, in the literary field, the Transcendentalists, among them Ralph Waldo Emerson and Henry David Thoreau, did borrow his vision on the goodness and benevolence of the natural world. Both nineteenth-century essayists shared his conceptions on the moral and religious virtues acquired by men living close to nature.

American Civil Religion Viewed by Alexis de Tocqueville

Before Bellah introduced the notion of civil religion in the 1960s and 1970s, it had been dealt with by the French historian Alexis de Tocqueville in his major work, *Democracy in America*. Tocqueville recalled that, as soon as he set foot on American soil, he was struck by the intermingling of politics and religion in the governmental arena. He tried to understand the crucial role played by religion in public affairs and its ensuing effect: "On my arrival in the United States it was the religious aspect of the country that first struck my eye. As I prolonged my stay, I perceived the great political consequences that flowed from these new facts."[4]

Tocqueville attempted to give his own explanation to this unexpected political situation. Since America, he argued, was peopled by Englishmen who had ceased to acknowledge the Pope's authority, they naturally adopted a new democratic and republican Christianity leading to the intermingling of Church and State. Attending a political meeting, the aim of which was to assist the Poles by providing them with arms and money, Tocqueville reported that he noticed a pastor moving forward to meet a crowd of people gathered in a vast room. To his surprise, the latter started to speak in these terms:

> God Almighty! God of hosts! Thou who did maintain the hearts and guide the arms of our fathers when they sustained the sacred rights of their national independence; Thou who made them triumph over an odious oppression and granted our people the benefits of peace and freedom, O Lord! Turn a favourable eye toward the other hemisphere; regard with pity an heroic people who today struggles as we did formerly for the defense of the same rights! Lord, who have created all men on the same model, do not permit despotism to come to deform Thy work and to maintain inequality on earth. God Almighty! Watch over the destiny of the Poles, render them worthy of being free; that Thy wisdom reign in their counsels, that Thy strength be in their arms; spread terror over their enemies, divide the powers that hatch their ruin, and do not permit the injustice to which the world has been witness for fifty years to be consummated today. Lord, who hold in Thy powerful hand the heart of peoples, like those of men, arouse allies to the sacred cause of right; make the French nation finally rise, and, leaving the repose in which its head keep it, come to fight once again for the freedom of the world.
> O Lord! Never turn Thy face away from us; permit us always to be the most religious people as well as the most free.
> God almighty, answer our prayer today; save the Poles. We ask this of Thee in the name of Thy much loved son, our Lord Jesus Christ, who died on the cross for the salvation of all men. Amen.[5]

This is a clear illustration of what Tocqueville called a "direct action" of the influence of religion on politics. But, according to him, there was also an "indirect action" which revealed itself to be more powerful. Referring to various religious denominations, he noticed that they all differed in the way their members worshiped their Creator, but agreed on their mutual duties and responsibilities. What mattered for the good organization of society was not so much the kind of religion citizens practiced, as the fact that they had one. In the end, Christian morality was the important unifying principle in America and it would be unthinkable, Tocqueville argued, for Americans to elect a president who did not acknowledge some kind of faith.

Thus, according to Tocqueville, religion could be viewed as the first institution in the social or political sphere. He could not say whether every American was a believer, since "who could read in the heart of men?" But he noted that, in America, religion stood as a necessary element to maintain the stability and righteousness of the republican institutions. Tocqueville related the story of a man who came forward as a witness in a New York State court and who declared he did not believe in God's existence and in the immortality of the soul. The judge declared that he could not hear his testimony, given that he could not trust a man who had "destroyed all credibility in advance." After grasping the essential religious components of political life, Tocqueville however questioned the validity of such interference:

> As long as religion is supported only by sentiments that are the consolation of all miseries, it can attract the hearts of the human race to it. Mixed with the bitter passions of this world, it is sometimes constrained to defend allies given by interest rather than love; and it must repel as adversaries men who often still love it, while they are combating those with whom it has united. Religion, therefore, cannot share the material force of those who govern without being burdened with a part of the hatreds to which they give rise.[6]

Civil Religion Interpreted by Twentieth-Century Religious Figures

Twentieth-century American religious figures attempted to redefine and explain the concept of civil religion. Facing the liberal evolution of Protestant churches and denominations in general, their purpose was to strengthen and rebuild the political community through strong ethical and religious principles.

For William McLoughlin (1922–1992), a historian of American religion, the expanding Pentecostal denominations did not constitute "a dynamic new force capable of replacing ... the old order." According to him, these new groups appeared rather as "a comment upon the confused state of religion and world affairs in this generation." However, America, he says, is a pluralistic and not an exclusively Protestant nation, implying that the ecumenical movement has a role to play and noting that the Catholic church has at last become Americanized.[7]

Martin Marty, an American Lutheran religious scholar born in 1928, emphasizes the fact that pluralism and ecumenism have changed the American religious experience, blending all the former spiritual elements into a single transcendental entity; he asks whether America is not in quest of a new "spiritual style." Marty regards civil rights marches as "epiphanies" led by new "charismatic spiritual leaders."[8]

According to Franklin H. Little, a Methodist minister, college professor and scholar who wrote in 1970 about "The Churches and the Body Politic," civil religion is a specific American concept that never existed in European countries. He noted that "the voluntary principle made it possible for churches to be what they had not generally been in Europe,"[9] and added that a new style of politics had to adapt to new religious requirements. What arises from these various reflections is a desire and search for unity inside the evolving American religious community so that politics rests on a firm and common religious basis, a kind of a spiritual Melting Pot.

Robert Bellah's "Civil Religion" (1967)

Robert Bellah's essay "Civil Religion in America" seems to be the best approach to understanding these terms from the American standpoint. Bellah asserts that civil religion "has its own seriousness and integrity and requires the same care in understanding that any other religion does."[10] This implies that the expression "civil religion" contains a whole concept in itself and should not be understood as two opposing terms. It appears rather as a unifying code of values tacitly respected by all citizens but not referring to a specific religion or God, "a word which almost all Americans can accept but which means so many different things to so many different people, that it is almost an empty sign." Bellah reminds us of Dwight D. Eisenhower's reflection that corroborates his own: "Our government makes no sense unless it is founded in a deeply felt religious faith — and I don't care what it is."[11]

The main idea expressed by Bellah is that, in American culture, there is a religious dimension which prevails over the separation of Church and State and binds all minds, on the grounds that they all share the basic elements of the Christian faith. Bellah tells us:

> Although matters of personal religious belief, worship, and association are considered to be strictly private affairs, there are, at the same time, certain common elements of religious orientation that the great majority of Americans share.... This public religious dimension is expressed in a set of beliefs, symbols, and rituals that I am calling the American civil religion.[12]

In addition, Bellah indicates that the phrase "civil religion" comes from Rousseau and that, indeed, there is some correlation between Rousseau's arguments and the American vision regarding Church and State. The main dogmas of the American civil religion seem to be modeled on recommendations of Rousseau's *Social Contract*, as cited by Bellah: "the existence of God, the life to come, the reward of virtue and the punishment of vice, and the exclusion of religious intolerance."[13] All these religious premises constitute integral parts of American institutions. Since the Revolutionary War all major leaders in the United States have embodied the same ideal based on the existence of God or a Deity and the observance of a moral conduct. George Washington's farewell address is a good example:

9—Civil Religion and American Messianism

Of all the dispositions and habits which lead the prosperity, Religion and Morality are indispensable supports. In vain, would that man claim the tribute of Patriotism, who should labor to subvert these great pillars of human happiness, these firmest props of the duties of men and citizens. The mere politician, equally with the pious man ought to respect and cherish them. A volume could not trace all their connections with private and public felicity. Let it simply be asked where is the security for property, for reputation, for life, if the sense of religious obligation deserts the oaths, which are the instruments of investigation in Courts of Justice? And let us with caution indulge the supposition, that morality can be maintained without religion. Whatever may be concede to the influence of refined education on minds of peculiar structure, reason and experience both forbid us to expect that National morality can prevail in exclusion of religious principle.[14]

In the end, the question this address raises is whether the principles of morality are directly linked to a belief in a Divine entity. In Washington's opinion, morality cannot be maintained without religion, and this appears to be a reductive argument as experience shows us that people may adhere to moral rules without professing a faith.

Another question concerns the nature of the "American" God, which leads us to a theological issue. To Bellah, "the God of the Civil Religion is not only rather 'Unitarian,' He is also on the austere side, much more related to order, law, and right than to salvation and love. Even though He is somewhat Deist in cast, He is by no means simply a watchmaker God. He is actively interested and involved in history, with a special concern for America."[15] Let us note that Jefferson himself had foretold that every American would, in the end, become Unitarian.

The role of civil religion in the United States is especially noticeable in biblical references that are an integral part of presidential and solemn speeches. However, as Bellah declared: "What people say on solemn occasions need not be taken at face value, but it is often indicative of deep-seated values and commitments that are not made explicit in the course of everyday life."[16] The strong emphasis on religious principles may also be perceived in the Declaration of Independence, which cites "the laws of Nature and Nature's God" and declares that "all people are endowed by their Creator with certain inalienable Rights," calling upon "the Supreme Judge of the world for the rectitude of (America)'s intentions," and advocating "a firm reliance on the protection of divine Providence."[17] The messianic idea encompassed in the doctrine of Manifest Destiny most probably derives from these institutional principles.

Bellah's civil religion, partly inspired by Roman and Greek writers, seeks to combine the temporal and the spiritual spheres into a modern frame of theocracy. To understand the origin of this attitude vis-à-vis other nations, he explains that by identifying with the "Chosen People," the American people identify themselves with Israel's history. Thus, the Revolutionary War could be compared to the escape from European domination; and the Civil War would correspond to a sorrowful experience sent by God to strengthen the Union. In this context, Washington becomes Moses, the savior of the American people, designated to take them to the Promised Land. As for Lincoln, he could be considered as a Christ like figure offering his sacrifice, "one who tragically dedicated himself to the destiny of a united nation and whose death summed up the sacrifices that redeemed the nation for that destiny."[18]

Given the great variety of denominations and churches in the United States, one could wonder whether this identification with the leading figures of the "Chosen People," regarded as archetypes and associated with biblical events, is shared by all religious groups. It seems that the differences are fused together into a kind of national credo since the references generally come from traditions which are recognized by most of these groups.

Conrad Cherry's *God's New Israel* (1971)

Conrad Cherry, distinguished professor emeritus at Indiana University, has been called "one of the foremost architects of the discipline of religious studies in the United States." Cherry's book *God's New Israel* gathers a collection of essays on American civil religion. Introducing the subject, he explains that this politico-religious concept is expressed by Americans twice a year on two important occasions, Memorial Day and Thanksgiving, which may be considered as moments of "sacred celebrations." On Memorial Day, Americans reiterate the idea of redemptive sacrifice in political speeches. Americans who gave their lives in wartime did so in the name of freedom against tyranny and oppression. The sacrifices were not vain: "The sacrifices are the sanctification of America's divine mission of preserving and dispensing freedom."[19] Every year, Memorial Day ceremonies recall that the United States has a mission to accomplish in the name of liberty and that it must not fail to accomplish this sacred duty. The intersection of the political and the religious is here well exemplified:

> The Memorial Day celebration is an American sacred ceremony, a religious ritual, a modern cult of the dead. Although it shares the theme of redemptive sacrifice with Christianity and other religions, and although its devotees would insist that the God called upon is the same God of their traditional religions, the Memorial Day rite is a civic service that aims to unite Americans beyond their separate religious differences.[20]

In his attempt to link politics to religion as his predecessors did, Cherry clearly defined the idea of civil religion, but nevertheless noted the weakness and fragility of the "theocratic" system:

> The civil religion, like any religion which becomes an established part of a culture, is always in danger of sanctifying the virtues of a society while ignoring its vices ... America's present position as a great world power intensifies the peril; Americans have long lived under the conviction that their nation always comes to the defense of other countries for the sake of "free institutions" and "democratic governments." Can we admit ... that we have also rushed to the aid of military dictatorships when we believe such action will serve our national interests?[21]

Cherry also noticed that, in the 1950s and early 1960s, criticism arose among Protestants, Catholics and Jews who felt that the true spirit of their own traditional religions was undermined by the "Americanization of their faiths" and that, in the end, it resulted in a vague religion based on a naïve and sentimental piety, without serious theological grounds. Corroborating the international community's main argument about religion in the United States, he added: "Much was made of the way in which God and religion were used in our culture by politicians, clergymen, popularizers of religion, and businessmen for their own higher ends: for the support of particular national tasks, for the swelling of church membership rolls, for gaining 'peace of mind' in a troubled world, for achieving success in a society of capitalistic competition."[22]

From Civil Religion to American Messianism

The idea of civil religion that lay deep in the American tradition was strongly linked to a sense of mission, since the reference to ancient Israel, as seen in Cherry's book, was often quoted. The term "our American Israel" was used as early as Jefferson who said in his Second Inaugural Speech: "I shall need, too, the favor of that Being whose hands we are, who led our fathers, as Israel of old, from their native land and planted them in a country flowing with all the necessary comforts of life." The theme of an elected nation, a light for the world, is anchored in the American mind. As we have already mentioned, the Founding Fathers shaped the tone of this messianic civil religion and were its first representatives.

Thus, over the centuries that followed the birth of their nation, American political leaders carried out their tasks and their responsibilities often unaware of the messianic aspects of their ancestral Puritan legacy. Americans were persuaded that their country was the greatest "alms" that God gave the world.[23] It was Ralph Waldo Emerson who voiced the messianic spirit of the time, deeply imbued with a nationalistic tone. His writings had a considerable influence on the readers of the time. Yet, according to Anders Stephanson, professor of history at Columbia University, the manner in which Emerson defined America "as a last effort of the Divine Providence on behalf of the human race seems to convey all the elements of an unorthodox kind of providentialism."[24] However, American messianism is an historical reality inasmuch as it perpetually evokes a sense of mission and destiny.

America's Special Place in History: Isaac Mayer Wise (1819–1900)

In this messianic and destinarian perspective, it may be interesting to note that a prominent rabbi from Cincinnati, Isaac Mayer Wise, strongly impressed the American mind in the late 1860s by emphasizing the idea of America as a new Promised Land. In a lecture he gave before the Theological and Religious Library Association of Cincinnati on January 7, 1869, he endeavored to explain America's role in history. His lecture, entitled "Our Country's Place in History," is an attempt to inscribe the historical course of America in a providential scheme. Wise stated that a "higher power" had shaped or preordained the whole history of America. His personal interpretation coincides, at times, with the Calvinist dogma of predestination not at an individual but at a national level.

Indeed, the opening line of his work "History is Providence realized"[25] left no room for secular interpretation of American historical events. Wise maintained that the nation's destiny was modeled on the elements of the universe that "are and will perpetually be formed by the same law, the same Word of God."[26] Consequently, the destiny of nations was bound to be regulated by the same universal and divine laws. Nonetheless, Wise argued, human beings live in a chaotic world and they have to "rise above this chaos to fulfill their destiny, to realize the designs of Providence."[27] Like the stars in the solar system, nations have to maintain their place near the Supreme Wisdom in order to realize His plan.

This analysis, he argued, leaves no room for fatalism. Still, people are free to choose their own course, but Wise announced that deviations from providential plans might lead to disillusion and failure. He explained that each individual had a specific role to play, a definite mission that must be accomplished or self-destruction will ensue. Likewise, "every nation has a destiny to which time, geographical location and the capacities of the race enable it."[28] Moreover, if a nation does not fulfill its destiny, that destiny may be fulfilled by another nation. As an example, he affirmed that the

Mexicans might have fulfilled the destiny of the United States, but failed as it had not been intended by the Higher Power, "and the succession was necessary to realize the design. There is no fatality."[29]

Now, how do nations know whether they have filled all the conditions to enter the circle of the Supreme Wisdom? Wise answered that progress is the only sign given by God's Providence: "Nations which contribute nothing to the progress of humanity fulfill no destiny. Nations contributing no longer to the progress of humanity have ceased to fulfill their destiny, and are in a state of dissolution. Nations which contribute most to the progress of humanity, fulfill the highest national destiny."[30] This approach to the study of universal history was thus based on the idea that each country had a particular destiny to accomplish, and that, in case of failure, progress of mankind would be curbed. The slowing down of progress was a visible sign that the nation's destiny had not been accomplished.

Wise tried to prove his arguments through historical examples. His study focused first on the European peasants' plight in the feudal system at the end of the fifteenth century. In these times, people having privileges imposed their rights, giving rise in the sixteenth and seventeenth centuries to the emergence of despotism in the church and state arenas. Wise deduced from this situation that those nations had not fulfilled their destiny. Europe, as the place which perpetrated "huge despotism," had reached a deadlock, which explained that a new nation had to be built.[31]

Thus, unaware of the "wonderful travail" that was being done, people were irresistibly drawn toward a new haven liable to favor their new holy desires and expectations. According to Wise, this unconscious driving force triggered the great migration to the New World, manifesting an "impulse from a higher power." Even the men who were responsible for the great departure from Old Europe were unaware of their acts, "popes and potentates and other mighty men, with the iron rod of oppression in one hand, assisted with the other in rearing a fortress to humanity, without knowing that they did."[32] The discovery of America was interpreted according to the same pattern. Columbus was "compelled" by an overwhelming power to land on a wrong spot, guided by the spirit of the Universe. Again, this impulse from a higher power was at work but to the knowledge of no one.

In the New World, Wise explained, a great mission lay with the colonists, as they were convinced of the greatness of their task to fight those who would oppose the fulfillment of their destiny. The American soldier developed a "martial spirit" since, in the course of events, he had to combat the Indians, the French and the British. However, in Wise's analysis, the Revolutionary War constituted the most patent example of America's messianic role. It was Washington and his daring companions who were "the chosen instruments in the hands of Providence, to turn the wheel of events in favor of liberty forever; and they proved worthy of their great mission, of their immortal work."

Wise also lay emphasis on the framers of the American Constitution who, while conceiving this document, respected the spirit of their people whose destiny had become the "palladium of liberty ... for the progress and redemption of mankind."[33] America's providential place in history was also due to these fathers of the country at the origin of an ideal symbolized by the "glowing sun of human prosperity." Wise described all these events unfolding according to the course of a natural process, shedding light on the notion of an inevitable messianic destiny.

Yet despite the irrevocable march of America's destiny, he insisted on people's freedom of choice and personal responsibility in the leadership over the nations of the world. Explaining that a "chain of natural causes and effects" existed in the building up of the nation, he nevertheless argued, "It can not be denied that every important step in the progress of our early history resulted from free choice, from personal freedom, demonstrating clearly the theory of individual freedom and universal necessity in the government of mankind."[34] In his opinion, the American Constitution became a universal and sacred document that should be respected and spread by zealous missionaries all over the world.

Finally, Wise placed American culture in such high esteem that he compared it to the Greek civilization, endowed with the blessings of a growing and prosperous economy. And indeed, there were similarities between the two countries. Greece, like America, was a country which received a large immigration from the surrounding regions and had to assimilate all the foreigners into one nation. In addition, the Greeks had a pedagogical role to perform all over the world. "Greece educated tens of thousands of emissaries to carry her wealth into Asia, Africa and Europe; so do we. We educate millions of free men, to carry our national wealth all over the earth."[35]

Commerce was, for Wise, one of the best channels to propagate ideas and help the world's countries to participate in the progress of mankind. And according to him, progress could not do without Liberty that stood as America's corollary: "Liberty is the cause, progenitor, preserver and protector of all blessings which we enjoy and impart to others. The chapter of Liberty in the modern record of nations is our country's place in history.... Liberty is our place in history, our national destiny, our ideal, the very soul of our existence."[36] These statements fully embodied the main strands of American ideology and its exceptional character. They revitalized the nationalistic enthusiasm advocated by the first settlers who obliterated from their memories their European or original ties entirely.

The expression of such strong feelings by the American community still bewilders foreign observers who also advocate some of these universal values, such as liberty, without seeking to define a "special place" for them in history. Wise's following reflection seems to emphasize this bewilderment: "Nothing can arrest our progress, nothing can drag down our own country from her high place in history, except our own wickedness working a willful desertion of our destiny, the desertion from the ideal of liberty. As long as we cling to this ideal, we will be in honor, glory, wealth and prosperity."[37]

Mission and Destiny of the Anglo-Saxons in the Reverend Josiah Strong (1847–1916)

Another pioneer of American messianism was the Reverend Josiah Strong, a Protestant clergyman and author who, in 1885, published a popular book, *Our Country: Its Possible Future and Its Present Crisis*, which sold 175,000 copies and was considered as a kind of bible of missionary expansionism. The Congregationalist pastor, founder of the Social Gospel movement, believed that all races could be improved and uplifted and that the Anglo-Saxon race had a responsibility to civilize and Christianize the world. Within that perspective, he was totally in phase with the philosopher John Fiske in his perception of the future for both American and British civilizations. Strong emphasized the idea of a mission for America and all over the world:

> Missionary activity, a defining trait of American church life, reached an organizational peak toward the end of the nineteenth century; at home, because of the need to maintain one's position amid the new urban realities of aliens, Romanism, corruption, and filth; abroad, because of the urgent desire to spread the blessings of the Word to non–Christian, uncivilized areas. Indeed, Christian missionaries were the one consistently "expansionist" feature of American foreign relations after the Civil War: there were boundaries to be crossed and spaces to be conquered.[38]

In *Our Country*, the issue of the Anglo-Saxons' divine mission as a politico-religious force was stressed through very evocative passages. Strong noted that England and America were the depository of two great blessings: "spiritual Christianity and civil liberty." These heavenly gifts allotted to both countries were intended to lift them up into the light of Christian civilization and to entrust them with the moral duty to elevate the human race. The destiny of Anglo-Saxonism, which according to him, ruled over one third of the earth's surface, was clearly exemplified in one of Strong's statements: "The Anglo-Saxon was destined by God and evolution to rule the world."[39]

Strong firmly adhered to Darwin's theory of evolution in the sense that he believed in the slogans "struggle for life" and "survival of the fittest." He maintained that, as a superior race, the Anglo-Saxons were "armed with the 'aggressive traits' of unequalled energy and indomitable perseverance." He stressed the fact that their language and civilization would spread around the globe just "as the Greek carried his language and civilization around the Mediterranean." [40] Strong's theory as expressed in *Our Country* rested on messianic argumentation, as his main objective was to evangelize the world. In a millenarian vein, he asserted that the Anglo-Saxon civilization was "more favorable than any other to the spread of those [Christian] principles whose universal triumph was necessary for the destined perfection of the world." He argued that the Anglo-Saxon race had been "pre-eminently fitted, and therefore chosen by God, to prepare the way for the full coming of His kingdom on the earth."[41]

He also advocated that the notion of the kingdom of God did not only refer to a spiritual world but to the present world. Before reaching the supernatural felicity, people living on this earth should endeavor to improve it and make it a perfect place. America was to lead the way toward social Christianity, given the supremacy of its institutions, its growing population and its wealth. During the expansionist period, Strong believed the developing economy would be controlled by principles based on ethics inherent to social Christianity. However, he asserted that these goals and objectives "could be fulfilled either through efforts to enlighten and instruct a nation, or, if prompt action were needed, through the benevolent use of force — international police duty."[42] This kingdom philosophy was an integral part of Strong's work and was largely transposed into the economic sphere in which the Anglo-Saxons excelled:

> Among the most striking features of the Anglo-Saxon is his money-making power — a power of increasing importance in the widening commerce of the world's future. We have seen ... that although England is by far the richest nation of Europe, we have already outstripped her in the race after wealth, and we have only begun the development of our vast resources.... Again, nothing more manifestly distinguishes the Anglo-Saxon than his intense and persistent energy, and he is developing in the United States an energy which, in eager activity and effectiveness, is peculiarly American.[43]

America's messianism has been highlighted by Strong's influential book which embodied the main nineteenth-century strands of thought. It has to be noted that most of these ideas were already ingrained in the national consciousness. Strong gave them more strength and vitality through his own enthusiasm filled with a nationalistic vision.

Anglo-Saxon Responsibility According to Reinhold Niebuhr (1892–1971)

Reinhold Niebuhr was another prominent Protestant figure who greatly influenced political thinking, insisting on the Anglo-Saxon role in religious and worldly affairs. An American theologian, he had an extensive impact on the public in the 1920s, and was widely read at home and abroad. He was one of the major thinkers who contributed to the shaping of American national identity during the postwar years. Despite his celebrity while alive, his popularity as far as his political theology was concerned declined after his death in 1971.

In an essay written in 1943, entitled "Anglo-Saxon Destiny and Responsibility," Niebuhr asserted that a British and American alliance would form the "cornerstone" that would restore peace and order to the world. He pointed out with some intuitive premonition that a partnership between these two nations could very well become a threat to international peace if they were left alone. Nevertheless, he declared that Anglo-Saxon solidarity was an essential corollary to pursue peaceful objectives.[44]

In his writings, he persistently emphasized the religious dimension underlining such international enterprise. Niebuhr maintained that the building of a world community could be understood only in religious terms: "The Anglo-Saxon peoples at the crucial and strategic point in the building of a world community is a fact of such tremendous significance that it can only be adequately comprehended in religious terms. It is a position of destiny and carries with it tremendous responsibilities. Without a religious sense of the meaning of destiny, such a position as Britain and America now holds is inevitably corrupted by pride and the lust of power."[45]

Niebuhr's notion of destiny was inscribed in a prophetic and biblical dimension. Although he stated that comparing the special destiny of the Anglo-Saxon peoples with that of Israel in ancient times would serve no purpose, he nevertheless thought that God's intervention could, at times, be revealed to some particular nations in order to entrust them with a mission. To him "some nation or group always has a higher degree of power and responsibility in the formation of community than others."[46] He added that, in our troubled times, America had been chosen to fulfill this divine mission.

To Niebuhr, the term "destiny" is wholly charged with implicit religious elements. The semantic meaning of "destiny" cannot be compared to the Greek notion of fate, as virtue and grace are the main components of all historical destiny. Acknowledging that people who do not believe in God's Providence may perceive the events of history as "pure accidents," he nevertheless focused on the religious man who "perceives them as gifts of grace.

The grace that determines the lives of men and nations is manifest in all special circumstances, favors, and fortunes of geography and climate, of history and fate that lead to eminence despite the weakness and sinfulness of the beneficiary of such eminence."[47] Yet, Niebuhr insisted on the fact that such divine favor was not devoid of responsibility and should not lead to Pharisaism because of the vicissitudes of human frailty.

As regards the moral concept of virtue, Niebuhr made it clear that, although he was convinced of his nation's superior virtue, this blessed gift should not be mistaken for power which would lead to a religious deviation and denature the alleged right to rule: "The idea that we have a right to rule because of our superior virtue is of a higher order than the amoral idea that we have a right to rule because of our power."[48] Virtue thus appeared as the paragon of pure religion, and even though the Anglo-Saxon world has been invested with the mission to establish a just order on earth, it should be careful not to fall into the trap of spiritual arrogance: "Thus a contrite recognition of our own sins destroys the illusion of eminence through virtue and lays the foundation for the apprehension of 'grace' in our national life."[49] To Niebuhr, a sense of responsibility should prevail over any form of pride.

Indeed, in the pastor's argument, the dangers brought about by all feelings of superiority were multifaceted and bound to eradicate the spiritual rewards of all good deeds and intentions. One may perceive in the following statement an echo of Governor Winthrop's recommendation on his first arrival on the American soil: "The real fact is that we are placed in a precarious moral and historical position by our special mission. It can be justified only if it results in good for the whole community of mankind. Woe unto us if we fail. For our failure will bring judgment upon both us and the world."[50] On racial pride, Niebuhr also maintained that the American nation had a leading role to play: "Our racial pride is incompatible with our responsibilities in the world community. If we do not succeed in chastening it, we shall fail in our task."[51]

Consequently, self-righteousness, Niebuhr noted, would undoubtedly lead to a spirit of vengeance but, well aware of the nations' incapacity to avoid evil in general, he foresaw the Anglo-Saxon world optimistically: "We may fairly be sure that the Anglo-Saxon world will not be good enough or sufficiently contrite to fulfill its historical mission with complete success. It nevertheless has a great opportunity to fulfill it with relative success."[52] Yet he contended that the British and the Americans should never forget that "an ascetic withdrawal" from the world of politics was destined to undermine the main purposes of their religious and historic mission. Relating to the world community, his last argument encapsulated all the components of America's idiosyncratic vision of history: "In both cases, the

Christian faith is still in sufficiently close relation to the national life to encourage the hope that it will help to purify the nations for their mission."[53]

Today's Messianism

Today, in spite of the past few centuries with their technological, economic, and social development, the United States still considers itself to be the bearer of a message for all nations, and it is in this sense that the world media speak of "American Messianism." Indeed, the word has a strong religious connotation and refers to an idea of redemption and salvation often related to Millenarianism.[54] Based on religious beliefs, several American leaders have felt invested with a worldwide mission to fight against all forms of violence and terrorism, seeking to guarantee a fundamental principle — liberty. This liberty, which the American people had fought for, constitutes the essence of their democracy, which is to be held up as a universal example.

As mentioned above, throughout its history, the United States' messianic vocation has inspired its foreign policy on many occasions. The American collective imagination still contains the idea that America was providentially chosen for a particular destiny. Conrad Cherry, in *God's New Israel*, also sees this messianic dimension when he notes, "It is an idea that still finds expression in our so-called secular age. It has resided at the heart of the attempt by Americans to understand their nation's responsibility at home and abroad."[55]

Given these reflections on civil religion and their implications in the emergence of American messianism, it is hoped that contemporary American thinking will take into account America's past in order to acknowledge the weaknesses and failures that are derived from a national ideology conceived by the first English religious dissenters, whose messianic "temptation" can still be felt today. Historian Clinton Rossiter (1917–1970) defined the role of the American mission with more moderation and wisdom: "The American Mission, a view of national destiny neither vulgar nor imperialistic, can certainly be squared with a healthy attitude of international cooperation." Cherry adds:

> We must free ourselves from these messianic illusions that wanted to persuade the world that Americans were saviors. International cooperation implies certain openness to choices and compromises. The crises issued from the foreign policy have darkened the sky of an America who believed too long in the exceptional character of her destiny.[56]

Thus, deep-rooted in the genesis of American culture, the Puritan theology, based on a reenactment of the Exodus narrative, seems to have resurfaced in the concept of civil religion and in the emergence of a messianic movement. It is interesting to note that, in the twentieth century, numerous American writers of the interwar period strongly criticized the Puritan-based American ideology, among them Hemingway, Faulkner, Steinbeck, Dos Passos, and many others who tried to convince Americans that Puritanism's obscure and deterministic forces undermined the social and spiritual well-being of American society. It is perilous, they said, for a country to adhere to a deviant and erroneous doctrine.

To that end, the statement of Ezra Stiles, president of Yale University in 1783, may still perplex and confuse international observers: "She will be a great, a very great nation when the Lord will have raised his American Israel very high, higher than other nations, in number and fame"[57] Yet it seems that America is gradually becoming aware of the lack of realism inscribed on the canvas of its founding myths since the concept of a messianic and manifest destiny is becoming less and less "politically correct"!

10

Evangelism and Millenarianism

The notion of "civil religion" in America, put forward by Robert Bellah, was further developed through a new religious movement, defined as neo-Evangelism, the aim of which was political involvement and Christian activism. According to one of its adepts, Francis Stiles, "Neo-evangelism is a religious philosophy. It attempts to reach and minister to man through his felt needs. It seeks to command man for his achievements and realign his energies for good. It emphasizes unity at the expense of truth and reduces the biblical requirements of purity and separation unto God until they are obscure. Man and his present circumstances, rather than God and His eternal precepts, are the core of its concern."[1] The movement, initiated by Harold Ockenga, emerged in the middle of the twentieth century as the National Association of Evangelicals and issued a journal, *Christianity Today*. At the beginning, it engendered controversies and dissensions among Protestants and tended to divide public opinion between liberal and fundamentalist tendencies. Nevertheless, this did not prevent the movement from growing rapidly, conducting traditional revivals and organizing large-scale evangelistic campaigns. One of its mentors and chief spokesmen, the influential preacher Billy Graham, came to the forefront of the national scene as he experienced considerable success during his campaigns.

Billy Graham carried his message throughout America and on to various parts of the world. Charismatic and impressive, he knew how to touch people's emotions, using religious rhetoric successfully and propagating a reassuring message at a time when the Cold War induced apprehensions and fears. As Tarek Mitri noted, in the United States, religion is never absent from politics. When John F. Kennedy ran for the presidency he met with resentment in Protestant circles. Graham and many other evangelical leaders met in Switzerland in an attempt to prevent his election. Their position contributed to awaken an old distrust towards the Catholic Church.[2]

Kennedy decided to stay away from religious and political intermixing while at the White House, preferring to invite Americans to gather in the name of their future as a nation. However, it was quite different with most of the following presidents. Indeed, Graham, "America's pastor," as George Bush Sr. used to call him, was an adviser to many American presidents. Up until his retirement, he was considered a privileged visitor to the White House and even had a bedroom reserved for him. Supported mostly by Republicans, Graham has often advocated the same positions as conservative politicians, even though he often declared himself aloof from political issues. An article in *Time* magazine (June 14, 1999) written by Harold Bloom, depicted him as the "nation's spiritual counselor":

> William Franklin Graham, Jr. known to all the world as Billy, is now 80 years old, and has been our religious revivalist for almost exactly 50 years, ever since his eight-week triumph in Los Angeles in the autumn of 1949. Graham's finest moment may have been when he appeared at President Bush's side, bible in hand, as we commenced our war against Iraq in 1991. The great revivalist's presence symbolized that the Gulf crusade was, if not Christian, at least biblical ... the aura of apostle still hovers around Graham.... He is an icon essential to the country in which, for two centuries now, religion has not been the opiate but the poetry of the people. In the U.S., 96 per cent of us believe in God, 90 percent pray, and 90 percent believe God loves them. Graham is totally representative of American religious universalism. You don't run for office among us by proclaiming your skepticism or by deprecating Billy Graham.[3]

Bloom ended his article by reminding the readers that politics could have been a "destructive element" for Graham, since he was a fervent red hunter. Indeed, in a radio broadcast in 1953, America's pastor had severely condemned those who he claimed had helped America's greatest enemy — communism. Nevertheless, Bloom added, in the 1980s Graham became a "preacher of world peace," refusing to adhere to the program of the Christian Right. Still, the pastor remained the principal leader of American evangelical Protestantism: "If there is an indigenous American religion — and I think there is, quite distinct from European Protestantism — then Graham remains its prime emblem."[4]

Thus, as symbolized by Billy Graham's iconic figure, the Evangelical movement has since grown to form an important segment of American society and has become very influential in politics. In 1980, it was reported that one American out of three claimed to be a born-again Christian.[5] Indeed, a growing number of Evangelical leaders gave a political color to the movement, leading to a strong revival of the destinarian concept, as seen through their crusades reported and broadcast on radio and television. Influential leaders of this movement, such as Pat Robertson and Jerry Falwell (founders respectively of the Christian Coalition and the Moral Majority), firmly encouraged their followers to become involved in public and political affairs.

This arrival of religious leaders in the political arena had tremendous consequences, since many Americans supported their views and ambition to act upon social and ethical issues. The aims of the Evangelical leaders were to defend what they saw as Christian values—for example, by combating abortion and gay rights, and restoring prayers that had been banned in public schools since the early 1960s. However, Congress has never officially paid much attention to most of their claims and never acted upon their program, but for the Defense of Marriage Act signed by President Bill Clinton on September 21, 1996. Evangelicals have consistently backed the Republican Party and have led its shift towards the right.

Yet lately several evangelical Christians have criticized the Evangelical movement for its close relationship with the Republican Party and its involvement in politics. Randall Balmer, for example, in his article "Jesus Is Not a Republican," published in the *Chronicle Review* (June 23, 2006), voiced his growing resentment:

> In terms of cultural and political influence, that alliance has been a bonanza for both sides.... And what has the religious right done with its political influence? Judging by the platform and the policies of the Republican Party — and I am aware of no way to disentangle the agenda of the Republican Party from the goals of the religious right — the purpose of all this grasping for power looks something like this an expansion of tax cuts for the wealthiest Americans, the continued prosecution of a war in the Middle East that enraged our long-time allies and would not meet even the barest of just-war criteria, to fray the social-safety net for the poorest among us.... The torture of human beings, God's creatures— some guilty of crimes, others not — has been justified by the Bush administration.... And what about abortion? ... Since January 2003, the Republican and religious right coalition has controlled the presidency and both houses of Congress— yet, curiously, it has not tried to outlaw abortion.... Such rhetoric and policies are a scandal, a reproach to the gospel.... The leaders of the religious right have led their sheep astray for the gospel of Jesus Christ to the false gospel of neoconservative ideology and into the maw of the Republican Party.... Jesus himself recognized that his followers held a dual citizenship. "Give back to Caesar what is Caesar's," he said, "and to God what is to God.... Religion functions best outside and often as a challenge to political order."[6]

Within the conjecture of the last few years, especially since 9/11, the distinctive religious feature of American politics has resurfaced. Indeed, the administration of George W. Bush frequently resorted to Puritan rhetoric as a reenactment of an old historical process. For example, the concept of "American exceptionalism," inscribed in the genes of the country's forbears, still appears linked to the myth of a historical redemptive mission. Many Americans are, as in the past, convinced that America has a divine mission, but, as in the past, this opinion is not shared by everyone worldwide. This, obviously, generates political tensions. In American historiography, the religious interpretation of many events may have denatured the core of the Christian faith and contradicted its truthfulness and its authenticity.

If American exceptionalism today gives rise to serious questioning, one must admit that such ideological patterns were largely reproduced in many other nations throughout the centuries. Since the origin of the world, nations and empires have claimed their supremacy over other countries or continents. However, what makes it quite original when it comes to America is the deep conviction that this supremacy is expressed in moral, religious and missionary terms.

The Millenarian Temptation

With the rise of the Evangelical movement over the past few decades came the resurgence of the millenarian concept. In the United States, from the beginning of European-American settlement, the millenarian doctrine has often been revived, and has undoubtedly underlain national and religious discourse. The newcomers found a favorable ground to nourish their messianic expectations, since a new era, a peaceful harmony, was to begin, far from the persecutions of England and the sinful Old Europe. Spiritual sons of English Puritanism, many American settlers soon adhered to the belief that the prophecies contained in the last chapter of the New Testament, the Book of Revelation, were about to occur in their own time and on their land. Like many Christians before them who expected Jesus Christ's return in glory, they thought America was "the first last chapter" in the history of the world. As Professor William Lamont has noted: "Puritanism and millenarianism come together in the creation of America."[7]

The fundamental idea of millenarianism derives from the Christian faith and may be expressed as follows:

> At the end of time Christ will return in all his splendor to gather together the just, to annihilate hostile powers, and to found a glorious kingdom on earth for the enjoyment of the highest spiritual and material blessing. He Himself will reign as a king, and the just, including the saints recalled to life, will participate in it. At the close of this kingdom, the saints will enter Heaven, while the wicked, who have also been resuscitated, will be condemned to eternal damnation. The duration of this glorious reign of Christ and His saints on earth is frequently given as one thousand years. Hence, it is commonly known as the "millennium," while the belief in the future realization of the kingdom is called "millenarianism" or "chiliasm."[8]

The triumph of Christ and His Saints is described in the Apocalypse of St. John (Revelation 20–21). Although the biblical pictures are very suggestive and evocative, they are allegoric, and the entire passage refers to the spiritual combat between Christ and the Church on the one hand and the powers of dark forces of evil on the other. Over the years, a large number of Christians misinterpreted the text, adopting a literal approach, leading to misconceptions which spread through the Christian world, denaturing the real spiritual meaning of the Millennium. Since the post–Apostolic era, many millenarian groups emerged, all referring to various prophecies contained in the Old Testament. In the Western world, a few religious movements adhered to this idea of a glorious kingdom on earth, focusing on the material accomplishment of this Golden Age. St. Augustine after adopting for a time the millenarian vision (*De Civitate Dei*, XX, 7), interpreted the prophecy in a more spiritual dimension (*Sermo*, CCLIX). His explanation convinced most Western theologians, and Chiliastic views were never set forth in the universal Church.[9]

However, the Reformation gave a new impulse to millenarian thinking. Protestant denominations such as the Anabaptists believed that the Golden Age would occur after the crumbling of the Papacy and the secular world. In their writings, other reformed theologians, such as Johann Alsted, a German Protestant divine, and Joseph Mede, an English scholar from Cambridge University, insisted on the promise of a literal kingdom of God. During the Puritan period in Great Britain, both believed that the new Advent of Christ would occur in England. Since then, the millennium concept has continued to reappear amid religious groups that expect Christ and His Second Advent on a specific date.

Indeed, many prominent Puritan rulers mentioned the apocalyptic prophecy as justification for their presence in the New World. John Winthrop, referring to the Holy Book, was the first to evoke the "City upon a Hill" and the New Jerusalem ("For we must consider that we shall be a shining city upon a hill," Matthew 5:14). However, as Christopher Findlay noted: "Winthrop's vision also carried within it portents of doom and divine retribution if the 'shining city' failed to match up to expectations: 'The eyes of the all people are upon us,' said Winthrop, 'so that if we shall fail falsely' with our God in this work we have undertaken, and so cause Him to withdraw His present help from us ... we shall be consumed out of the good land whither we are agoing."[10]

Increase Mather, another seventeenth-century Puritan minister and major political and religious figure in New England also held a belief in a future millennium. Best known for his involvement in the Salem witch trials and as the first president of Harvard University, Mather witnessed a natural phenomenon that led him to express his millenarian views: A comet had appeared in 1680 above Boston. Mather gave a sermon, entitled "Heaven's Alarm to the World," claiming that such an event was the sign of God's wrath. Giving a theological meaning to the phenomenon, he warned the faithful of some imminent danger, resorting to a Doomsday rhetoric. At the time, comets, meteors and eclipses were regarded as religious omens, and American preachers observed them closely, interpreting them as apocalyptic signs.

Thomas Stoppard, another significant figure in colonial New England, sought to contain this apocalyptic fever among New England's inhabitants: "Some think that all this time may be the days of the Coming of Christ ... we ought to live in a daily expectation of His coming ... we are not yet in the latter part of those last days."[11] However, his arguments did not convince the majority of the preachers, who continued to announce the millenarian promise of the Old Testament. John Cotton, a theologian of great repute who led the Boston Church, believed that the children of the first Puritans, who had signed a covenant with God, should inherit their spiritual blessings: "Too many of the founders' children did not have the 'saving experience' which would qualify them for church membership. The clergy found the answer in the 'first principles of New England.' In their case, they decided, the churches would grant provisional membership by inference of conversion. The spiritual legacy had to continue from one generation to the next, until this second flight from Babylon would issue in the Second Coming."[12]

In the eighteenth century, Jonathan Edwards was the great revivalist of Millenarianism. Born into a Puritan household on October 5, 1703, in East Windsor, Connecticut, he became one of the most illustrious preachers and theologians in America. He believed this new land was the place where the biblical prophecies of the Book of Revelation would occur; in other words, the Golden Age would begin in America. He was the inspirer of the Great Awakening of 1740 described by Perry Miller, who defined this spiritual event as "the point at which the wilderness took over the task of defining the objectives of the Puritan errand. I am the more prepared to say this because Jonathan Edwards was a child of the wilderness as well as Puritanism."[13] Edwards' millenarian orations were vivid and thundering and conveyed his personal interpretation of the biblical sentence "new heavens and new earth." He believed the discovery of the New World meant that this "new and most glorious state of God's Church on earth might commence here," for "when God is about to turn the earth into a Paradise, he does not begin his work where there is some good growth already but in a wilderness."[14] To revive the dormant faith of the New Englanders, Edwards embraced a very evocative style: "But we know the spring is coming when God shall say, Behold, I make all things new, and there shall be a new heaven and a new earth ... the sun of Righteousness ... shall rise in the west, contrary to the course of ... things in the old heaven and earth, ... until it shines through the world.... America is a brighter type of heaven."[15] At the dawn of the Revolutionary War, these sermons, imbued with apocalyptic overtones, tended to extol patriotic and national ideals.

10—Evangelism and Millenarianism

During the Revolutionary War, religious fervor blended with an implicit yearning for independence. Throughout the "Golden Age of Oratory," American ministers delivered a plethoric number of sermons which dealt not only with the issue of individual redemption, but also with the material well-being of God's chosen people. Most denominations were from Reformed or Calvinist origin, believing that all events were parts of a providential design. Religious congregations, in spite of their spiritual divergences with the British, had remained faithful to their Motherland. When economic problems developed due to restrictive British trade laws, the issue of religion came to the forefront. The apocalyptic rhetoric resurfaced in Samuel Sherwood's sermon *The Church's Flight into the Wilderness: An address on the Times, containing Some very Interesting and Important Observations on Scriptures Prophecies* (1776).[16] Sherwood was a Congregational clergyman from Weston, Connecticut, who used scriptural metaphors to identify America's ordeal with passages of the Book of Revelation. He called his fellow countrymen to arms, believing that an American victory would initiate Christ's thousand-year reign. This prophetic theme took shape in people's minds, since it seemed to fit with their vision of America's historic role. Quoting the text of Revelation 12:14–17, Sherwood compared the destiny of America to the "woman clothed with the sun":

> And to the woman were given two wings of a great eagle, that she might fly into the wilderness, into her place; where she is nourished for a time, and times, and half a time, from the face of the serpent; And the serpent cast out of his mouth water as a flood, after the woman; that he might cause her to be carried away of the flood. And the earth helped the woman, and the earth opened her mouth, and swallowed up the flood which the dragon cast out of his mouth. And the dragon was wroth with the woman, and went to make war with the remnant of her seed, which keep the commandments of God, and have the testimony of Jesus-Christ" [Revelation xii, 14, 15, 16].[17]

Sherwood articulated his reflections through these metaphoric images to illustrate his views on freedom. He observed that the prophecies of St. John could mirror and explain the new hostilities between England and the American colonies: "We may conjecture at least, without a spirit of vanity or enthusiasm, that some of those prophecies of St. John, not unaptly, be applied to our case, and receive their fulfillment in such providence as are passing over us." For him, the woman in a pregnant state represented the true Church of Christ, the "king's daughter, all glorious within." This emblematic woman stood as the American Church which fled the red dragon, with its seven heads and ten horns, representing the tyrannical and persecution powers of the earth—the British Parliament. The "purified" Church was carried on eagles' wings to a distant and remote wilderness—America, "her new abode for unadultered Christianity, liberty and peace."

God, from immemorial times, had prepared a place for his new American bride, giving her civil and religious liberties "that no power on earth can have any right to invade, much less to dispossess of them." In Sherwood's imagination, the serpent symbolized British administration and the unrighteous decrees such as the Stamp Act: "The colonies of America will not soon forget the cruel and tyrannical administration of Sir Edmond Andross, at Boston, and his evil designs against them in general." The symbol of the earth related to God's prodigality which assisted the woman since her arrival on the shores of America.

The figure of the dragon embodied the despotic and arbitrary rule of the English, who shut ports and harbors, paralyzing trade and commerce. It also incarnated spiritual warfare "that is carrying on with such heat and fury against us; which is chiefly leveled against those who most strictly and conscientiously adhere to the pure, uncorrupted doctrine and worship of our pious forefathers; and have not been seduced nor perverted from the right ways of the Lord, but still keep God's commandments, and have the testimony of Jesus-Christ, in his pure gospel."

But the time is near, Sherman warned his audience, when Babylon the Great would fall to rise no more, since the unjust attacks of the British Empire would cease to struggle with the "woman in the wilderness." The downfall of its wicked tyrants and oppressors would be a sign of the fulfillment of St. John's prophecies, entailing the future glory and prosperity of Christ's Church, since the "vials of God's wrath begin to be poured out his enemies and adversaries." Sherwood's language, intertwining apocalyptic images with political ideals, viewed the contemporary events in the Manichean perspective of good and evil. He inherited this dual vision of the world from his Puritan forbears.

The Book of Revelation, according to which Christ would personally come again to reign a thousand years on earth before the Judgment Day, had a crucial importance for several Puritan clergymen who were convinced that He would return in America. However, they were also aware that human understanding could not totally grasp the expression of the Divine act. Nonetheless, they expected signs and heavenly wonders to support their claims. As noted above, when the Puritans wrote about the New World, they very often alluded to God's will acting and revealing itself through the events of American history.

Although Puritan millenarianism remained in the dark recesses of people's minds, many American religious leaders believed it would fulfill all providential promises, God participating in all stages of American experience. They knew that hardship and trouble would tarnish their Edenic vision of the New World, but their enthusiasm did not deter them from the prospect of building a heavenly city in the wilderness: "The writers' urgent task was to displace the traditional center of historical significance in Europe and direct it onto the small band of spiritual pioneers who, for the world's sake has accepted God's injunction to establish His kingdom in the wilderness."[18]

Puritanism took on many forms through the centuries, but the millenarian spirit always permeated American consciousness, even though it seemed to fade under the influence of the Age of Enlightenment when the notion of providential history lost ground. Similarly, Emerson's Transcendentalism gave the Puritan doctrine a Romantic color with his personal idea of Revelation. Emerson, as the most influential nineteenth-century American thinker, did not refer to the stern Jehovah of the Old Testament, but rather to the "Universal One," a timeless Divine Force transcending Puritan hermeneutics. His praise of Revelation contributed to the exaltation of both individual and collective ideals and to romantic naturalism preached by the members of Brook Farm, a social utopian community founded by the Transcendentalist and former Unitarian minister George Ripley and his wife, Sophia Ripley. The theological approach of Transcendentalism spurred the feeling that America was ready for the coming of the Apocalypse.

The nineteenth century also witnessed the emergence of a new religious line of thought, which exerted a great influence on the way certain Christians regarded the doctrine of eschatology—dispensationalism. It was the Anglo-Irish John Nelson Darby (1800–1882), Evangelist and precursor of modern Christian fundamentalism, who set forth the main tenets of dispensationalism while at University College in Dublin. This new approach to theology appeared in the mid–1800s in the United States under the influence of Cyrus Ingerson Scofield, an American theologian, minister and writer, who adhered to the dispensational theology. Scofield defined the main lines of his eschatological doctrine in his writings and produced a new translation of the Bible, the Scofield Reference Bible, the notes of which explained the scriptural texts from a dispensational perspective. The Brethren Movement took shape under his guidance and popularized these ideas.

Dispensationalism advanced the idea that the whole history of humanity, from its creation to Judgment Day, is divided into seven periods or epochs, that is, dispensations. Literally, the term "dispensation" refers to the Divine intervention in human events through time. Within the biblical framework, these seven dispensations related to:

1. The Creation to the Fall, corresponding to the dispensation of innocence (Genesis 1:1–3:7).
2. The Fall to the Flood, relating to the dispensation of conscience (Genesis 3:8–8:22).

3. The Flood to Abraham, referring to the dispensation of government (Genesis 9:1–11:32).
4. Abraham to Moses, the dispensation of the patriarchal rule (Genesis 12:1–Exodus 19:25).
5. Moses to Christ, the dispensation of the Mosaic Law (Exodus 20:1–Acts 2:4).
6. Church Age, the dispensation of Grace (Acts 2:4–Revelation 20:3).
7. The Millennium, the dispensation of the Millennial Kingdom.

This new theological approach had a broad impact on evangelical Protestantism. Ministers who believed in Dispensationalism gave many Bible conferences on the subject and founded several Bible institutes to promote this new vision of the eschatological doctrine. Generally, the main features of Dispensationalism reside in a few tenets; among them, it sustains a literal interpretation of biblical texts and declares that all the promises made to Israel should be fulfilled, including the return of the Jews to Israel. This last tenet is very important in the sense that, in the twentieth century, it incited American policy makers, influenced by the powerful evangelical movement, to send American Jewish nationals back to their country.

Indeed, the twentieth century witnessed the portentous impact of Dispensationalism on Evangelicals, giving strength to their millenarian vision, especially among American preachers. Millenarianism, or post–Millenarianism, became the dominant feature of Evangelical Protestant beliefs. One of its most prominent representatives was Jerry Falwell, an American pastor and televangelist, founder of the Thomas Road Baptist, a megachurch in Lynchburg, Virginia. Falwell was best known for founding a political lobby that gathered Evangelicals during the 1980s, the Moral Majority. The main targets of the Moral Majority included outlawing abortion, opposition to state recognition and acceptance of homosexuality, opposition to the Equal Rights Amendment and Strategic Arms Limitation Talks, enforcement of what members saw as a traditional vision of family life and censorship of media outlets that promoted an "anti-family" program.[19]

Falwell expressed his millenarian views and apocalyptic beliefs in his book *Nuclear War and the Second Coming of Jesus Christ*, published in 1983, in which he wrote: "Biblical Prophecy tells of a glorious time for all believers but there will come a time when God will unleash his wrath and judgment upon unbelievers. He will crush them beneath his thumb."[20] Referring to the Tribulation, a period preceding the Second Coming of Christ, Falwell added, "a powerful ruler led by Satan and referred to as the antichrist will rise to power.... God will be pouring out his wrath upon the earth and mankind, unlike anything that has ever taken place. It will be a time of terrible persecution and suffering.... At the end of the Great Tribulation, Jesus Christ will come in great glory and power to defeat the forces of Satan at the battle of Armageddon."[21]

Falwell, as a dispensationalist, insisted on the notion of pre-millenarianism. Pre–millenarians believe that Christ's Second Coming will occur before the new millennium, whereas post-millenarians think that Christ's Second Coming will occur after the millennium. According to Struan Hellier, "The distinction between pre-millenarianism and post-millenarianism is of vital importance to the way groups interact with the outside world. For the post-millenarian, the thousand year's peace on earth will be instituted by man with Christ arriving only at the end to take up His throne in order to fight the Apocalypse. For the pre-millenarians, Christ will institute the millennium Himself. This has great political consequence in that, for the post-millenarians, politics is an active tool for change. If man is to institute the millennium, then he must actively work towards this."[22] Falwell declared: "I believe in the pre-millennial, pre-tribulational Coming of Christ for all his Church, and to summarize that, your first poll, do you believe Jesus coming the second time will be in the future, I would vote yes with the 59 percent and with Billy Graham and most evangelicals."[23]

Remembering the biblical corollary on the fate of "God's elected people," Billy Graham was one of the first Evangelicals to encourage Jews to return to Israel with a view to "precipitate" the Millennium, and his son Franklin Graham stated in a recent interview that it was a means for the Bible to "become alive."[24] Many of these emblematic figures tried to convince Christians of the Second Coming of Christ, a spiritual reality instilled at the core of the Christian theology according to their own reading and interpretations. Still today, some Protestant denominations such as the Shakers, Seventh-day Adventists, Jehovah's Witnesses, and Latter-day Saints (Mormons) tend to adapt their activities to the eventual coming of the Apocalyptic era.[25] This belief in biblical prophecy has had a strong impact on American culture, as witness the million-selling book *The Late Great Planet Earth* by Hal Lindsey, a work on pre-millenarian Christian eschatology published in 1970, or the science fiction film *Armageddon*, which came out in 1998 and became an international box-office success.

The Millenarian Concept in American Foreign Policy

The millennium was not confined to the religious and political spheres of the United States, but extended also to its foreign policy. In *The Last Crusade*, the journalist Barbara Victor[26] asserts that, during the last decades of the twentieth century, many members of the Evangelical movement have brought their ideas into the highest ranks of the American government, resorting to the millenarian doctrine for religious and political ends, particularly on the question of the Jews' return to Israel. Since the creation of Israel, various political and private organizations have been founded to tighten the bonds between the United States and Israel. Several Evangelicals, such as Billy Graham, Franklin Graham, Pat Robertson and Jerry Falwell, have established close ties with Jewish organizations which granted financial help to Jews to incite them to return to Israel with the aim of "reviving the Bible."[27] The main objectives of neo-conservatives and Zionist Evangelicals are, in Barbara Victor's opinion, to maintain and expand Israel's territories, even though they are slowly losing ground.

Their political action is widely influenced by the deterministic tenets of Dispensationalism, and by its important corollary — the return of the Jewish people to Israel. According to this doctrine, the world has already undergone six dispensations and is at the eve of the Millennium, due to occur when all the Jews are back in their country. Although the Book of Revelation does not precisely identify the place nor the time of Christ's Second Coming, according to the sixth pre-millenarian dispensation His return will occur on the Israeli soil, which would entail the destruction of all the Jews refusing to convert to Christianity.[28]

Millenarianism was first advocated by the Pilgrim Fathers, who believed that Boston would be the New Jerusalem. It resurfaced during the Great Awakening revivals and at other times. During the 1890s, for example, Eugene Blackstone, an American evangelical and Christian Zionist born in New York in 1841, held Christian Zionist conferences in Chicago and was hailed as "the Father of American Zionism." Deeply involved in the pre-millenarian movement, he became an overt advocate of the resettlement of Jews in Palestine, as he wished to reestablish the nation of Israel, thus complying with the Bible prophecy. In 1887, he founded the Chicago Hebrew Mission for the evangelization of the Jews, and in 1890 he organized the first conference between Christians and Jews to expound his pre-millenarian views on the restoration of Israel. Blackstone also drafted a petition addressed to President Harrison to promote the resettlement of Jews in Palestine. Part of it read:

> Why not give Palestine back to them? According to God's distribution of nations, it is their home — an inalienable possession from which they were expelled by force. Under their cultivation, it was a remarkably fruitful land, sustaining millions of Israelites, who industriously tilled its hillsides and valleys. They were agriculturists and producers as well as a nation of great commercial importance — the center of civilization and religion.... We believe this an appropriate time for all nations, and especially the Christian nations of Europe, to show kindness to Israel. A million of exiles, by their terrible suffering are piteously appealing to our sym-

pathy, justice and humanity. Let us restore to them the land of which they were so cruelly despoiled by our Roman ancestors.[29]

The "Blackstone Memorial" gathered 413 signatures of highly influential leaders, among them the mayors of Chicago, Boston, New York, Philadelphia and Baltimore; many leading churchmen and rabbis; and, notably, William McKinley, future president of the United States. In 1906, Blackstone published a bestseller, *Jesus Is Coming*, which sold over a million copies and was translated into thirty-six languages. All in all, "it is not surprising," reported Dr. Thomas Ice, that a "1918 Zionist Conference in Philadelphia acclaimed Blackstone as 'Father of Zionism,' and in 1956, on the seventy-fifth anniversary of the Blackstone Memorial to President Harrison, the citizens of the state of Israel dedicated a forest in his honor."[30] Blackstone continued to work for the cause of Israel and died in 1935, without seeing his wish realized.[31]

In 1948, the state of Israel was established while Harry Truman was president of the United States. Truman was a Baptist who, according to his daughter, Margaret Truman Daniel, had read the Bible four times before the age of fourteen. After a friendly encounter with Billy Graham, Truman became the first president to invite him to the White House. For Truman, the recognition of Israel as a nation was a significant and personal event, as it was reported that he often read Psalm 137: "Weeping, we sat beside the rivers of Babylon thinking of Jerusalem."[32]

In May 1949, when Israel was admitted to the United Nations, Louis T. Talbot, a dispensational Evangelical and head of the Bible Institute of Los Angeles, declared that it was the "greatest event from a prophetic standpoint that has taken place within the last one hundred years, perhaps even since 70 A.D., when Jerusalem was destroyed." As for Washington leaders, their support for Israel was based on the Christian Zionist agreement to sustain the country for geopolitical reasons. From then on, the United States and Israel's mutual interests began to merge, at least on the surface.

To strengthen the ties between the United States and Israel, powerful organizations have been set up, such as the American Israel Public Affairs Committee (AIPAC), founded in 1953 by Isaiah L. "Si" Kenen. Today America's major pro-Israel lobby, from a small organization "it has grown into a 100,000-member national grass-roots movement."[33] Its aim and activities are to lobby the Congress of the United States on various social, economic and political issues.

Historian Michael Oren, in his bestseller "Power, Faith, and Fantasy" (2007), observed that the United States' unwavering support for Israel can be traced back to Puritan times. During an interview with Joanne Myers on January 18, 2007, he explained what the theme of Faith meant in his book:

By faith, I mean the impact of Christianity, largely Protestant Christianity, on American Middle Eastern involvement. We are talking about an almost irrepressible missionary urge to impart Christianity; but on the other side of the coin, is the civic version of the idea, of bringing democracy and republican government to the world. They exist side by side. Now, this is the faith of the Colonial Americans, who viewed themselves as the settlers of a new Promised Land. They proceeded to give no less than 1,000 biblical place names to their towns and cities, particularly along the eastern Seaboard — those of you who live in New Canaan; Connecticut, or in Bethlehem, or in Jericho. They considered themselves the "new Jews," who were divinely enjoined to help restore the "old Jews" to the Promised Land.[34]

It was mainly during the government of Menachem Begin that the bonds between Evangelical Christians and the conservative leaders of Israel began to tighten more firmly. From 1977, Begin and his Likud Party justified the takeover of Arab land by resorting to a "biblical" right. Relationships became deeper, and Begin's gift of a private Learjet to Falwell for his help in favor of the Jewish people is a secret to no one. Moreover, many other organizations developed rapidly. According to Barbara Victor, the National Unity Coalition for Israel gathered more than two hundred Jewish and Christian organizations, numbering millions of Americans. In April 2003, a symposium was held at the Mayflower Hotel in Washington to reinforce the American political alliance with Israel. Many key American and Jewish figures attended the symposium, among them Jerry Falwell. One of them declared that they had supported Israel for a long time because they believed that God bequeathed the land of Israel to the Jews. Everyone in the assembly was convinced that Israel should be restored to God's "Chosen People."[35]

In addition, in 1996 Israeli Prime Minister Benjamin Netanyahu founded the Israel Christian Advocacy Council. To celebrate the event, he invited to Israel a group of Christian leaders, who swore that America would never abandon Israel. Since the events of September 11, 2001, Barbara Victor notes, Christian conservatives have made the backing of Israel one of their priorities.[36] This is why many organizations have set up offices in Jerusalem, such as Bridges for Peace, which provides grants to conservative Israeli economic and financial leaders. The organization also helps people from Europe, Russia, South America and Canada by issuing resident visas to Christians wishing to live and work in the Holy Land.[37]

Today, Evangelical Christians who decide to live in Israel are involved not only in projects to support the Jewish state but also to put pressure on American political leaders. This explains why the Christian Right has had a prominent impact on the U.S. foreign policy, and with it, worldwide consequences. For born-again Christians, the return of the Jewish people to Palestine is tangible proof that the prophecies in the Book of Revelation are about to become true. In one of his bestsellers, *Armageddon, Oil and the Middle East Crisis,* John F. Walvoord writes:

> The purpose of Christ's return to the Mount of Olives will be to establish Jerusalem as the capital of His new world kingdom. The law will once more go forth from Zion (Isa. 2:3). Christ's return will save Jerusalem and the nation of Israel from complete annihilation. This direct intervention of God in saving Israel and returning Jews from all nations was predicted as early as the promise recorded in Deuteronomy 30:3: "the Lord your God will restore your fortunes and have compassion on you and gather you again from all the nations where He scattered you."[38]

Two striking elements seem to fully illustrate the political and religious interference in American foreign policy. The first concerns the persistent influence of a national myth, largely recognized by foreign observers, namely the constant and recurrent identification of America with the people of Israel; the second refers to Christian millenarianism. Both biblical events, on which American history was fashioned, tend to belong either to the past or to the future. The concept of destiny, entailing the creation of a "historical" future, acts as a link that binds them: as a chosen people, America has to fulfill a messianic role at home and abroad, in an eschatological perspective.

Conclusion

American nationalism, deeply based on a religious culture, was molded in the name of principles which imposed themselves with an irresistible force on American political leaders and on people as a whole, even though all citizens did not approve of these principles. It is necessary to understand and analyze the notion of "inescapable force." Indeed, if geopolitical considerations have guided American statesmen with a certain logic and efficiency, it seems quite bold to justify an expansionist policy by resorting to a supposedly Divine and Providential Will.

The notion of a particular destiny, specially reserved and chosen for the United States, began to take root in the minds of Puritan men and women as they fled England following the mistreatment and persecution inflicted upon them, making them victims of intolerance. In their desire to "purify" a religion, which from their point of view had deviated from its true source, the new immigrants, mostly of Calvinist origin, identified themselves with the Hebrews on their way to the land of "milk and honey." Their imaginations, nurtured by an Edenic vision of a New Jerusalem, engendered a utopia whose metamorphosis has not ceased to mark the canvas of their collective consciousness. The New England town of Salem bears an iconic sign in the history of this anointed nation and embodies all aspects of this idea.

Although the influence of the seventeenth-century English philosopher John Locke and the era of Enlightenment brought to an end the stern and severe religion of colonial times, the American nation never abandoned its religious fervor. New liberal ideas were naturally taken into consideration, and were especially reflected in the American Declaration of Independence. Alexander Hamilton, James Madison, Thomas Jefferson, and other Founding Fathers of the United States believed that reason and tolerance were the two pillars of American politics. They all argued that Church and civil powers should be separated. However, they needed a transcendental power to gather the different denominations, which had broken with traditional Protestantism. While certain Christians remained attached to the concept of an Abrahamic God, the idea of a cosmic divine figure was then elaborated by others to maintain social and spiritual cohesion.

Conclusion

Indeed, America is a "Nation-Idea,"[1] as Jacques Andréani has suggested. Americans are more idealists than realists in the sense that their aspirations are "grafted" onto a common dream for a better world. Putting strong emphasis on the notion of commonwealth, the New World's citizens escaped the abuses and hierarchical rigidity of the Old World. One should bear in mind that, at the origin, they were geographically uprooted Europeans who, for the great majority, had been psychologically wounded. This Garden of Eden that the Lord had reserved for them was a necessity to compensate for their painful experiences. This idea of an American Eldorado was best exemplified by the "poet of Democracy," Walt Whitman, whose poetry conveyed an illuminated vision of a sacred land and blissful destiny for Americans.

This was the recurrent leitmotif that underlay the period of the western conquest. Even though political objectives seemed to prevail over ideological ones, the spirit of Manifest Destiny remained ever-present as it was regarded as an infallible sign of God's concern for His chosen people. Economic and commercial interests are, of course, not to be neglected in the territorial expansion, and certain people have justifiably contested the spiritual aspect of the adventurous enterprise. But given the numerous documents on the question, it appears quite evident that the religious arguments carried a heavy weight in the interpretation of these historical events. Placed under God's Providence or God's Nature, the American Western Conquest was predetermined to fulfill a supernatural plan. Once this plan was accomplished, other territorial opportunities were seized abroad to reiterate the same deterministic, religiously inclined pattern.

The most emblematic American figures who supported these idealistic views had a common vision of their nation. Although they were different in their approach to the political and religious issues, they were ardent patriots with ambitious goals. Their passionate and vibrant discourse inflamed the masses, thus enhancing the dominant spirit of nationalism. Gradually, American minds became imbued with evocative symbols and meaningful metaphors that upheld their faith in an invincible nation. All through the nineteenth century, the idea of America as a worldwide model of democracy was propagated in schools, churches and other social organizations, to such an extent that the notion of "exceptionalism" could be applied to all fields. Yet this specific character of the national identity could best be apprehended in Turner's thesis and the emergence of Social Darwinism.

However, Turner, the historian who best exalted intense national feeling, assured that the American had become a man of exception through the unusual virtues of the pioneer. Boasting of the Puritan ideals, Turner drew an attractive portrait of his fellow men, who had to endure pains and hardships to become the finest specimens of all humanity. Endowed with superior qualities in the understanding of human experience and life in society, the "new man" alone could envision and implement the best political system, democracy. True democracy was, in Turner's opinion, deeply rooted in pioneering. Survival of the fittest was the basic argument of Social Darwinism, which spread through the United States in the mid–nineteenth century, often undermining the attempted influence of humans in the social sphere.

This feeling of exceptionalism — based on religious assumptions, reinforced by the strong appeal of natural laws which led to the survival of the fittest — allowed the American mind to feel confident and self-assured. The United States could now consider itself as a great international power, able to stand beside the European nations and to defend its own interests. Before the mid–nineteenth century, the Monroe Doctrine had already imposed limits to the territorial ambitions of Europe in a clear and firm tone. Even though difficult to apprehend and controversial, the Monroe message was a tacit acknowledgment of American hegemony in North America and South America. With its idiosyncratic vision of world relationships U.S. diplomacy began to take shape and put forward its own policy and interests. "America for Americans" became the motto of a people who wanted to break with the outside world. At the time, the melting-pot phenomenon was at a peak. Yet the principles of 1823 remained confined to political circles as a safeguard against European intrusion in American affairs. At the close of the territorial conquest, other issues developed as the United States had to absorb into the white community native populations which had been subdued.

This was an acute problem, as these people had been regarded as inferior races, who, in their "struggle for life" had been defeated. The notion of "superior races" had yet to be defined in an attempt to elucidate the biological origin of the different "categories" of human species. The ethnocentric debate endeavored to explain the various genetic factors that differentiated the races. To most social theorists, heredity was a crucial element in the evolution of man. This gave rise to pseudo-theories that deeply affected currents of thought in nineteenth-century America. Reinforced by the theory of natural selection, then much in vogue, the racial theories perpetuated discrimination against minorities and created social turmoil. However, liberals of the later nineteenth century denied the role of social determinism and condemned the implications of such theories based on racial prejudices.

Amid these ethnocentric polemics, a growing number of American citizens denounced racial discrimination, which opposed the fundamental principles of the Declaration of Independence as well as the intrinsic values of Christianity underlying the text. In this perspective, to establish a more visible link between the secular and the religious (contrary to the American Constitution, founded on secular principles), certain intellectuals elaborated the notion of "civil religion." This ambiguous designation seeks to gather under the same cloak political and religious ideals to guarantee a certain harmony within the national frame, bearing in mind that religion may be a priceless shield against ill deeds and corruption. J. Miller sums up this idea through a clever reflection in *Theology and the Political: The New Debate*: "There is no need to join theology and social theory, for theology is already included in social theory, and social theory is already theology."[2] This formula clearly expresses the concept of "civil religion."

However, the idea of an interaction between the secular and the spiritual involves a whole range of questioning as far as political action is concerned. It appears quite comprehensible when the question of personal ethics is raised, but, at the collective level, it becomes a delicate problem, given the convictions of each individual regarding faith. When religious motives overlie political motives, the main risks reside in the occurrence of dissensions among different people or communities. It seems to be the case with religious movements imposing their vision on the political body, which sometimes thwart the arguments of the democratic majority. A good illustration of such a dilemma is the actual millenarian tendency, popular among politically influential believers. The credibility of their actions is often challenged by their opponents, who wish to reestablish (or maintain) the wall of separation between Church and State.

Although over the years a considerable number of academics and public figures have come forward against this ideological view, it seems that today the religiously inclined movements are weakening. However, when confronted recently by major international threats,[3] the reaction of the majority of Americans and the discourse from Washington political leaders constitute tangible proof that the old Puritan syndrome is still ready to resurface. Prayer meetings of the Republican and Democratic administrations in the Oval Office led by preachers, singularly recalled the Pilgrim Fathers' religious plea, in the form of a pact of alliance with a benevolent Divinity.

In this context, the expression "Axis of Evil" also brings to mind the doctrine of predestination, a basic principle of the Puritan doctrine. The recurrent American authoritarian warning, "Evil has to be tracked and men who support it must be punished" did not spare European countries. The idea of a privileged destiny often seemed alive, even if at times it lay dormant in the recesses of the American mind. Any event related to religion, nationalism, the defense of democracy or America's quasi-sacred mission, seemed to be an opportunity to revive it.

Conclusion 191

The presence of religious arguments in U.S. foreign policy shows that the United States frequently draws its inspiration from these ideological axioms. Missionary diplomacy is still highly influential in America's methods of settling international conflicts. As Michael Hunt, professor at the University of North Carolina, Chapel Hill, justly observed:

> By exposing Americans to the yawning gap between our own national experience and ideals and those of most of the other inhabitants of the globe, we might curb the arrogant and ethnocentric impulses evident in our long-standing view on international affairs.... It is time Americans made the discovery and accepted the limits of our power to shape other societies, time we pondered the contradiction we have long perpetrated by seeking to impose our conception of self-determination and development on peoples with aspirations quite different from our own...While proclaiming the cause of freedom and cheering on those who struggled for it, America should not go roaming overseas "in search of monsters to destroy,"... Can Americans behave as true believers at home and agnostics before the world?[4]

It seems that over the past few years, the awareness of this contradiction is gradually filtering into a large part of American public opinion which, still influenced by pioneer spirit, always seeks a greater good, being able to call itself into question, recognizing its errors and correcting them. Achieving success in all fields, not only on a professional level but also on moral and spiritual levels, constitutes one of the oldest values of the American mind. Endowed with uncurtailed dynamism, *Homo Americanus* often overcomes and transcends his failures in a positive manner. He or she thus moves forward, using the theme of "the Fall," so exalted in modern American literature, as a means to advance in the sphere of knowledge and truth. Intellectuals and technocrats exemplify this method according to which success and failure sustain the upward movement of the nation's human progress, illuminating the positive elements of its identity, among others, its qualities of adaptability, optimism, endurance, creative genius, and sense of quest.

Chapter Notes

Preface

1. The selective competitive examination to qualify as a teacher in the French Higher Education System.

Introduction

1. John Winthrop, *A Modell of Christian Charity (1630)*, Boston: collections of the Historical Society of Massachusetts, 1838, third series, pp. 333–348.
2. Cotton Mather, *Magnalia Christi Americana*, in *The Puritans*, Perry Miller and Thomas H. Johnson, eds., vol. I, New York: Harper & Row, 1963, p. 163.
3. John O'Sullivan, *Democratic Review* 6, 426–430 in Robert W. Johannsen, "The Meaning of Manifest Destiny," *Manifest Destiny and Empire*, Sam W. Haynes and Christopher Morris, eds., Arlington, Texas, 1997, p. 11.
4. John L. O'Sullivan, "The Great Nation of Futurity," *Democratic Review*, vol. VI, (November 1839) 2–3, 6 in Bernard Vincent, *La Destinée manifeste des Etats-Unis au dix-neuvième siècle*, Paris: Editions Messene, 1999, p. 43.
5. *Ibid.*, p. 41.
6. *Ibid.*, p. 46.
7. *Dictionary of American History*, vol. IV, New York: Scribner's Sons, 1976.
8. Robert W. Johannsen, "The Meaning of Manifest Destiny," *Manifest Destiny and Empire*, Sam W. Haynes and Christopher Morris, eds., Arlington, Texas, 1997, p. 11.
9. *Ibid.*, p. 12.
10. John Fiske, "Manifest Destiny" (1885) *Harper's New Monthly Magazine*, (March 1885): 587–590, in Vincent, *La Destinée manifeste des Etats-Unis au dix-neuvième siècle*, p. 118.

Chapter 1

1. William Larmont, *Puritanism and Historical Controversy*, London: UCL Press, 1996, p. 7.
2. The Prayer Book is linked to the name of Thomas Cranmer (1489–1556), Archbishop of Canterbury under the reign of Henry VIII. The history of this book relates the difficulties of a compromise between moderates (essentially Anglicans) and radical Puritans: Armand Himy, *Le Puritanisme*, Presses Universitaires de France, 1987, p. 11.
3. Armand Himy, *Le Puritanisme*, Presses Universitaires de France, 1987, p.13.
4. *Ibid.*, p. 14.
5. Geoffrey Robertson, *Crimes Against Humanity: The Struggle for Global Justice*, New York: Penguin Books, 2002, p. 5.
6. Larmont, p. 153.
7. Théodore Maynard, *Histoire du catholicisme américain*, Paris: Le Portulan, 1948, pp. 76–77.
8. Sacvan Bercovitch, *The Puritan Origins of the American Self*, New Haven and London: Yale University Press, 1975, p. 79.
9. Maynard, p. 66.
10. *Ibid.*, p. 69.
11. *Ibid.*, p. 78.
12. Perry Miller and Thomas H. Johnson, eds., *The Puritans*, New York, Harper & Row, 1963, p. 1.

13. *Ibid.*, p. 12.
14. *Ibid.*, p.12.
15. *Ibid.*, p. 9.
16. *Ibid.*, p. 10.
17. *Ibid.*, p. 10.
18. Doris Faber, *Anne Hutchinson*, Champaign: Garrard Publishing, 1970, p. 391.
19. Bernard Bailey, *The Peopling of British North America*, New York: Random House, 1986, p. 92.
20. New settlers, coming from Massachusetts arrived in the region in 1636. Rhode Island was the first colony to declare its independence in 1776 and joined the Union in 1790.
21. Selma Williams, *Divine Rebel: The Life of Anne Marbury Hutchinson*, New York: Holt, Rinehart and Winston, 1975, p. 131.
22. Roger Williams, *Complete Writings*, VII, 159; I, 141; III, 250; VI, 278–279; VII, 37, quoted in Bercovich, *The Puritan Origin of the American Self*, p.110.
23. The Baptist Church, founded by John Smith in seventeenth-century England, constitutes an important branch of Protestantism and was originally regarded with much suspicion because of its rejection of infant baptism and its insistence on baptism of adult believers by immersion. In 1620, a large number of Baptists embarked on the Mayflower. Today Baptists are the most numerous in the United States, where more than a third of Americans identify themselves as Baptists.
24. Perry Miller, *Errand in the Wilderness*, Cambridge, Massachusetts, London, England: The Belknap Press of Harvard University Press, 1984, p. 114.
25. *Ibid.*, p. 142.
26. *Ibid.*, p. 143.
27. The Levellers were a mid–17th century English political movement. During the English Civil War, John Lilburne (1614–1657) was their prominent representative. They advocated equal rights for all.
28. Jonathan Edwards: "The First Awakening" (Northampton), 1735, quoted in Jean Pierre Martin, *La religion aux Etats-Unis*, Nancy: Presses Universitaires de Nancy, 1989, p.51.

29. Bercovitch, *The Puritan Origin of the American Self*, p.154.
30. Winthrop S. Hudson, *Nationalism and Religion in America*, New York: Harper & Row, 1970, p. 55.
31. *Ibid.*, p. 55.
32. *Ibid.*, p. 56.
33. *Ibid.*, p. 56.
34. *Ibid.*, p. 57.
35. *Ibid.*, p. 58.
36. Timothy Dwight, Yale College, July 25 1776, in Winthrop S. Hudson, *Nationalism and Religion in America*, New York: Harper & Row, 1970, p. 59.
37. *Ibid.*, p. 73.
38. Isaiah, 52: 13–53: 12.
39. M. G. J. de Crèvecoeur, *Letters from an American Farmer*, Philadelphia: Matthew Carey, 1793, pp. 46–47.

Chapter 2

1. Yvon Belaval et Dominique Bourel, *Le Siècle des Lumières et la Bible*, Paris, Beauchesnes, 1986, p. 555.
2. Saughton Lynd, *Intellectual Origins of American Radicalism*, London: Wildwood, 1973, p. 18.
3. John Locke, *Writings on Religion*, Victor Nuovo, ed., Oxford: Oxford University Press, 2002, p. xv.
4. *Ibid.*, p. xx.
5. Saughton Lynd, p. 20.
6. *Ibid.*, p. 23.
7. *Ibid.*, p. 20.
8. *Ibid.*, p. 18
9. François Marie Voltaire, *Treatise on Tolerance* (1763), ed. Simon Harvey, Cambridge: Cambridge University Press, 2000, p. 27.
10. *Ibid.*, p. 49. See Locke's *Letter on Tolerance*. (*Voltaire's notes*).
11. *Ibid.*, p. 93.
12. Charles de Montesquieu, *The Spirit of the Laws* (1748), Book 1.1, *Of Laws in General*, translated by Thomas Nugent and revised by J.V. Prichard, London: G. Bell & Sons Ltd., 1914.
13. *Ibid.*, Book 1.1.
14. *Ibid.*, Book 1.3.
15. Bernard Vincent, "Circonstances historiques et origines intellectuelles de la Constitution américaine," Université

d'Orléans, 2001, printemps sources, p. 138.
16. Leonard Labaree, ed., *Autobiography of Benjamin Franklin*, New Haven: Yale University Press, 1964, p. 66.
17. *Ibid.*, p. 66.
18. *Ibid.* p. 67.
19. Franklin to Mary Stevenson Hewson, January 27, 1783; cf. Franklin to Richard Price, February 6, 1780.
20. Max Farrand, *The Records of the Federal Convention of 1787*, 4 vols. (New Haven: Yale University Press, 1966), 3:540 in (Loraine) Smith Pangle, *The Political Philosophy of Benjamin Franklin*, p. 170.
21. Smith Pangle, *The Political Philosophy of Benjamin Franklin*, Baltimore: The Johns Hopkins University Press, 2007, p. 170.
22. *Poor Richard Improved*, 1748, in Benjamin Franklin, *Writings*, ed. J.A. Leo Lemay (New York, Library of America, 1987), 1246 in Pangle, p. 188.
23. "A Dialogue between Two Presbyterians" April 10, 1735, in Pangle, p. 189.
24. Ian Ousby, ed., *The Wordsworth Companion to Literature in English*, Hertfordshire, England: Wordsworth Edition Limited, 1994, p. 76.
25. *Letter to the Pennsylvania Gazette*, April 10, 1730, Writing (Lemay), 145–148, in Smith Pangle, p. 191.
26. Smith Pangle, p. 200.
27. Speech on Prayer, June 28, 1787, Max Farrand, *The Records*, 1:451, Smith Pangle p. 213.
28. Thomas Jefferson, *Writings*, New York: The Literary Classics of the United States, 1984, p. 1466.
29. *Ibid.*, p. 510.
30. Thomas Jefferson, to the Virginia Baptists (1808) ME 16:320. This is his second known use of the term "wall of separation," here quoting his own use in the Danbury Baptist letter. This wording of the original was several times upheld by the Supreme Court as an accurate description of the Establishment Clause: *Reynolds* (98 US at 164, 1879); *Everson* (330 US at 59, 1947); *McCollum* (333 US at 232, 1948).
31. Alexis de Tocqueville, "Essay on American Government and Religion," in Wilson Pierson, *Tocqueville in America*, New York: Doubleday, 1969, p. 100.

Chapter 3

1. Miller and Johnson, eds., *The Puritans*, p. 4.
2. *Ibid.*, p. 3.
3. After his conversion in 1738, the Reverend John Wesley, M.A, decided not to go to Oxford. For more than 50 years he evangelized Great Britain, disregarding rules and customs to save souls. He preached everywhere, even in the middle of fields when necessary (Jean-Claude Bertrand, *Le Méthodisme*, Paris: Armand Colin, 1971, p. 5.)
4. With the design to bring about a Religious Revival which spread into the Anglo-Saxon world, Methodism was characterized by a concern for Christian life and the evangelization of crowds. Inspired by certain aspects of the primitive Reformation, Methodism maintained its orthodox theology, insisting on Calvinist predestination. (*Grand Larousse Encyclopédique*, 1970.)
5. Protestant religious gatherings in the 18th and 19th centuries. Starting in 1737, Methodism triggered the first wave of Protestant revivals that spread to the United States of America.
6. Anders Stephanson, *Manifest Destiny: American Expansion and the Empire of Right*, New York: Hill and Wang, 1995, p. 50.
7. Richard Drinnon, *Facing West, The Metaphysics of Indian-Hating & Empire-Building*, Herman Melville, Norman and London: University of Oklahoma Press, 1980, Introduction, p. xxv.
8. Herman Melville, "Hawthorne and His Mosses," *The Literary World*, August 17 and 24, 1850.
9. Ralph Waldo Emerson, *Essays and Lectures*, New York: Literary Classics of the United States, 1983, p. 226–230.
10. Henry David Thoreau, *Walden and Civil Disobedience*, New York: Penguin Books, 1986, p. 402.
11. Alfred Kazin, *On Native Grounds* (1942) in Richard Ruland and Malcolm Bradbury, *From Puritanism to Postmod-*

ernism. A History of American Literature, New York: Penguin Books, 1992, pp. 348–49.
12. Philip Callow, *Walt Whitman: From Noon to Starry Night* Chicago, London: Allison & Busby, 1992, p. 83.
13. Walt Whitman, *Leaves of Grass*, New York, 1972, p. xxviii.
14. David S. Reynolds, *Walt Whitman's America: A Cultural Biography*, New York: Vintage Books, 1995, p. 5.
15. Walt Whitman, p. 734.
16. *Ibid.*, p. 735.
17. *Ibid.*, p. 735.
18. *Ibid.*, p. 736.
19. *Ibid.*, p. 741.
20. Walt Whitman, *Prose Works 1892*, ed. Floyd Stovall. 2 vols. New York, New York University Press, 1963, p. 372 (Italics are mine).
21. Walt Whitman, *Leaves of Grass: Comprehensive Reader's Edition*, eds. Harold W. Blodgett and Scully Bradley, New York: New York University Press, 1965, p. 745.
22. Walt Whitman, p. 743.
23. Whitman, *Democratic Vistas*, New York: The Liberal Arts Press, 1949, p. 2.
24. *Ibid.*, p. 5.
25. *Ibid.*, p. 22.
26. *Ibid.*, p. 25–26.
27. *Ibid.*, p. 28.
28. *Ibid.*, p. 29.
29. *Ibid.*, p. 30.
30. *Ibid.*, p. 33.
31. *Ibid.*, p. 65.
32. Albert Boime, *The Magisterial Gaze: Manifest Destiny and Landscape Painting*, Washington, D.C: Smithsonian Press, 1991.
33. *Ibid.*, p. 23.
34. *Ibid.*, pp. 4–5.
35. Henderson, John and Roger E. Belson, Thomas Cole (1801–1848), "White Mountain Art & Artists," 14 April, 2008, Cole Biography, 21 July 2008.
36. John Gast's *American Progress*, 1872.
37. Bils Büttner, *Landscape Painting: A History*, New York: Abbeville Press Publishers, 2006, pp. 283–285.
38. Gerald L. Carr quoted by Carter B. Horsley, "In search of the Promise Land: Frederic Edwin Church," 19 June 2008 <http://www.thecityreview.com/fechurch.html>.

Chapter 4

1. American statesman (1743–1826). Delegate to the Continental Congress in Philadelphia, Thomas Jefferson authored the Declaration of Independence (July 4, 1776). Minister to Paris from 1785 to 1789. As President of the United States, Jefferson played an important role in the creation of the new architectural style that replaced the old colonial architecture in North America. The new style, called "Young America," was influenced by European classical monuments; Jefferson drew up the plans for the Capitol building in Richmond, Virginia (1785), inspired by the "Maison Carrée" in Nîmes, France.
2. Thomas Jefferson, *Notes on the State of Virginia*, New York, W.W. Norton, 1954, Query XIX: Manufactures, 164–165, quoted in Smith Pangle, *The Political Philosophy of Benjamin Franklin*, p. 49.
3. Shomer S. Zwelling, *Expansion and Imperialism*, Chicago: Loyola University Press, 1969, p. 3.
4. Richard W. Vanalstyne, *The Rising American Empire*, New York: W. W. Norton and Company, 1974, p. 86.
5. Richard Drinnon, *Facing West: The Metaphysics of Indian-Hating & Empire Building,* Norman and London: University of Oklahoma Press, 1997, p. 108.
6. Vanalstyne, p. 86.
7. Albert Weinberg, *Manifest Destiny, A Study of Nationalist Expansionism in American History*, Chicago: Quadrangle Paperback, 1963, pp. 74–75.
8. *Ibid.*, p. 75.
9. *Ibid.*, p. 79.
10. Weinberg, p. 80.
11. Serge Ricard, "The Exceptionalist Syndrome in U.S Continental and Overseas Expansionism," in Adams, David K., and van Minnen, Cornelis A., *Reflections on American Exceptionalism*. European papers on American History. Keele, England: Ryburn Publishing-Keele U. P., 1994. p. 75.
12. *Ibid.*, p. 82.
13. John L. O'Sullivan, *Democratic Re-*

view, vol. VI (November, 1839). Italics are mine.
14. Stephanson, p. 43.
15. *Ibid.*, p. 38.
16. *Ibid.*, pp. 39–40.
17. James D. Richardson, ed., *Messages and Papers of the Presidents*, vol. IV (Washington, D.C.: Government Printing Office), p. 381.
18. Zwelling, p. 54.
19. Stephanson, p. 43.
20. Bradford Perkins, *American Foreign Relations*, New York: Cambridge University Press, vol. 1, 1993, p. 176.
21. *Ibid.*, p. 206.
22. Thomas Hietala, *Manifest Destiny, Anxious Aggrandizement in Late Jacksonian America*, Ithaca and London: Cornell University Press, 1985, p. 205.
23. *Ibid.*, p. 207.
24. *Ibid.*, p. 207.
25. Weinberg, 161.
26. *Ibid.*, p. 163.
27. *Ibid.*, p. 167.
28. *Ibid.*, p. 168.
29. *Ibid.*, p. 254.
30. Frederick Merk, *Manifest Destiny and Mission in American History: A Reinterpretation.* 1963. 1st Harvard University Press Paperback, Cambridge, Mass: Harvard University Press, 1995, p. 232.
31. Lewis L. Gould, *The Spanish-American War and McKinley*, Lawrence, Kansas: University Press of Kansas, 1980, p. 14.
32. Weinberg, pp. 252–253.
33. *Ibid.*, p. 254.
34. *Ibid.*, p. 255.
35. *Ibid.*, p. 255.
36. H. Wayne Morgan, *America's Road to Empire*, New York: McGraw-Hill, 1965, p. 4.
37. *Ibid.*, p. 9.
38. Weinberg, p. 281.
39. Bernard Vincent, *La Destinée manifeste des États-Unis au dix-neuvième siècle: Textes et documents*, Paris: Éditions Messène, 1999, p. 96.
40. David Healey, *U.S Expansionism*, Madison, Milwaukee: University of Wisconsin Press, 1970, p. 57.
41. *Ibid.*, p. 65.
42. Gould, pp. 108–109.
43. Stephanson, p. 118.

Chapter 5

1. Jean Béranger et Robert Rougé, *Histoire des idées aux U.S.A.*, Paris: Presses Universitaires de France, 1981, p. 113.
2. Jean-Pierre Martin et Daniel Royot, *Histoire et civilisation des Etats-Unis*, Paris, Nathan, 1995, p. 78.
3. Richard Drinnon, *Facing West: The Metaphysics of Indian-Hating and Empire-Building*, Norman and London: University of Oklahoma Press, 1997, p. 108.
4. John A. Garraty, *The American Nation*, Volume I, New York: Longman, 1998, p. 241.
5. James D. Richardson, ed., *Messages and Papers of the President*, vol. II (Washington, D.C.: Government Printing Office, 1887) pp. 519–523.
6. *Ibid.*, pp. 519–523.
7. *Ibid.*, pp. 519–523.
8. Frederick Robinson, "An Oration Delivered Before the Trades Union of Boston and Vicinity, July 4, 1834," in *Social Theories of Jackson Democracy*, Joseph L. Blau, ed., New York, 1947, p. 325, quoted in Staughton Lynd, *Intellectual Origins of American Radicalism*, London: Wildwood House, 1973, p. 141.
9. Seth Luther, *An Address to the Working Men of New England*, delivered in Boston, Charlestown, Cambridgeport, Waltham, Dorchester, Mass., Portland, Saco, Me., and Dover, N.H., New York, 1833, p. 9, quoted in Lynd, p. 141.
10. President Andrew Jackson's Farewell Address, 1837.
11. Frédéric Robert, *L'Histoire américaine à travers les présidents américains et leurs discours d'investiture* (1789–2001), Paris: Ellipse, 2001, pp. 70–72.
12. John Tyler, letter, 10 July 1843. Web page: *The Religion of John Tyler, 10th U.S. President*, created 23 November 2005. Last modified 30 November 2005, p.1.
13. Stephanson, p. 44.
14. Vincent, p. 56.
15. Frederick Merk, *Manifest Destiny and Mission in American History*, Cambridge, Massachusetts: Harvard University Press, 1963, p. 88.
16. Daniel Clifton, ed., *Chronicle of*

America, Farnborough, Hampshire: Jol International Publishing, 1989, p. 324.
   17. James D. Richardson, ed., *Messages and Papers of the President,* vol. IV, Washington D.C.: Government Printing, pp. 472–487.
   18. *Ibid.,* pp. 472–487.
   19. Stephanson, p. 46.
   20. Merril D. Peterson, *The Great Triumvirate,* New York, Oxford: Oxford University Press, 1987, p. 5.
   21. Henry Thomas and Dana Lee Thomas, *American Statesmen,* New York: Garden City Publishing Co, 1942, p. 190.
   22. *Ibid.,* p. 190.
   23. Robert Remini, *Henry Clay,* New York: W. W. Norton and Company, 1991, p. 618.
   24. Ibid, p. 619.
   25. Lincoln, *Eulogy on Henry Clay,* July 6, 1852.
   26. Quoted by Lincoln in *Eulogy on Henry Clay.*
   27. John Niven, *John C. Calhoun and the Price of Union: A Biography,* Baton Rouge, Louisiana: State University Press, 1988, p. 306.
   28. Peterson, p. 20.
   29. *Ibid.,* p. 27.
   30. Niven, p. 325.
   31. *Ibid.,* p. 312.
   32. *Ibid.,* p. 316.
   33. John Calhoun, *The Oregon Bill Speech,* 1848.
   34. Peterson, p. 36.
   35. *Ibid.,* p. 36.
   36. Peterson, p. 27.
   37. John Calhoun, *The Second Reply to Hayne,* January 26–27, 1830. Source: Webster, 113–121.
   38. "Moment with the Book," *Daniel Webster's Greatest Thought,* 7 July 2008, .
   39. Peterson, p. 5.
   40. Hans Kohn, *American Nationalism,* New York: Macmillan, 1957, p. 13.

Chapter 6

   1. Frederick Jackson Turner, *The Frontier in American History,* New York: Holt, Rinehart and Winston, 1962, p. 253.
   2. Report of the American Historical Association for 1893, pp. 199–227, in Vincent p. 88.
   3. Drinnon, p. 460.
   4. Eliza Lee, *The Cult of the Vanishing American,* quoted in Nelcya Delanoë and Joëlle Rostkowski, *Les Indiens dans l'histoire américaine,* Nancy: Presses Universitaires de Nancy, 1991, p. 79.
   5. David M. Potter, *People of Plenty,* Chicago: University of Chicago Press, 1954, p. 150.
   6. Vincent, p. 86.
   7. *Ibid.,* p. 87.
   8. *Ibid.,* p. 89.
   9. *Ibid.,* p. 90.
   10. *Ibid.,* p. 90.
   11. Drinnon, p. 467.
   12. James Mooney, *The Ghost-dance Religion and the Sioux Outbreak of 1890,* 14th Annual Report of the Bureau of American Ethnology, Part 2 (1896).
   13. National Historic Landmarks Program: Wounded Knee. National Park Service.
   14. Jan Willem Schulte Nordholt, *Reflections on American Exceptionalism,* David K. Adams and Cornelis A. van Minnen, eds., Staffordshire, England: Keele University Press, 1994, p. 9.
   15. *Ibid.,* p. 9.
   16. *Ibid.,* p. 10.
   17. Michel de Montaigne, *Michel de Montaigne: The Complete Work,* New York: Randolph House, 2003, p. 185. (*Of Cannibals.* This is an excerpt from *Reading About the World,* volume 2, eds. Paul Brians, Mary Gallwey, Douglas Hughes, Azfar Hussain, Richard Law, Michael Myers, Michael Neville, Roger Schlesinger, Alice Spitzer, and Susan Swan and published by Harcourt Brace Custom Books.)
   18. Montaigne quoted in Nordholt. (Nordholt, p. 10.)
   19. Nordholt p. 11. (*Ibid.,* p. 11.)
   20. *Ibid.,* p. 12.
   21. *Ibid.,* p. 12.
   22. *Ibid.,* p. 9.
   23. Serge Ricard, "The Exceptionalist Syndrome in U.S. Continental and Overseas Expansionism," in *Reflections on American Exceptionalism,* David K. Adams and Cornelis A. van Minnen, eds., p. 73.

24. *Ibid.*, p. 5
25. Weinberg, quoted in Ricard, p. 74.
26. *Ibid.*, p. 74.
27. *Ibid.*, p. 75.
28. Thomas Hietala, *Manifest Design, Anxious aggrandizement in Late Jacksonian America,* Ithaca and London: Cornell University Press, 1985, p. 173.
29. *Ibid.*, p. 196.
30. "A Greater England with a Nobler Destiny," Albert Beveridge, the Indianapolis Journal (September 17, 1898).
31. Richard Hofstadter, *Social Darwinism in American Thought,* New York: George Braziller, Inc., 1959, p. 10.
32. John Fiske, "Manifest Destiny," New York: Harper & Brothers, Publishers, 1885, p. 583.
33. *Ibid.*, p. 588.
34. *Ibid.*, p. 589.
35. *Ibid.*, p. 178.
36. Josiah Strong, *Our Country: Its Possible Future and Its Present Crisis,* New York: Baker and Taylor, 1885, pp. 159–161, 165, 170, 178–180.
37. Hofstadter, p. 178.
38. *Ibid.*, p. 179.
39. *Ibid.*, p. 180.
40. *Ibid.*, p. 192.

Chapter 7

1. James Monroe (1758–1831), American Minister to Paris (1794–1796), statesman, and senator. He was appointed by Jefferson to negotiate the purchase of the Louisiana Territory from France (1803). Elected President twice as the Democratic-Republican candidate, his terms were regarded as the "Era of Good Feelings."
2. Vincent, p. 14.
3. Thomas Jefferson, *Writings,* New York: Literary Classics of the United States, 1984, p; 1481.
4. James D. and Henry Steele Commager, eds., *Documents of American History,* New York: Meredith Corporation, 1973, p. 236.
5. *Ibid.*, p. 236.
6. *Ibid.*
7. *Ibid.*, p. 237.
8. Michael H. Hunt, *Ideology and U.S. Foreign Policy,* New Haven and London: Yale University Press, 1987, p. xi.
9. *Ibid.*, p. 4.
10. *Ibid.*, p. 5.
11. *Ibid.*, p. 10.
12. *Ibid.*, p. 9.
13. *Ibid.*, p. 15.
14. *Ibid.*, p. 16.
15. Dexter Perkins, *The Monroe Doctrine,* 1867–1907, Gloucester, Mass: Peter Smith, 1966, p. 254.
16. *Ibid.*
17. H. Wayne Morgan, *America's Road to Empire, The War with Spain and Overseas Expansion,* New York: Wiley, 1965, p. 9.
18. *Ibid.*, p. 35.
19. Perkins, p. 271.
20. Maurice de Beaumarchais, *La Doctrine de Monroe: l'évolution de la politique des États-Unis au XIXe siècle,* Paris: Académie des Sciences Politiques, 1898, p. 192, in Perkins, p. 272.
21. Perkins, pp. 275–76.
22. LaFeber, *The Cambridge History of American Foreign Relations,* vol. II, Cambridge: Cambridge University Press, 1993, p. 91.
23. *Ibid.*, p. 279.
24. Cong. Record., 55th Cong., 2nd Sess., p. 6634, quoted in Perkins, p. 280.
25. *Ibid.*, p. 282.
26. LaFeber, p. 147.
27. *Ibid.*, p. 148.
28. *Ibid.*
29. Report Philippine Commission, vol. I, p. 183. On November 2, 1900, Dr. Schurman signed the above statement.
30. Halstead, 1918, p. 318 Ch.28. 10 December 2008, http://en.wikipedia.org/History_of the_Philippines_(1898–1946).
31. Perkins, p. 282.
32. Stanley Karnow, *In Our Image: America's Empire in the Philippines,* Headline Series 288, New York: Foreign Policy Association, Spring 1989, p. 16.
33. Perkins, p. 283.
34. George Frisbie Hoar, from a speech in the United States Senate, May 1902. Originally published in Bryan, William Jennings, ed. *The World's Famous Orations.* Volume X, America III. New York: Funk and Wagnalls, 1906.

35. Perkins, p. 283.
36. Ibid., p. 284.
37. Ibid., p. 286.
38. Ibid., p. 287.
39. Ibid., p. 289.
40. Carl Schurz, *Harper's New Monthly Magazine*, vol. 87, issue 521 (October, 1893).
41. Healey, p. 215.
42. Stephanson, p. 103.
43. Morrison I. Swift, *Imperialism and Liberty*, Los Angeles: Ronbroke Press, 1899, Part IV p. 464.
44. William Jennings Bryan, Official Proceedings of the Democratic National Convention, held in Kansas City, Mo., July 4, 5 and 6, Chicago, 1900, pp. 205–227.
45. Mark Twain, *New York Herald*, Oct. 1900.
46. Healey p. 230.

Chapter 8

1. Rubin Francis Weston, Columbia, South Carolina: University of South Carolina Press, 1972, p. xiii.
2. Drinnon, Introduction, p. xxvii.
3. Speech of John W. Daniels of Virginia, ibid, 55 Cong., 3 Sess., XXXII, pt.2:1430 (February 3, 1899), quoted in Weston, p. 2.
4. Nelson M. Blake, quoted in Weston, *Racism in U.S Imperialism*, p. xi.
5. Richard E. Welch, Jr., *Response to Imperialism: The United States and the Philippine-American War*, 1899–19002, Chapel Hill: University of North Carolina Press, 1979, p. 101.
6. Ibid., p. 103.
7. Reginald Horsman, *Race and Manifest Destiny: The Origins of American Racial Anglo-Saxonism*, Cambridge, Mass: Harvard University Press, 1981, p. 331.
8. John B. Watson quoted in Samuel L. Blumenfeld, *NEA: Trojan Horse in American Education*, 1984, Chap 9, "Behaviorism in Watson's Own Words," 2 September 2008, <http://www.sntp.net/behaviorism.htm>
9. Richard Hofstadter, *Social Darwinism in American Thought*, New York: George Braziller, Inc., 1959, p. 10.
10. Blake and Bark, *United States in Its World Relations*, p. 354, quoted in Weston, p. 35.
11. Theory explaining the mechanism of evolution proposed by Charles Darwin and applied to social sciences.
12. Thomas F. Gossett, *Race: The History of an Idea in America*, 2nd ed., New York: Oxford University Press, 1997, p. 146.
13. Ibid., p. 146.
14. Ibid., p. 149.
15. Ibid., p. 151.
16. Ibid., p. 151.
17. Herbert Spencer, "Progress: Its Law and Cause," *The Westminster Review*, vol. 67 (April 1857), pp. 445–447, 454–456, 464–65.
18. William Graham Sumner, *What Social Classes Owe to Each Other*, New Haven, 1925, p. 21, cited in Hofstadter, p. 210.
19. William Graham Sumner, *What Social Classes Owe to Each Other*, Caldwell, Idaho: The Caxton Printers, Ltd, 1974, p. 114.
20. William Graham Sumner quoted in Gossett, p. 154.
21. Eugenics: science which studies the methods liable to improve the specific characteristics of human populations, essentially founded on knowledge acquired on heredity.
22. Daniel J. Kiele, *In the Name of Eugenics*, Boston: Harvard University Press, 1995, Preface, p. ix-xiii.
23. Francis Galton, *Hereditary Genius*, London and New York: Macmillan, 1892, p. 15.
24. Gossets, p. 156
25. Ibid., p. 157.
26. Ibid., p. 159.
27. Ibid., p. 159.
28. Lester. F. Ward, *The Psychic Factors of Civilization*, Boston: Ginn & Company, 1893, p. 92.
29. Ibid., p. 163.
30. Charles H. Cooley, *Human Nature and Social Order*, New York: Charles Scribner's Sons, 1902, p. 2.
31. Ibid., p. 171.
32. Ibid., p. 229.
33. Ibid., p. 230.
34. Ibid., p. 233.

35. *Ibid.*, p. 241.
36. *Ibid.*, p. 235.
37. *Ibid.*, p. 241.
38. *Ibid.*, p. 239.
39. *Congressional Record*, 56 Cong., 1 Sess., XXXIII, pt. 1: 673–74 (January 8, 1900), quoted in Weston, *Racism in U.S Imperialism* p. 11.
40. "The Caste Notion of Suffrage," Nation, LXXVII (September 3, 1903), 182, quoted in Weston, *Racism in U.S Imperialism* p. 12.
41. Welch, p. 106.
42. Constitutional Rights Foundation.
43. Booker T. Washington, "Democracy and Education," Address before the Institute of Arts and Sciences, September, 30, 1896.
44. W.E.B. Du Bois, "The Soul of Black Folk," 1. *Of Our Spiritual Strivings*, Chicago: Herbert Aptheker, 1973, p. 3.
45. *Ibid.*, p. 5–6.
46. W.E.D. Du Bois, "To the Nations of the World," Alexander Walters, *My Life and Work*, New York: Fleming H. Revell, 1917, pp. 257–260.
47. UNIA Declaration of Rights of the Negro Peoples of the World, New York, August 13, 1920. Reprinted in Robert Hill, ed., *The Marcus Garvey and Universal Negro Improvement Association Papers*; vol 2, Berkeley: University of California Press, 1983, pp. 571–580.
48. Gossett, p. 316.
49. *Ibid.*, p. 315.
50. *Ibid.*, p. 318.
51. *Ibid.*, p. 321.
52. *Ibid.*, p. 324.
53. *Ibid.*, p. 324.
54. *Ibid.*, p. 326.
55. *Ibid.*, p. 329.
56. *Ibid.*, p. 329.

Chapter 9

1. Robert N. Bellah, "Civil Religion in America," in Stephen R. Graubard, ed., *Daedalus*, Journal of the Academy of Arts and Science, 1967, p. 12.
2. Susan Dunn ed., *Jean-Jacques Rousseau, Social Contract*, Book 4, Chapter 8 (Civil Religion), New Haven and London: Yale University Press, 2002, p. 252–253.
3. *Ibid.*, p. 250.
4. Alexis de Tocqueville, *Democracy in America*, vol. I, Chicago and London: The University of Chicago Press, 2000, p. 282.
5. *Ibid.*, p. 277.
6. *Ibid.*, p. 440.
7. Stephen R. Graubard ed., *Daedalus*, Journal of the Academy of Arts and Science, preface to the Issue "Civil Religion in America," 1967, p. iv.
8. *Ibid.*, p. iv-v.
9. *Ibid.*, p. iv.
10. Robert N. Bellah, "Civil Religion in America," *Daedalus*, p. 1.
11. *Ibid.*, p. 3.
12. *Ibid.*, p. 4.
13. *Ibid.*, p. 5.
14. *Ibid.*, p. 6.
15. *Ibid.*, p.7.
16. *Ibid.*, p. 2.
17. *Ibid.*, p. 6.
18. Conrad Cherry ed., *God's New Israel, Religious interpretations of American Destiny*, Chapel Hill and London: The University of North Carolina Press, 1998, p. 11.
19. *Ibid.*, p.3.
20. *Ibid.*, p. 3.
21. *Ibid.*, p. 17.
22. *Ibid.*, p. 15.
23. Jean-Pierre Fichou, *La Civilisation américaine*, Paris: Presses Universitaires de France, 1987, p. 103.
24. Stephanson, p. 53.
25. Isaac Mayer Wise, "Our Country's Place in History," in Cherry, p. 224.
26. *Ibid.*, p. 225.
27. *Ibid.*, p. 225.
28. *Ibid.*, p. 226.
29. *Ibid.*, p. 226.
30. *Ibid.*, p. 226.
31. *Ibid.*, p. 227.
32. *Ibid.*, p. 228.
33. *Ibid.*, p. 231.
34. *Ibid.*, p. 231.
35. *Ibid.*, p. 233.
36. *Ibid.*, p. 233.
37. *Ibid.*, p. 234.
38. *Ibid.*, p. 79.
39. Dorothea R. Muller, "Josiah Strong and American Nationalism: A Re-evaluation," *The Journal of American History*,

vol. LIII, June 1966 to March 1967, p. 488.
40. *Ibid.*, p. 489.
41. *Ibid.*, p. 493.
42. *Ibid.*, p. 497.
43. Josiah Strong, "Anglo-Saxon Predominance" 1885, in Vincent, *La Destinée manifeste des Etats-Unis au dix-neuvième siècle*, p. 117.
44. Reinhold Niebuhr, "Anglo-Saxon Destiny and Responsibility," in Cherry, *God's New Israel*, p. 296.
45. *Ibid.*, p. 296.
46. *Ibid.*, p. 297.
47. *Ibid.*, p. 298.
48. *Ibid.*, p. 298.
49. *Ibid.*, p. 299.
50. *Ibid.*, p. 299.
51. *Ibid.*, p. 299.
52. *Ibid.*, p. 300.
53. *Ibid.*, p. 300.
54. Millenarianism is the belief that Christ will reign for a thousand years (the millennium) before the Last Judgment. The Apostle John speaks of the millennium in the Apocalypse. It was both the early Christians' and the Apostle Paul's belief since they were waiting for a near return of Christ. It became an accepted doctrine claiming the extermination of the wicked and the salvation of a very small number of people. The doctrine was advocated by certain Fathers of the Church such as Papias, Tertullian and Lactantius. Origen fought against it. It came back during troubled times, especially in the twelfth century with Joachim of Fiore, in the sixteenth century with the Anabaptists, in the seventeenth century with a Protestant theologian, Jurieu, and finally, in the eighteenth century among Anglo-Saxons like Burnet and Whiston. Several sects of Biblical origin, notably Adventists, Mormons, and Jehovah's Witnesses (generally originated in the United States in the nineteenth century) hold this belief of Christ's return (some say on American soil) at the core of their faith.
55. Cherry, p. 1.
56. *Ibid.*, p. 21.
57. Jean Béranger et Robert Rougé, p. 151.

Chapter 10

1. Francis Stiles, quoted in "Neo-Evangelicalism," Neo- Evangelicalism — CharacteristicsandPositions,6June2006,< http://www.rapidnet.com/~jbeard/bdm/Psychology/neoe.htm>.
2. Tarek Mitri, *Au nom de la Bible, au nom de l'Amérique*, Genève : Labor and Fides, 2004, p. 50.
3. Harold Bloom, "Heroes and Icons," *Time Magazine*, June 14, 1999.
4. *Ibid.*
5. Barbara Victor, *La Dernière Croisade: les fous de Dieu version américaine*, Paris: Plon, 2004, p. 227.
6. Randall Balmer, "Jesus Is Not a Republican," *The Chronicle Review*, June 23, 2006, vol. 52, Issue 42, p. B6.
7. Larmont, p. 129.
8. Johann Peter, "Millennium and Millenarianism." *The Catholic Encyclopedia*. Vol. 10. New York: Robert Appleton Company, 1911, 17 June 2008, p. 1.
9. *Ibid.* pp.1–4.
10. Christopher Findlay, "Millenarism in US Domestic Policy." ISN Security Watch, Millenarism in US Domestic Policy, 17 June 2008, <http://www.isn.ethz.chz.ch/news/sw/details.cfm?ID=11158>.
11. Andrew Delbanco, *The Puritan Ordeal*, Boston: Harvard University Press, 1989, p. 89.
12. Bercovitch, p. 94.
13. Miller and Johnson eds., p. 153.
14. Jonathan Edwards, *Thoughts on the Revival of Religion in New England*, 1740, quoted in Bercovitch, *The Puritan Origins of the American Self*, p. 154.
15. Jonathan Edwards, *Images*, pp. 104–05, 86, 92, 116, quoted in Bercovitch, *The Puritan Origins of the American Self*, p. 155.
16. Samuel Sherwood, *The Church's Flight into the Wilderness: An Address Containing Some Very Interesting and Important Observations on Scriptures Prophecies*, in Ellis Sandoz, *Political Sermons of the American Founding Era*, vol. I (1730–1788), Indianapolis: Liberty Fund, 1991.
17. Samuel Sherwood, *The Church's Flight into the Wilderness: An Address on the Times*, in Ellis Sandoz, *Political Sermons of*

the American Founding Era, vol. 1 (1730–1788), 1991. Online Library of Liberty—16: Samuel Sherwood, THE CHURCH'S-FLIGHTINTO…18June2008,<http://oll.libertyfund.org/index.php?option=staticxt&staticfile=show.php&title=>.

18. Ibid.

19. "Moral Majority." *Columbia Encyclopedia*, 6th ed., (2004). Columbia University Press. Retrieved on 8 November 2007.

20. Jerry Falwell, *Nuclear War and the Second Coming of Jesus Christ*, United States, 1983, p. 14.

21. Ibid., pp. 6–8.

22. Struan Hellier, "An Inquiry into the term 'Fundamentalism' and its transportability from the North American Protestant Context," 22 June 2008, <http://www.shellier.co.uk./fundamentalism.htm>.

23. Jerry Falwell, CNN, *Media Matters for America*. Aug. 1, 2006.

24. Victor, p. 190.

25. Kirsh, Johann Peter, "Millennium and Millenarianism." *The Catholic Encyclopedia*, vol. 10, New York: Robert Appleton Company, 1911. 17 June <http://www.newadvent.org/cathen/10307a.htm>.

26. Victor, p. 190.

27. Ibid., p. 190.

28. Ibid., p. 193.

29. Carl F. Ehle, Jr., "Prolegomena to Christian Zionism in America: The Views of Increase Mather and William E. Blackstone Concerning the Doctrine of the Restoration of Israel," Ph.D. Dissertation at New York University, 1977, pp. 204–244.

30. Thomas Ice, "William Blackstone and American Christian Zionism," Pre-Trib Research Center, 20 June 2008 <http://www.pre-trib.org/article-view.php?id=311>.

31. Ibid.

32. Victor, p. 185.

33. AIPAC, "The American Israel Public Affair Committee," AIPAC — Learn About AIPAC, 20 June 2008 < >

34. Michael Oren, interviewed by Joannes Myers, Director of Public Affairs Programs and on behalf of the Carnegie Council, January 18, 2007, about his book, *Power, Faith, and Fantasy: America in the Middle East, 1776 to the Present*, New York: W.W. Norton & Company, 2007 <http://www.ccela.org/resources/transcript/5413.html>.

35. Victor, pp. 106–107.

36. Victor, p. 113.

37. Ibid., p. 182.

38. John F. Walvoord, *Armageddon, Oil and the Middle East Crisis, What the Bible Says about the Future of the Middle East and the End of Western Civilization*, Grand Rapids, MI: Zondervan Publishing House, 1990, p. 195.

Conclusion

1. Jacques Andréani, *L'Amérique et nous*, Paris: Editions Odile Jacob, 2000, p. 19.

2. Creston Davis, John Milbank, and Slavo Zizek, *Theology and the Political: The New Debate*, Durham: Duke University Press, 2005, quoted in Franck Damour, "Radical Orthodoxy," *Etudes-Paris* 408, no. 6, June 2008, p. 805.

3. The Iraqi War.

4. Michael H. Hunt, *Ideology and U.S. Foreign Policy*, New Haven and London: Yale University Press, 1987, pp. 193–198.

Bibliography

Andreani, Jacques. *L'Amérique et nous.* Paris: Editions Odile Jacob, 2000.
Bailyn, Bernard. *The Peopling of British North America*, New York: Random House, 1986.
Balmer, Randall. "Jesus Is Not a Republican," *The Chronicle Review*, June 23, 2006, Vol. 52, Issue 42.
Beaumarchais, Maurice de. *La doctrine de Monroe: l'évolution de la politique des Etats-Unis au XIXe siècle*, Paris: Académie des Sciences Politiques, 1898, in D. Perkins.
Belaval, Yvon, and Dominique Bourel. *Le siècle des Lumières et la Bible*, Paris: Beauchesnes, 1986.
Bellah, Robert N. "Civil Religion in America." In Stephen R. Graubard, ed., *Daedalus*, Journal of the Academy of Arts and Science, 1967.
Beranger, Jean, and Robert Rouge. *Histoire des idées aux U.S.A*, Paris: Presses Universitaires de France, 1981.
Bercovitch, Sacvan. *The Puritan Origins of the American Self.* New Haven and London: Yale University Press, 1975.
Blake, Nelson Manfred, and Oscar Theodore Barck. *The United States in Its World Relations.* New York: McGraw-Hill, 1960.
Bloom, Harold. "Heroes and Icons," *Time Magazine*, June 14, 1999.
Boime, Albert. *The Magisterial Gaze: Manifest Destiny and Landscape Painting.* Washington, D.C.: Smithsonian Press, 1991.
Bryan, William Jennings. *Official Proceedings of the Democratic National Convention, held in Kansas City, Mo., July 4, 5 and 6.* Chicago: s.n., 1900: www.globalpolicy.org/empire/history/1900/1900paralyzing.htm.
Buttner, Bils. *Landscape Painting: A History.* New York: Abbeville Press, 2006.
Callow, Philip. *From Noon to Starry Night: A Life of Walt Whitman.* Chicago: Ivan R. Dee, 1996.
Cherry, Conrad, ed. *God's New Israel: Religious Interpretations of American Destiny.* Chapel Hill and London: The University of North Carolina Press, 1998.
Clifton, Daniel, ed. *Chronicle of America.* Farnborough, Hampshire: Jol International Publishing, 1989
Cooley, Charles H. *Human Nature and Social Order.* New York: Charles Scribner's Sons, 1902.
Crèvecoeur, M.G.J. de. *Letters from an American Farmer*: Philadelphia: Matthew Carey, 1793.
Davis, Creston, John Milbank, and Slavo Zizek. *Theology and the Political: The New Debate*, in Franck Damour, "Radical Orthodoxy," *Etudes-Paris* 408, no. 6, June 2008.

Delbanco, Andrew. *The Puritan Ordeal.* Boston: Harvard University Press, 1989.
Dictionary of American History. Vol. IV. New York: Charles Scribner's Sons, 1976.
Drinnon, Richard. *Facing West: The Metaphysics of Indian-Hating & Empire–Building,* Norman and London: University of Oklahoma Press, 1997.
Du Bois, W. E. B. "To the Nations of the World," Alexander Walters, *My Life and Work,* New York: Fleming H. Revell, 1917.
_____. *The Souls of Black Folk.* Millwood, N.Y.: Kraus-Thomson Organization Ltd., [1973].
Dwight, Timothy. Valedictory address. Yale College, July 25, 1776. In Winthrop S. Hudson, *Nationalism and Religion in America,* New York: Harper & Row, 1970.
Edwards, Jonathan. "The First Awakening" (Northampton, 1735). Quoted in Jean Pierre Martin, *La religion aux Etats-Unis,* Nancy: Presses Universitaires de Nancy, 1989.
_____. *Images.* Quoted in Bercovitch, *The Puritan Origins of the American Self.*
_____. *Thoughts on the Revival of Religion in New England* (1740). Quoted in Bercovitch, *The Puritan Origins of the American Self.*
Emerson, Raph Waldo. "The Young American," *Emerson, Essays and Lectures.* New York: Literary Classics of the United States, 1983.
Faber, Doris. *Anne Hutchinson.* Champaign: Garrard Publishing, 1970.
Falwell, Jerry. *Nuclear War and the Second Coming of Jesus Christ.* United States, 1983.
Farrand, Max. *The Records of the Federal Convention of 1787.* 4 vols. (New Haven: Yale University Press, 1966), 3:540, in Lorraine Smith Pangle, *The Political Philosophy of Benjamin Franklin.* Baltimore: Johns Hopkins University Press, 2007.
Fichou, Jean-Pierre. *La Civilisation américaine.* Paris: Presses Universitaires de France, 1987.
Fiske, John. "Manifest Destiny," *Harper's New Monthly Magazine,* March 1885.
Franklin, Benjamin. *Poor Richard Improved* (1748). In *Benjamin Franklin, Writings,* ed. J. A. Leo Lemay (New York, Library of America, 1987), in Lorraine Smith Pangle, *The Political Philosophy of Benjamin Franklin.*
Galton, Francis. *Hereditary Genius.* London and New York: Macmillan and Co, 1892.
Garraty, John A. *The American Nation.* Vol. I. New York: Longman, 1998.
Gossett, Thomas F. *Race: The History of an Idea in America.* 2nd ed. New York: Oxford University Press, 1997.
Gould, Lewis L. *The Spanish-American War and McKinley.* Lawrence: University Press of Kansas, 1980.
Graubard, Stephen R., ed. *Daedalus, Journal of the Academy of Arts and Sciences,* preface to the issue "Religion in America," 1967.
Halstead, Murat. *Our New Possessions Natural Riches, Industrial Resources ... of Cuba, Porto Rico [Sic], Hawaii, the Ladrones and the Philippine Islands, with Episodes of Their Early History.* Chicago: Dominion Co, 1898.
Healey, David. *U.S. Expansionism.* Madison: University of Wisconsin Press, 1970.
Hietala, Thomas. *Manifest Destiny: Anxious Aggrandizement in Late Jacksonian America.* Ithaca and London: Cornell University Press, 1985.
Hill, Robert, ed. *The Marcus Garvey and Universal Improvement Papers.* Vol. 2. Berkeley: University of California Press, 1983.
Himy, Armand. *Le Puritanisme.* Paris: Presses Universitaires de France, 1987.
Hoar, George Frisbie, from a speech in the United States Senate, May 1902. Originally published in Bryan, William Jennings, ed. *The World's Famous Orations.* Vol. X, America III. New York: Funk and Wagnalls, 1906.
Hofstadter, Richard. *Social Darwinism in American Thought.* New York: George Braziller, 1959.

Horsman, Reginald. *Race and Manifest Destiny: The Origins of American Racial Anglo-Saxonism.* Cambridge, Mass.: Harvard University Press, 1981.
Hunt, Michael H. *Ideology and U.S. Foreign Policy.* New Haven and London: Yale University Press, 1987.
Jefferson, Thomas. "Letter to John Adams." Quoted in Lester Cappon, ed., *The Adams-Jefferson Letters,* 1959.
_____. *Notes on the State of Virginia,* New York: W.W. Norton, 1954. Quoted in Lorraine Smith Pangle, *The Political Philosophy of Benjamin Franklin.*
Johannsen, Robert W. "The Meaning of Manifest Destiny." In Sam W. Haynes and Christopher Morris, eds., *Manifest Destiny and Empire.* College Station: Texas A&M University Press, 1997.
Karnow, Stanley. *In Our Image: America's Empire in the Philippines.* Headlines Series 288. New York: Foreign Policy Association, Spring 1989.
Kazin, Alfred. *On Native Grounds* (1942), in Richard Ruland and Malcolm Bradbury, *From Puritanism to Postmodernism: A History of American Literature,* New York: Penguin Books, 1992, pp. 348–349.
Kevles, Daniel J. *In the Name of Eugenics.* Cambridge, Mass.: Harvard University Press, 1995.
Kirsh, J. P. *The Catholic Encyclopedia.* Vol. X. New York: Robert Appleton Company, 1911.
Kohn, Hans. *American Nationalism.* New York: Macmillan, 1957.
Labaree, Leonard, ed. *Autobiography of Benjamin Franklin.* New Haven: Yale University Press, 1964.
LaFeber, Walter. *The Cambridge History of American Foreign Relations.* Vol II. Cambridge, U.K.: Cambridge University Press, 1993.
Lamont, William. *Puritanism and Historical Controversy.* London: UCL Press, 1996.
Larousse, Pierre. *Grand Larousse Encyclopédique.* Paris: Librarire Larousse, 1960.
Lee, Eliza. *The Cult of the Vanishing American.* Quoted in Nelcya Delanoë and Joëlle Rostkowski, *Les Indiens dans l'histoire américaine.* Nancy: Presses Universitaires de Nancy, 1991.
Locke, John. *Writings on Religion.* Edited by Victor Nuovo. Oxford, U.K.: Oxford University Press, 2002.
Luther, Seth. *An Address to the Working Men of New England* (1833). Quoted in Lynd, *Intellectual Origins of American Radicalism.*
Lynd, Staughton. *Intellectual Origins of American Radicalism.* London: Wildwood, 1973.
Martin, Jean Pierre, and Daniel Royot. *Histoire et Civilisation des Etats-Unis,* Paris: Nathan, 1995.
Mather, Cotton. *Magnalia Christi Americana.* Quoted in Perry Miller and Thomas H. Johnson, *The Puritans.*
Maynard, Théodore. *Histoire du catholicisme américain.* Paris: Le Portulan, 1948.
Melville, Herman. "Hawthorne and His Mosses," *The Literary World,* August 17 and 24, 1850.
Merk, Frederick. *Manifest Destiny and Mission in American History: A Reinterpretation.* Cambridge, Mass.: Harvard University Press, 1995.
Miller, Perry. *Errand in the Wilderness.* Cambridge, Mass., London, England: The Belknap Press of Harvard University Press, 1984.
_____, and Thomas H. Johnson, eds. *The Puritans.* New York: Harper & Row, 1963.
Mitri, Tarek. *Au nom de la Bible, au nom de l'Amérique.* Genève: Labor and Fides, 2004.

Montaigne, Michel de. *Michel de Montaigne, The Complete Works*. Translated by Donald F. Frame. New York: Random House, 2003.
Montesquieu, Charles de. *The Spirit of the Laws* (1748), Book 1.1, *Of Laws in General*, translated by Thomas Nugent (1752) and revised by J. V. Prichard. London: Liberty Library of Constitutional Classics, G. Bell & Sons Ltd., 1914.
Morgan, H. Wayne. *America's Road to Empire: The War with Spain and Overseas Expansion*. New York: Wiley, 1965.
Muller, Dorothea R. "Josiah Strong and American Nationalism: A Re-evaluation," *The Journal of American History 53*, June 1966–March 1967.
Niebuhr, Reinhold. "Anglo-Saxon Destiny and Responsibility." In Cherry, *God's New Israel*.
Niven, John. *John C. Calhoun and the Price of Union: A Biography*. Baton Rouge: Louisiana State University Press, 1988.
Nordholt, Jan Willem Schulte. *Reflections on American Exceptionalism*. Edited by David K. Adams and Cornelis A. van Minnen. Keele, U.K.: Keele University Press, 1994.
O'Sullivan, John L. "The Meaning of Manifest Destiny." In Sam W. Haynes and Christopher Morris, eds., *Manifest Destiny and Empire*. College Station: Texas A&M University Press, 1997.
———. "The Great Nation of Futurity," *Democratic Review* (November, 1839). In Vincent, *La destinée manifeste des Etats-Unis au dix-neuvième siècle*, Paris: éditions Messene, 1999.
Ousby, Ian, ed. *The Wordsworth Companion to Literature in English*. Hertfordshire, U.K.: Wordsworth Editions Limited, 1994.
Pangle, Lorraine Smith. *The Political Philosophy of Benjamin Franklin*. Baltimore: Johns Hopkins University Press, 2007.
Perkins, Bradford. *American Foreign Relations*. Vol. 1. New York: Cambridge University Press, 1993.
Perkins, Dexter. *The Monroe Doctrine, 1867–1907,* Gloucester, Mass.: Peter Smith, 1966.
Peter, Johann. "Millennium and Millenarianism." *The Catholic Encyclopedia*. Vol. X. New York: Robert Appleton Company, 1911.
Peterson, Merril D. *The Great Triumvirate*. New York, Oxford: Oxford University Press, 1987.
Potter, David M. *People of Plenty*. Chicago: University of Chicago Press, 1954.
Remini, Robert. *Henry Clay*. New York: W. W. Norton and Company, 1991.
Reynolds, David S. *Walt Whitman's America: A Cultural Biography*. New York: Vintage Books, 1995.
Ricard, Serge. "The Exceptionalist Syndrome in U.S Continental and Overseas Expansionism." In David K. Adams and Cornelis A. van Minnen, *Reflections on American Exceptionalism*. Keele, U.K.: Keele University Press, 1994.
Richardson, James D. *A Compilation of the Messages and Papers of the Presidents, 1789–1897*. Washington, D.C.: Government Printing Office, 1896.
Robert, Frédéric. *L'histoire américaine à travers les présidents américains et leurs discours d'investiture* (1789–2001), Paris: Ellipse, 2001.
Roberson, Geoffrey. *Crimes Against Humanity: The Struggle for Global Justice*. New York: Penguin Books, 2002.
Robinson, Frederick. "An Oration Delivered Before the Trades Union of Boston and Vicinity" (July 4, 1834). In *Social Theories of Jackson Democracy*, ed. Joseph L. Blau, New York, 1947, quoted in Lynd, *Intellectual Origins of American Radicalism*.

Rousseau, Jean-Jacques. *The Social Contract*. Edited by Susan Dunn. New Haven and London: Yale University Press, 2002.
Ruland, Richard, and Malcolm Bradbury. *From Puritanism to Postmodernism: A History of American Literature*. New York: Penguin Books, 1992.
Schurz, Carl. "Manifest Destiny," *Harper's New Monthly Magazine*, vol. 87, issue 521 October 1893.
Segal, Haggai. *Dear Brothers*. Jerusalem: Keter Press, 1987.
Sherwood, Samuel. *The Church's Flight into the Wilderness: An Address Containing Some Very Interesting and Important Observations on Scriptures Prophecies*. In Ellis Sandoz, *Political Sermons of the American Founding Era, Vol. I (1730–1788)*. Indianapolis: Liberty Press, 1991.
Spencer, Herbert. "Progress: Its Law and Cause," *The Westminster Review*, vol. 67, April 1857.
Stephanson, Anders. *Manifest Destiny: American Expansion and the Empire of Right*. New York: Hill and Wang, 1995.
Strong, Josiah. "Anglo-Saxon Predominance, 1891." In Vincent, *La Destinée manifeste des Etats-Unis au dix-neuvième siècle*.
_____. *Our Country: Its Possible Future and Its Present Crisis*. New York: Baker and Taylor, 1885.
Sumner, William Graham. *The Forgotten Man and Other Essays*. Edited by Albert Galloway. New Haven: Yale University Press, 1918.
Swift, Morrison I. *Imperialism and Liberty*. Los Angeles: Ronbroke Press, 1899.
Thomas, Henry, and Dana Lee Thomas. *American Statesmen*. New York: Garden City Publishing Co., 1942.
Thoreau, Henry David. *Walden and Civil Disobedience*. New York: Penguin Books, 1986.
Tocqueville, Alexis de. *Democracy in America*. Vol. I. Chicago and London: The University of Chicago Press, 2000.
_____. "Essay on American Government and Religion." In Wilson Pierson, *Tocqueville in America*, Balitmore: Johns Hopkins University Press, 1996.
Van Alstyne, Richard W. *The Rising American Empire*. New York: W. W. Norton and Company, 1974.
Victor, Barbara. *La dernière croisade: les fous de Dieu, version américaine*. Paris: Plon, 2004.
Vincent, Bernard. "Circonstances historiques et origines intellectuelles de la Constitution américaine," Université d'Orléans, 2001.
_____. *La Destinée manifeste des Etats-Unis au dix-neuvième siècle: Textes et documents*. Paris: Editions Messene, 1999.
Voltaire, François Marie. *Treatise on Tolerance* (1763). Edited by Simon Harvey. Cambridge, U.K.: Cambridge University Press, 2000.
Walwoord, John F. *Armageddon, Oil and the Middle East Crisis: What the Bible Says About the Future of the Middle East and the End of Western Civilization*. Grand Rapids, Mich.: Zondervan Publishing House, 1990.
Ward, Lester F. *The Psychic Factors of Civilization*. Boston: Ginn & Company, 1893.
Washington, Booker T. "Democracy and Education." Address before the Institute of Arts and Sciences, Brooklyn, NY, September 30, 1896.
Wayne, Morgan H. *America's Road to Empire*. New York: McGraw-Hill, 1965.
Webster, Daniel, Kenneth E. Shewmaker, Richard Nelson Current, and Daniel Webster. *Daniel Webster, "the Completest Man."* Hanover, NH: Dartmouth College, 1990.

Weinberg, Albert. *Manifest Destiny: A Study of Nationalist Expansionism in American History.* Chicago: Quadrangle Paperback, 1963.

Welch, Richard E., Jr. *Response to Imperialism: The United States and the Philippine-American War (1899–1902).* Chapel Hill: University of North Carolina Press, 1979.

Weston, Rubin Francis. "Racism in U.S. Imperialism: The Influence of Racial Assumption on American Foreign Policy, 1896–1946," *The Journal of Southern History* 4, November 1972.

Whitman, Walt. *Leaves of Grass: Comprehensive Reader's Edition.* Edited by Harold W. Blodgett and Scully Bradley. New York: New York University Press, 1965.

———. *Leaves of Grass.* New York: W. W. Norton & Co., 1972.

———. *Democratic Vistas* (1871). New York: The Liberal Arts Press, 1949.

———. *Prose Works* (1892). Edited by Floyd Stovall. New York: New York University Press, 1963.

Williams, Selma. *Divine Rebel: The Life of Anne Marbury Hutchinson.* New York: Holt, Rinehart and Winston, 1975.

Williams, William. *Complete Writings.* Quoted in Bercovitch, *The Puritan Origin of the American Self.*

Winthrop, Hudson S. *Nationalism and Religion in America.* New York: Harper & Row, 1970.

Winthrop, John. *A Modell of Christian Charity* (1630). Boston: Collections of the Historical Society of Massachusetts, 1838.

Zwelling, Shomer S. *Expansion and Imperialism.* Chicago: Loyola University Press, 1969.

Index

Act of Uniformity 15
Adams, John 26, 42, 69, 86, 96, 106, 115, 121, 127, 136, 144
Adams-Onis Treaty 69
Aguinaldo, Emilio 125, 126, 127
American-Israel Public Affairs Committee 183
Anglican 15, 16, 19, 21, 22, 41, 193
Anglo-Saxonism 3, 147, 165
Anti-imperialism 131
Archbishop of Canterbury 13, 14, 15
Austin, Stephen F. 70

Babylon 18, 20, 176–178, 183
Beaumarchais, Maurice de 122
Begin, Menachem 184
Bellah, Robert N. 154, 158, 159, 171
Beveridge, Albert J. 77, 107, 111, 135, 141, 152
Boime, Albert 59
born-again Christians 184
Boston 9, 21, 22, 48, 51, 52, 151, 175, 176, 178, 182, 183
Boston Herald 127
Bridges for Peace 184
Brooks, John Graham 142
Brown, Dee 146
Bryan, William, Jennings 80, 132
Bush, George W. 172

Cabot Lodge, Henry 71, 127, 128
Calhoun, John 58, 86, 87, 88, 89, 90, 91, 94, 95, 96
California 34, 75, 76, 78, 125
Calvin, John 19, 47
Calvinism 6, 16, 17, 18, 19, 25, 38, 42, 47, 48, 49, 50, 108, 137, 162, 177, 187
Cambridge 21, 22, 175
Canaan 23, 25, 184
Canada 5, 146, 184

Carlyle, Thomas 151
Carnegie, Andrew 131, 132
Catholicism 13–20, 34, 37, 45, 57, 70, 137, 157, 171
Chamberlain, Joseph 152
Channing, William Ellery 48, 49
Charles I 17, 18
Cherokees 145
Cherry, Conrad 160, 161, 169
Chicago Chronicle 128
Chosen People 20, 25, 26, 82, 90, 159, 160, 184
Christian Advocacy Council 184
Christian Coalition 172
Christian Right 172, 184
Church, Frederick Edwin 60
Church of England 13, 16, 17, 24, 31
Civil War 5, 27, 28, 44, 61, 74, 101, 118, 147, 160, 165
Clark, William 48
Clay, Henry 49, 58, 74, 87, 88, 89
Cleveland, Grover 77, 71, 123
Clinton, Bill 173
Cold War 171
Cole, Thomas 59, 60
Concord 9, 51, 53
Cooley, Charles H. 143
Cooper, James Fenimore 145
Cooper, Samuel 27
Cortelyou, George B. 78
Cotton, John 19, 21, 176
Cranmer, Thomas 13, 14, 15
Creek 94, 103, 159, 164, 158, 167
Crèvecoeur, Hector de 28, 104
Cromwell, Oliver 18
Cuba 69, 77–80, 120, 121–123, 130, 151

Daniel, John 111
Darby, John, Nelson 171
Darwin, Charles 108, 110, 111

211

Index

Darwinism 112, 128, 137, 140, 142, 143, 144, 188, 189
Declaration of Independence 26, 28, 30, 31, 32, 33, 34, 35, 41, 44, 65, 81, 84, 86, 91, 92, 94, 105, 131, 159, 187, 189
Defense of Marriage Act 173
Deism 41, 44, 45, 57
Democratic Review 6, 7, 8, 9, 70, 74, 77
Dewey, George 71, 128
Dos Passos, John 2
Du Bois, W.E.B. 148, 149
Dwight, Timothy 27

Eden 27, 188
Edwards, Jonathan 24, 176
Elizabeth I 14, 15, 16, 17
Emerson, Ralph Waldo 9, 50, 51 155, 161
Enlightenment 32, 33, 34, 35, 36, 40, 41, 43, 44, 46, 49, 81, 85, 155, 171, 187
Eugenics 140, 143
Europe 116, 117, 122, 125, 128, 130, 140, 157, 163, 164, 158, 174, 171, 182, 184, 189
Evangelical Christians 184
Evangelicals 171, 173, 180, 181
Exceptionalism 97, 99, 101, 103, 105, 107, 109, 111
Exodus 19, 170, 180

Falwell, Jerry 172, 180, 182, 184
Faulkner, William 25
Fiske, John 9, 109, 151, 165
Fitzgerald, F. Scott 2
Florida 58, 67, 68, 69, 78
France 28, 31, 32, 34, 36, 38, 40, 44, 65, 67, 76, 80, 95, 104, 105, 109, 116, 118, 124, 128, 138, 141, 154, 155, 156, 163
Franklin, Benjamin 44, 106

Galton, Francis 140
Garvey, Marcus 148, 149
Godkin, Edwin, Lawrence 130, 131
Gompers, Samuel 131
Graham, Billy 171, 172, 181, 182, 183
Great Awakening 24, 47, 176, 182
Great Britain 13, 35, 108, 116, 140, 151, 152, 176

Hawthorne, Nathaniel 9, 50, 51
Hay, John 71, 128, 152
Hebrews 19, 20, 22, 25, 131, 187
Hemingway, Ernest 2, 25
Henry VIII 13, 15
Hoar, George Frisbie 127, 147

Houston, Sam 145
Howells, William Dean 153
Hudson Bay 72
Hudson River School 59, 60
Hutchinson, Anne 21, 22

Illinois State Register 76
Imperialism 123, 131, 132, 150
Indians 82, 83, 84, 90, 91, 98, 101, 102, 103, 144, 145, 146, 163
Isaiah 27, 183
Israel 167, 169, 170, 180, 181, 182, 183, 184, 185

Jackson, Andrew 8, 26, 58, 68, 70, 82, 88, 97, 101, 106
Jackson, Helen Hunt 145
Jacksonian democracy 8
James I 16, 17
Japan 77, 71
Jefferson, Thomas 41, 58, 81, 103, 106, 187
Jerusalem 20, 61, 175, 182, 183, 184, 185, 187
Jews 23, 37, 161, 180–182, 184, 185
Johns Hopkins 97, 104, 135
Johnson, Andrew 27, 118

King James 16, 17
Kipling, Rudyard 98, 153
Knox, John 15, 19

Leaves of Grass 55, 57
Lee, Eliza 98
Levellers 24
Lincoln, Abraham 26, 76, 129
Lindsey, Theophilus 48
Little, Franklin, H. 157
Locke, John 30, 187
Lodge, Henry Cabot 71, 127, 128, 142
Louis XIII 17
Louisiana 5, 65, 58, 67, 81
Luminism 60

Madison, James 35, 187
Magisterial Gaze 59
Manifest Destiny 118, 127, 129, 130, 134, 159, 188
Marty, Martin 157
Mary Tudor 14
Massachusetts 6, 21, 22, 23, 27, 51, 139
Massachusetts Bay Colony 6, 23
Mather, Cotton 6, 144

Index

Mather, Increase 20, 175
Mayflower 6, 19, 184
Maynard, Theodore 20
McKinley, William 77, 120, 126, 183
McLaughlin, William 157
Melting pot 5, 189
Mencken, H.L. 20
Merk, Frederick 2
Messianism 154, 155, 157, 159, 161, 163, 165, 167, 169
Methodism 46–49, 157
Mexican War 54, 74, 76, 85, 86, 91, 145
Mexico 16, 49, 54, 58, 70, 72–77, 85–87, 91, 117, 118, 145
Mexico City 76
Millenarianism 169, 171, 173, 175, 176, 177, 171, 180, 181, 182, 183, 185
Miller, Oliver C. 151
Miller, Perry 20, 21, 24
Milton, John 17
Mississippi River 69, 82, 83, 145
Mobile Bay 68
Monroe, James 106, 115, 121, 127
Monroe Doctrine 115, 117, 118, 119, 120, 121, 122, 123, 124, 125, 127, 128, 129, 131, 133, 189
Monroeism 125, 128, 129
Montaigne, Michel de 104
Montesquieu, Charles, Baron de 32, 34, 35
Moral Majority 172, 180
Morning News 7, 8
Morrison, Isaac Swift 131
Morse, Jedidiah 146
Moses 6, 131, 160, 180

Napoleon 67, 118, 128
Napoleon III 118
National Unity Coalition for Israel 184
Netanyahu, Benjamin 184
New Testament 28, 174
Niebuhr, Reinhold 167, 168
Nordholt, Jan Willem Schulte 103

Ohio 71, 94, 145
Old Europe 5, 20, 50, 109, 163, 174
Old Testament 20, 175, 176
Oregon 73, 74, 76, 85, 91, 116, 117, 125
Oren, Michael 183
O'Sullivan, John L. 7, 8, 9, 69, 71

Pacific 59, 67, 69, 72, 73, 77, 78, 71, 117, 124, 125, 147
Pact of Union 6

Palestine 182, 184
Panama Canal 71
Paredes, Mariona 75
Parliament 14, 17, 18, 19, 26, 38, 177
Perdido River 68
Pétin, Hector 128
Pettygrew, Richard Franklin 130
Philippines 80, 111, 120, 121, 125, 126, 128, 131, 132, 134, 135, 151
Pilgrim Fathers 6, 19, 25, 52, 107, 190
Poe, Edgar Allan 9
Polk, James K. 58, 72, 73, 74, 75, 76, 85, 86, 87, 95, 117
Predestination 25, 42, 49, 69, 162, 190
Presbyterian 16, 18, 19, 31, 36, 90, 101, 124, 132
Promised Land 6, 20, 58, 60, 149, 160, 162, 184
Puerto Rico 58
Puritanism 28, 29, 31, 36, 37, 46–50, 52, 53, 67, 68, 69, 70, 83, 90, 94, 96, 98, 139, 144, 150, 161, 170, 173–176, 178, 171, 183, 187, 188, 190

Quaker 88, 89, 137, 140

Reformation 13, 15, 16, 19, 21, 23, 31, 48, 175
Reid, Whitelaw 152
Removal Act 82, 101
Removal Bill 145
Revivals 47, 48, 171, 182
Revolutionary War 19, 26, 28, 30, 38, 58, 158, 163
Rhode Island 22, 23
Rio Grande 75, 76
Robertson, Pat 172, 182
Rocky Mountains 69, 73
Roosevelt, Theodore 127, 152
Ross, E. A. 143
Rossiter, Clinton 169
Rousseau, Jean-Jacques 31, 32, 33, 104, 154, 155, 158
Russia 71, 116, 184

Sacramento 74
Salem 23, 24, 50, 175, 187
Salem Witch Trials 42
Samoa 71
San Diego, CA 74
San Francisco, CA 74, 151
Santa Fe Trail 74
Scarlet Letter 50, 51

Schurz, Carl 78, 129, 130, 132
Scofield, Cyrus Ingerson 171
Scots 18
Scott, Winfield 76, 145
Scriptures 15, 19, 32, 49, 98, 137, 177
Seward, William 78
Sherman, John 71, 178
Sherwood, Samuel 177
Sioux 101, 102, 146
Slidell, John 75, 76, 86
Smith, Justin 76
Social Darwinism 108, 109, 110, 111, 128, 137, 142, 143, 144, 188, 189
Spain 14, 16, 26, 69, 70, 74, 76, 78–80, 87, 116, 118, 120–122, 125, 126, 129, 132, 152
Spanish-American War 71, 132, 152
Spencer, H. 108, 137, 138, 139, 140
The Spirit of Laws 34
Steinbeck, John 25, 170
Stiles, Ezra 42, 170
Stoppard, Thomas 176
Strong, Josiah 110, 111, 124, 151, 165, 158
Strother, George 69
Sumner, William Graham 137, 139

Talbot, Louis 183
Taylor, Zachary 75
Tennyson, Alfred 151
Teutonic 104, 111, 135
Texas 72, 74, 75, 76, 85, 86, 87, 117
Thoreau, Henry David 9, 50, 51, 53, 54, 58, 155
Tocqueville, Alexis de 44, 103
Transcendentalism 9, 51, 52, 54, 56, 60, 171

Treaty of Guadalupe Hidalgo 76
Trimble, David 26
Turner, Frederick Jackson 97, 98, 99, 100, 101, 103, 104, 105, 108, 188
Twain, Mark 132, 152
Tyler, John 85, 123

Unitarianism 41, 46–49, 51, 159, 171
United Kingdom 25

Van Buren, Martin 84
Victor, Barbara 182, 184
Virginia 35, 41, 88, 148, 180
Voltaire 31, 32, 33, 34, 35

Walden 53
Ward, Lester F. 142, 143
Washington, Booker T. 148
Washington, George 36, 160, 163
Washington Union 73
Webster, Daniel 58, 87, 94, 95, 123
Weinberg, Albert K. 67
Wesley, John 47
West, Nathaniel 28
Whigs 74
Whitefield, George 40, 47
Whitelaw 152
Williams, Roger 22
Winthrop, John 22, 24, 40, 68, 175
Wise, Isaac, Meyer 162, 163, 164
Wounded Knee 101, 102, 146

Yale 26, 35, 90, 139, 170

Zionism 182, 183

www.ingramcontent.com/pod-product-compliance
Ingram Content Group UK Ltd.
Pitfield, Milton Keynes, MK11 3LW, UK
UKHW041957140426
5217IPUK00015B/842